T. S. Eliot and American Poetry

Lee Oser

D0209814

University of Missouri Press
Columbia and London

Library of Congress Cataloging-in-Publication Data

Oser, Lee, 1958–

   T. S. Eliot and American poetry / Lee Oser.

     p.   cm.

   Includes bibliographical references and index.

   ISBN 0-8262-1181-X (alk. paper)

    1. Eliot, T. S. (Thomas Stearns), 1888-1965—Criticism and
interpretation.   2. National characteristics, American, in
literature.   3. American poetry—History and criticism.
4. Influence (Literarty, artistic, etc.).   I. Title

PS3509.L43Z7975   1998

821'.912—dc21   98-21589

                                      CIP

Designer: Stephanie Foley

Typesetter: BookComp, Inc.

Printer and binder: Thomson-Shore, Inc.

Typefaces: Imago Extra Bold and Minion

For Brian Patrick Oser

I'd say that my poetry has obviously more in common with my distinguished contemporaries in America than with anything written in my generation in England. That I'm sure of. . . . In its sources, in its emotional springs, it comes from America.

—T. S. Eliot, 1959 interview

Contents

Preface

OVER THE PAST TWENTY YEARS, a shift has occurred in Eliot studies, away from a predominantly English and European Eliot, and toward a predominantly American one. Building on work by Lyndall Gordon, Eric Sigg, and others, I have set out to consolidate the basic argument for Eliot's Americanness as a poet and then, while observing ways in which English and French writers engage Eliot's native sensibility, to offer an original picture of Eliot from the vantage of American literary history. In method, this book issues from the broad tradition of critical scholarship: part history of ideas, part aesthetic criticism, part biographical, historical, and cultural reference, with an awareness of the theoretical positions that support and challenge one's work. Viewing the job of the literary historian as an effort at persuasion, I craft my argument using all the "common topics" of classical rhetoric: definition of terms, comparison, relationship (cause and effect, contraries, contradictions), testimony of authorities (such as poets and leading critics), and appeal to the historical record.

Studies by Gordon and Sigg have addressed Eliot's Americanness at some length, and I am indebted to them. Here I would note briefly how this book differs from theirs. Gordon's *Eliot's Early Years* and *Eliot's New Life* are critical biographies, with a strong psychological take on their subject. Though she discusses the poetry and is sensitive to Eliot's American background, Gordon does not offer detailed close readings of the poems against that background. In my extended analyses of individual poems, my more limited—and less psychologizing—interest in Eliot's biography, and my specific concern with Eliot as an American poet, I differ from Gordon in scope and method.

Sigg's *The American T. S. Eliot* is a fine book. I have benefited from his research into Eliot's cultural milieu and find his placement of Eliot in the American aestheticist tradition of Henry Adams, William James, and George Santayana to be compelling and important. But Sigg and I are pursuing different ends. Concentrating solely on the early Eliot (i.e., through 1922), Sigg evaluates Eliot's philosophical training at length; his emphasis on F. H. Bradley seems surprising given the suggestion of his title. My concern is with the connection of major literary figures—Emerson, Poe, Whitman, Robert Lowell, and others—to Eliot's poetry, and with the literary influence of Charlotte Eliot upon her son, all of which Sigg leaves very largely untouched. Moreover, I follow Eliot through *Four Quartets* and beyond.

If this book is in any way original, it is through my interest in Eliot's intense and fruitful dialogue with other American poets. In attempting to trace this dialogue, I aim to rediscover the richness—multivalent, unpredictable—of the American poetic tradition, and to show how, in their original ways, our writers claim their poetic citizenship. The American poetic art has been for the most part (notwithstanding its difficulty) a very public-oriented medium. Since the deaths of Eliot, in 1965, and Lowell, in 1977, the development of a highly process-oriented, metalinguistic poetry may be signaling the end of this public-mindedness, or it may only mark the tastes and market power of an ultraprofessionalized generation of poets, critics, and students. I offer this book to those, younger readers in particular, who are dissatisfied with our corporate-academic culture, and who want to explore what is good and serviceable in our literary past.

L. O.
October 24, 1997
Decatur, Illinois

Acknowledgments

PERMISSIONS COSTS FOR THIS book were generously provided by Provost Thomas Flynn and Millikin University.

Many friends, teachers, and colleagues read the manuscript and offered advice. It gives me deep pleasure to thank my mentors, Paul Fry and Marie Borroff, both of whom provided crucial insights into Eliot and the art of poetry. Of course, my mistakes are my own. Jewel Spears Brooker, Langdon Hammer, David Kleinbard, Louis Menand, Steven Monte, Christopher Ricks ("in the captain's tower"), and Sanford Schwartz helped me to improve particular sections; I can hardly thank them enough for their personal generosity. I have benefitted from literary conversations with Ian Baucom, Fr. Robert Beloin, Leslie Brisman, Adam Cox, Vinnie-Marie D'Ambrosio, Donald Gallup, Gregory Jones, Bruce and Adele King, Douglas Levin, Seth Lobis, James Najarian, Linda Peterson, Ronald Schuchard, and Jeffrey Shoulson.

Jane Lago and Julie Schroeder of the University of Missouri Press provided invaluable editorial help.

My mother, Maureen Waters, helped me immeasurably in developing the manuscript. To my wife, Kate, any formal expression of gratitude is a memento of other things.

A version of Chapter 2 has appeared in *Modern Philology,* copyright 1996 by The University of Chicago Press, all rights reserved.

Excerpts from uncollected prose by T. S. Eliot are reprinted by the kind permission of Mrs. Valerie Eliot and Faber and Faber Ltd.

Excerpts from *The Waste Land, Ash-Wednesday,* "Choruses from *The Rock*" in *Collected Poems 1909–1962,* by T. S. Eliot, copyright 1936 by Harcourt Brace & Company, copyright 1964, 1963 by T. S. Eliot, reprinted by permission of Faber and Faber Ltd. and Harcourt Brace & Company.

Excerpts from "Burnt Norton," "East Coker," "The Dry Salvages," and "Little Gidding" in *Four Quartets,* copyright 1943 by T. S. Eliot and renewed 1971 by Esme Valerie Eliot, are reprinted by permission of Faber and Faber Ltd. and Harcourt Brace & Company.

Excerpts from *Collected Poems 1909–1962,* by T. S. Eliot, reprinted by permission of Faber and Faber Ltd.

Excerpts from *Selected Essays,* by T. S. Eliot, copyright 1950 by Faber and Faber Ltd. and by Harcourt Brace & Company, renewed 1978 by Esme Valerie Eliot, are reprinted by permission of the publishers.

Excerpts from *The Waste Land: A Facsimile and Transcript of the Original Drafts Including the Annotations of Ezra Pound,* by T. S. Eliot, copyright 1971 by Esme Valerie Eliot, reprinted by permission of Faber and Faber Ltd. and Harcourt Brace & Company.

Excerpt from *Inventions of the March Hare: Poems 1909–1917,* by T. S. Eliot, copyright 1996 by Esme Valerie Eliot, reprinted by permission of Faber and Faber Ltd. and Harcourt Brace & Company.

Excerpts from *The Use of Poetry and the Use of Criticism,* by T. S. Eliot, copyright 1933 by the President and Fellows of Harvard College, renewed copyright 1961 by T. S. Eliot.

Excerpts from *The Poems of Hart Crane,* by Marc Simon, editor, copyright 1933, 1958, 1966 by Liveright Publishing Corporation, copyright 1986 by Marc Simon. Reprinted by permission of Liveright Publishing Corporation.

Excerpts from "The System," by John Ashbery, as published in *Three Poems,* are reprinted by permission of Georges Borchardt, Inc., for the author, and by Carcanet Press Limited. Copyright 1977 by John Ashbery.

Excerpts from "Self-Portrait in a Convex Mirror," copyright 1974 by John Ashbery, from *Self-Portrait in a Convex Mirror,* by John Ashbery. Used by permission of Viking Penguin, a division of Penguin Books USA Inc.

The following are reprinted by permission of Farrar, Straus, & Giroux, Inc.:

Excerpts from "At the Fishhouses," from *The Complete Poems 1927–1979,* by Elizabeth Bishop, copyright 1979, 1983 by Alice Helen Methfessel.

Excerpts from *Knowledge and Experience in the Philosophy of F. H. Bradley,* by T. S. Eliot, copyright 1964 by T. S. Eliot. Copyright renewed 1992 by Mrs. Valerie Eliot.

Excerpts from *To Criticize the Critic,* by T. S. Eliot, copyright 1965 by T. S. Eliot. Copyright renewed 1993 by Valerie Eliot.

Excerpts from "T. S. Eliot," from *Collected Prose,* by Robert Lowell, copyright 1987 by Caroline Lowell, Harriet Lowell, and Sheridan Lowell.

Excerpts from "My Last Afternoon with Uncle Devereux Winslow," and "Words for Hart Crane," from *Life Studies,* by Robert Lowell, copyright 1956, 1959 by Robert Lowell. Copyright renewed 1987 by Harriet Lowell, Sheridan Lowell, and Caroline Lowell.

Abbreviations

The following abbreviations are used in parenthetical citations throughout *T. S. Eliot and American Poetry*. Full information concerning these texts is given in Works Cited.

WORKS BY T. S. ELIOT

ASG	*After Strange Gods*
CP	*Collected Poems 1909–1962*
FLA	*For Lancelot Andrewes*
ICS	*The Idea of a Christian Society*
IMH	*Inventions of the March Hare*
KE	*Knowledge and Experience in the Philosophy of F. H. Bradley*
LTSE	*The Letters of T. S. Eliot 1898–1922*, vol. 1
NDC	*Notes towards the Definition of Culture*
OPP	*On Poetry and Poets*
PWEY	*Poems Written in Early Youth*
SE	*Selected Essays*
SP	*Selected Prose of T. S. Eliot*
TCTC	*To Criticize the Critic and Other Writings*
UPUC	*The Use of Poetry and the Use of Criticism*
VMP	*The Varieties of Metaphysical Poetry*
WLF	*The Waste Land: A Facsimile and Transcript of the Original Drafts*

Poems in *CP*

AW	*Ash-Wednesday*
	Four Quartets
BN	"Burnt Norton"
DS	"The Dry Salvages"
EC	"East Coker"
HM	"The Hollow Men"
LG	"Little Gidding"
WL	*The Waste Land*

WORKS BY OTHER AUTHORS

Ralph Waldo Emerson

Works	*The Complete Works of Ralph Waldo Emerson*

Edgar Allan Poe

ER	*Essays and Reviews*
PT	*Poetry and Tales*

Walt Whitman

CPCP	*Complete Poetry and Collected Prose*

Note: following a title, a date in parentheses refers to the year of first publication in a volume (not to periodical publication).

**T. S. Eliot
and
American Poetry**

1 | Introduction
From Poe to Whitman

POE RECEIVES HIS ANNUAL TRIBUTE of passing references from Eliot scholars, but recent criticism has ignored his relation, as an American, to Eliot and American modernism.[1] In consequence, a large gap exists in our picture of Eliot, a gap that I would like to rectify, beginning with a few small points about Eliot's youth.

It appears that the young Eliot first encountered Poe during visits to a dentist's office. This is notable because it suggests that Poe was absent from the family library; he may have been among those authors, such as Mark Twain, who were contraband in the Eliot home. In 1906, the year he graduated from the Milton Academy and entered Harvard College, Eliot obtained a personal copy of *The Poems of Edgar Allan Poe*.[2] Three years later, Poe's centenary was commemorated by an unsigned editorial in the *Harvard Advocate*:

> Having barely finished with celebrating the tercentenary of Milton we
> are now come to that lonely and ill-starred genius, the "only Ishmael"

1. Grover Smith's topic differs from my own, but his essay, "The Ghost of Poe," in *T. S. Eliot and the Use of Memory*, offers trenchant insights into the "psychology of horror" in both writers. On the relation of Poe's aesthetic to *The Waste Land*, see F. O. Matthiessen, *The Achievement of T. S. Eliot*, 40–41.

2. Peter Ackroyd, *T. S. Eliot: A Life*, 27. "I suspect that a fear on the part of my parents lest I should acquire a premature taste for tobacco, and perhaps other habits of the hero of the story, kept [*Huckleberry Finn*] out of my way" (T. S. Eliot, introduction to *The Adventures of Huckleberry Finn*, 198). On Eliot's acquisition of the Poe volume, see John Soldo, *The Tempering of T. S. Eliot*, 67.

of American literature—Poe. It is curious how consistently we disavow Poe, and exalt Whitman, for instance. Both were revolters: yet through the magazines the one is exalted, while the other is hunted. So much for the wonderful consistency of the Puritan temperament. With the passing of the Puritan, and the evolution of the future American type of national character, we shall hope to see poetic justice, at least, done to Poe.[3]

This issue of the *Advocate* saw Eliot's promotion to the editorial board, where he was reputed to have been among the journal's "leading lights." Below the commentary, one finds a sample of his juvenilia, entitled "Song" (*PWEY*, 22), a pre-Laforguian poem that is suggestively placed, in tacit support of Poe's aesthetic and the decadent poetry it inspired. Conrad Aiken, Eliot's friend and coeditor, probably contributed to the editorial,[4] and it may be that the two young men collaborated on the production of this interesting page.

A dentist's office, a 1906 bookplate, an unsigned editorial, and a not un-Poe-like poem: not much to go on, but they do hint at a pattern. In Eliot's circle, Poe was the "only Ishmael," a figure of lost patrimony, an author consigned to the margins both at home and at school. Moreover, Eliot's purchase of Poe's volume coincided with his physical separation from his family and first taste of personal independence. This evidence of Eliot's unfostered receptivity to Poe gains significance in the context of Eliot's continuing attempts at self-definition, such as his pointed comment of 1922: "And how tardy, and still how deficient, has been the English appreciation of one of the greatest and least local [of poets]: Edgar Poe."[5] In the *Advocate* piece of 1909, the editors desired to nationalize Poe; in 1922, the year of *The Waste Land*, Eliot laid claim to Poe as a fellow exile, an important forerunner who was by coincidence American. For much of his career, Eliot would seek to resolve these contradictory positions: the American and the fugitive Poe.

Though it tends to impress us less than his French incarnation, Poe's direct impact on American modernism was substantial. Marianne Moore praises "The Rationale of Verse" in a 1916 issue of the *Egoist;* William Carlos

---

3. Conrad Aiken? [Editorial], 130.
4. Haniel Long, quoted in H. W. H. Powel Jr., "Notes on the Life of T. S. Eliot 1888–1910," 59. See Edward Butscher, *Conrad Aiken, Poet of White Horse Vale*, 116.
5. T. S. Eliot, "The Three Provincialities," 13.

Williams names Poe the "first American poet" in *Spring and All* (1923); and Poe rides the subway in Hart Crane's *The Bridge* (1930), in the penultimate section, "The Tunnel." In two letters of 1938 (one being to Moore), Elizabeth Bishop writes of "doing nothing much but reread[ing] Poe" for a theory of writing based on "a combination of Poe's theories and . . . 17th-century prose." These writers draw diverse if generally related conclusions about Poe's significance; of chief concern for Eliot, much as for Moore and the early Bishop, is Poe's technical emphasis, which encourages an impersonal aesthetic.[6]

In "The Rationale of Verse" (1848), Poe writes: "It would require a high degree, indeed, both of cultivation and of courage, on the part of any versifier, to enable him to place his rhymes—and let them remain—at unquestionably their best position, that of unusual and unanticipated intervals" (*ER*, 41). A passage from "Reflections on *Vers Libre*," Eliot's profoundly influential article of 1917, follows Poe closely:[7] "[The] liberation from rhyme might mean as well a liberation *of* rhyme. Freed from its exacting task of supporting lame verse, it could be applied with greater effect where it is most needed. There are often passages in an unrhymed poem where rhyme is wanted for some special effect, for a sudden tightening-up, for a cumulative insistence, or for an abrupt change of mood" (*TCTC*, 189). Recalling Poe's idea of the "best position" and "unusual and unanticipated intervals," much of Eliot's poetry exemplifies the "liberation of rhyme" described here. This singular pursuit of effects has earned the wrath of moralizing critics but should not be construed as undiluted aestheticism. In Poe as in Eliot, the cultivation of prosodic and other poetic effects signals a revolt against the literary culture of the United States, and of New England in particular.

A case in point is Poe's "The City in the Sea," subtitled "A Prophecy," a seminal poem that dates in its earliest version from Poe's 1831 volume. On the level of auditory stimulus, "The City in the Sea" aims to entrance its

6. Marianne Moore, "The Accented Syllable"; William Carlos Williams, *Spring and All*, 111; Hart Crane, *The Poems of Hart Crane*, 99. Elizabeth Bishop, *One Art: Letters*, 71 and 73. Cf. Matthiessen in his classic of American literary criticism: "The two fundamental ways of regarding the poet, either as inspired genius or as craftsman, may divide American poetry between the descendants of Whitman and Poe" (F. O. Matthiessen, *American Renaissance*, 578–79).

7. On the influence of this essay, see Grosvenor Powell, "The Two Paradigms for Iambic Pentameter and Twentieth-Century Metrical Experimentation."

reader. Intense assonance and alliteration, end-rhyme and internal rhyme, a fluid four-beat line, a refrain, and a full ensemble of rhetorical devices contribute to its incantatory power, though the fourth line is, as Allen Tate remarked, a descent into doggerel. On the level of social critique, "The City in the Sea" pays ironic homage to the prophetic traditions that it subverts. I quote the opening stanzas:

> Lo! Death has reared himself a throne
> In a strange city lying alone
> Far down within the dim West,
> Where the good and the bad and the worst and the best
> Have gone to their eternal rest.
> There shrines and palaces and towers
> (Time-eaten towers that tremble not!)
> Resemble nothing that is ours.
> Around, by lifting winds forgot,
> Resignedly beneath the sky
> The melancholy waters lie.
>
> No rays from the holy heaven come down
> On the long night-time of that town;
> But light from out the lurid sea
> Streams up the turrets silently—
> Gleams up the pinnacles far and free—
> Up domes—up spires—up kingly halls—
> Up fanes—up Babylon-like walls—
> Up shadowy long-forgotten bowers
> Of sculptured ivy and stone flowers—
> Up many and many a marvellous shrine
> Whose wreathèd friezes intertwine
> The viol, the violet, and the vine.

(PT, 67)

As the vehicle for what Eliot would call Poe's "*sounding*" lines (*UPUC*, 49), the poem depicts a city "lying alone / Far down within the dim West." Poe was responding in his geography to a body of English and American literature that had adopted the traditional theme of the *translatio imperii et studii*, the western movement of empire and learning, to give expression to America's utopian destiny. An eighteenth-century commonplace, the *translatio* theme would be extended and amplified in American poetry by leading figures such as Philip Freneau, in many poems, including "On the Emigration to America and Peopling the Western Country" (1785); by William Cullen Bryant, in his Harvard Phi Beta Kappa poem of 1821, "The Ages"; by Whitman, in such works as "Passage to India" (1871); and by Crane, in *The Bridge.*[8] Rebelling against the poetic legacy of New England, Poe travesties America's founding mythologies of western movement and the city on the hill. He denies American redemptive history, and is defiantly independent of the culture he portrays: "There shrines and palaces and towers / (Time eaten towers that tremble not!) / Resemble nothing that is ours." "Ours" brings in a note of ostentatious satire, but Poe is seriously contesting American socializing rituals and the ubiquitous cry of progress.[9]

Many models have been cited for Eliot's urban landscapes. Poe has been overlooked, but his example is uniquely revealing. While they share a knowledge of such precursor texts as Byron's "Darkness" and Shelley's "Lines Written among the Euganean Hills," Eliot's gothic sensationalism forsakes the meditative approach of these poets and recalls the hallucinatory directness of Poe:

> A woman drew her long black hair out tight
> And fiddled whisper music on those strings

8. Crane adumbrates my own reading of "The City in the Sea" by quoting it (while alluding to "The Raven") in "The Tunnel": "And Death, aloft,—gigantically down / Probing through you—toward me, O evermore!" (*Poems of Hart Crane*, 99). For Crane, Poe's dystopian prophecy had to be assimilated and transcended by the higher, redemptive vision of *The Bridge.*

9. Poe's reaction against the nineteenth-century culture of progress makes him a forebear of Eliot's modernist reaction against the same. In "The Colloquy of Monos and Una," Monos says: "You will remember that one or two of the wise among our forefathers— wise in fact, although not in the world's esteem—had ventured to doubt the propriety of the term 'improvement,' as applied to the progress of our civilization." Along similar lines, Poe commented in *Graham's Magazine:* "The world is infested, just now, by a new sect of philosophers. . . . They are the *Believers in every thing Odd*. Their High Priest in the East, is Charles Fourier—in the West, Horace Greely. . . . The only common bond among the sect, is Credulity:—let us call it Insanity at once, and be done with it" (*PT,* 450, and *ER,* 1,303; quoted in Ernest Marchand, "Poe as Social Critic," 40, 35). Marchand's essay, which shows that Poe's writings consistently and deliberately address the social history of his time, remains indispensable. More recently, Benjamin Fisher has observed of Poe's cities, "they suggest none of the American optimism concerning urban growth and expansion during the second quarter of the nineteenth century" (Benjamin Fisher, "The Urban Scene and Edgar Allan Poe," 46).

And bats with baby faces in the violet light
Whistled, and beat their wings
And crawled head downward down a blackened wall
And upside down in air were towers
Tolling reminiscent bells, that kept the hours
And voices singing out of empty cisterns and exhausted wells
(*WL* 378–85)[10]

Like "The City in the Sea," the passage conveys its vision with immediate force. There is no initial conceit for the Americans, such as one finds in Byron or Shelley. The link between Poe and Eliot is strengthened by comparing the texts at hand: they have in common an infernal atmosphere of collapse, intense rhyming, a richly inflected melancholy, and similar diction, with "wall[s]", "air," "violet," "hours," and "towers" appearing in each. Aiken wrote of having "long been familiar with" the above lines as a fragment or poem in their own right, before he found them, in 1922, "inserted into *The Waste Land* as into a mosaic."[11] Preceding that poem's conception entirely, they show Eliot assuming a Poe-like manner to depict the unreal city that haunted his imagination.

The anonymous city life of the nineteenth and twentieth centuries had a magnetic fascination for Poe and Eliot, whose art profited from its engagement with the urban masses. Eliot may be said to follow Poe, as well as Europeans like Baudelaire, Laforgue, Tennyson, and James Thomson, in the achievement of new effects that were made possible by the appearance of modern urban society. However, unlike European writers, Poe and the early Eliot encounter cities with little or no history, local traditions of art, archaeological interest, or resonating, mythical past. In his *Harvard Advocate* review of Van Wyck Brooks's *The Wine of the Puritans* (discussed more fully in the next chapter), Eliot reflected on this situation by quoting what he called Brooks's "expressed hope": "I think that a day will come when the names of Denver and Sioux City will have a traditional and antique dignity like Damascus and Perugia—and when it will not seem

---

10. Unless stated otherwise, quotations from Eliot's poetry are from *CP*. Following quotations of Eliot's poetry, numbers in parentheses generally refer to line numbers; for some shorter poems, I have cited only the page numbers in *CP*.

11. Conrad Aiken, "Prefatory Note" to "Anatomy of Melancholy," 196. Valerie Eliot gives the date "1914 or even earlier" for the surviving draft, which begins "So through the evening, through the violet air" (*WLF*, 113, 130).

grotesque to us that it is so." Eliot felt a brief shiver of sympathy for this prediction but could find no empirical support for it. Critical of the culture of progress, unpersuaded by the American city's sociohistorical rhetoric, he followed Poe in turning inward, to his own psychological and artistic resources, in order to orient himself in the world.[12] European models, with their familiar *genius loci,* provided only limited assistance in this process; where Baudelaire could discover a mythic texture in Paris construction sites, the Americans lacked an atmosphere. In addition, neither Poe nor Eliot felt quite at home with blank verse, which had established a permanent residence in New England. Both writers responded to this last problem with brilliant displays of artifice; though Eliot's innovations were more radical and genuinely rebellious, the heightened technique of the "poem written solely for the poem's sake" (*ER,* 76) became for both a measure of social distance and aristocratic *hauteur.*

Eliot tempers certain qualities that he receives from Poe with a more mature sense of irony. "Preludes," which was composed intermittently during the years 1910–1911 (possibly as late as 1912), helps suggest why this is so—why Eliot, to his poetry's advantage, moved beyond Poe's mocking bravura. Like "The City in the Sea," the work hinges on a positioning strategy that offers no historical grounding. But instead of gothic ambience, Eliot in this case describes the play of consciousness through parataxis, that is, through an arrangement of clauses independently, without subordination. In the absence of causal connectives, the act of observation itself dominates the opening:

12. I build on the work of Denis Donoghue, who has suggested, "A distinctive modern literature arose not from the development of cities as such, but from the experience of crowds on city streets; or rather, from the friction between the individual mind and appearances—city streets, crowds, anonymity—over which it had little control" (Denis Donoghue, *Being Modern Together,* 12). T. S. Eliot, review of *The Wine of the Puritans,* 80. One can only speculate on the impression made upon Eliot by the Louisiana Purchase Exposition of 1904, with its stupendous "Column of Progress," vast crowds, and endless exhibits; his juvenilia shows an adolescent sympathy for the national progressivism from which he broke dramatically in early adulthood (see Chapter 2). Summarizing the St. Louis world's fair, cultural historian Robert Rydell writes: "Above all, the Louisiana Purchase Exposition gave a utopian dimension to American imperialism" (Rydell, *All the World's a Fair: Visions of Empire at American International Expositions, 1876–1916,* 183). Perhaps it is no accident, then, that in 1922 Eliot would satirize the U.S. presence in "old Manila Harbour" (see note 35 below): the St. Louis fair featured a Philippine Reservation and a Philippine Day (see Rydell, *All the World's a Fair,* 155–78).

> The winter evening settles down
> With smell of steaks in passageways.
> Six o'clock.
> The burnt-out ends of smoky days.
>   ("Preludes" 1.1–4)

The poet doesn't refer to a dream or fancy or provide any reason or occasion for this place. Nor is the title of the work very helpful in directing the reader: the deletion of American signposts, "Dorchester" and "Roxbury" in successive drafts, adds to the effect of stepping into another world entirely. The poem's strange immediacy is enhanced by the interplay of an object-centered vision ("grimy scraps," "withered leaves") with a more subjective point of view (the winter evening "settles down"; morning then "comes to consciousness"). Similarly, gritty realism mingles with a highly refined sense of the absurd: "Six o'clock," the speaker punctually informs us— things are on schedule. And throughout, a series of quasi-personifications, of inanimate objects acting and abstractions coming to life, dramatizes the mind's curious awareness of its surroundings. This world yoked into a sensibility, with its disjunctive pattern of consciousness, bears ultimately on questions of spirit that are not without large historical consequence for Eliot.

After the daily sordor of the second "Prelude," one might expect Eliot to develop the idea of life's mechanical repetition, an idea that would serve to deny historical progress. Yet, as the poet turns his attention to an isolated woman, arguably an aspect of his own self, the poem hovers momentarily between repetitions and beginnings:

> And when all the world came back
> And the light crept up between the shutters
> And you heard the sparrows in the gutters,
> You had such a vision of the street
> As the street hardly understands; . . .
>   ("Preludes" 3.7–11)

In a brief aubade, which recalls "The City in the Sea" and looks forward to Bishop's "Love Lies Sleeping," the poet reveals a world where spirit and matter, the vision and the street, are at odds, and matter has the upper hand. The city will not admit the woman's vision, and remains opaque to spiritual frames of reference that would make sense of "all the world."

The "vision of the street" breaks "Preludes" apart, as perceiver and perceived begin a radical divergence. In pointing out the street's lack of understanding, a dramatic subjectivity intrudes upon and fractures the more impersonal sensibility of the first and second "Preludes." These two narrative modes (impersonal unity and intimate disunity) compete in the work's final section, where the visionary woman is succeeded by a man's soul and then the poet speaking in his own voice:

> His soul stretched tight across the skies
> That fade behind a city block,
> Or trampled by insistent feet
> At four and five and six o'clock;
> And short square fingers stuffing pipes,
> And evening newspapers, and eyes
> Assured of certain certainties,
> The conscience of a blackened street
> Impatient to assume the world.
>
> I am moved by fancies that are curled
> Around these images, and cling:
> The notion of some infinitely gentle
> Infinitely suffering thing.
>
> Wipe your hands across your mouth, and laugh;
> The worlds revolve like ancient women
> Gathering fuel in vacant lots.
>
> ("Preludes" 4.1–16)

If I follow correctly, the "soul" is alternately "stretched" and "trampled" (though it is possible to read the soul as "trampling" or tramping about the busy street); in being trampled, the soul itself becomes the street's "conscience." Along with the city's soul-crushing force, the wrenched syntax that opens the final "Prelude" implies that the unity of perceiver and perceived cannot hold. The "images" also suggest as much: insofar as unity exists, it verges increasingly on the demonic, with eyes that are habitually blind and grotesque animal habits marking the senses and physical extension, respectively, of the amoral conscience. In the conclusion, which is in effect two conclusions, perceiver and perceived fall mercilessly apart. There is an apparent or false ending, which in its pathos and sentimentality creates a foil to the unexpected suppression of feeling in the final stanza. Trying to resolve the tensions of the poem, Eliot moves in opposite directions over the course of seven lines, toward the spiritual and then the material world. He suffers from what Emerson in his essay "Fate" called "the double consciousness"; with Laforgue, he thus "repeats the theme of Baudelaire and Emerson: *'je ne suis qu'un faux accord . . .'*" (*VMP*, 214).

Eliot is said to have associated the "infinitely gentle / Infinitely suffering thing" with his older brother, Henry Ware Eliot Jr. (*LTSE*, 1:54 n). This bears, I think, upon a late remark of his: "My urban imagery was that of St. Louis, upon which that of Paris and London have been superimposed." As youngsters, the brothers lived in a St. Louis neighborhood that "had become shabby to a degree approaching slumminess,"[13] but where stood relics of a bygone era: their grandmother's house, and the Unitarian Church of the Messiah, which memorialized the career of the boys' grandfather, Reverend William Eliot (*TCTC*, 44). In growing more and more alien as the young poet entered manhood, Eliot's ancestral landscape whispered the truth, that his family's history had ended in spiritual defeat. Because those St. Louis blocks must have radiated with a familial sacredness for him, the "infinitely gentle / Infinitely suffering thing" harbors a christological significance, which I connect to his family's missionary heritage.

Admittedly, I am seeking to recover what Eliot has all but erased from "Preludes," but I am also trying to make sense of his emotional content. Perhaps, the poet suggests, it would be best only to record the impersonal sensorium, but certain associations "cling" whether one likes them or not—the emotional life cannot be fully repressed. The poet doesn't specify the nature of his emotions: because the "vision" is neither described nor understood, it translates into abstracted emotional tension; the "soul" undertakes a vague spiritual odyssey, with feelings adrift; the "fancies" that "move" the speaker are unnamed; and a mere "notion" of feeling indicates an intelligence at odds with itself. This flatness in Eliot's emotional content is of profound interest. The demonic came naturally enough, for Poe (among others) had supplied a serviceable model; but when Eliot approached feelings of gentleness and suffering, he responded with a detachment that remains genuinely disconcerting.

"Preludes" not only breaks from American optimism and U.S. locales, as Poe had done, but discards the bourgeois and by extension nationalist

---

13. Both remarks from T. S. Eliot, "The Influence of Landscape upon the Poet," 422.

norms of American lyric and narrative poetry: the poem is deliberately unprettified, mimetically contorted, and spiritually abnormal. Like much of Eliot's early work, it ends in anticlimax. Yeats, in his famous introduction to *The Oxford Book of Modern Verse* (1936), would prefer to call Eliot a "satirist rather than poet."[14] I would say that while Eliot's preconversion work is at once too rich in symbolism, too hallucinatory, and too particular to be compared, as Yeats would suggest, with Pope's *An Essay on Man,* it does subvert the kind of heroic, national consciousness that Yeats sought for Irish literature. Perhaps Yeats sensed, with good cause, that Eliot's was the very opposite of a nationalistic art.

In the 1950s, Eliot's thinking about Poe underwent a climactic change. But while his earlier statements, with their emphasis on Poe's isolation and his influence on French poets, became the capital of academic modernism, Eliot's later statements, which try to place Poe as a distinctly American writer, have been neglected. I will look at some of the early remarks first. In "American Literature," written in 1919, Eliot defended Poe's criticism and his art. By calling him "the directest, the least pedantic, the least pedagogical of the critics writing in his time in either America or England," Eliot advanced terms that the author of "The Poetic Principle" would have appreciated. Poe's literary enemies were the "Frogpondians," the Boston literati whom he berated for being pedants, and in response to whose didacticism and lack of taste he expressly directed his aesthetic theories. A disaffected New Englander and Harvard graduate, Eliot relished this aspect of Poe. But Poe was also "the *reductio ad absurdum*" of the "romantic movement," a diabolist who ended that movement insofar as Tennyson and Whitman transformed the romanticism they inherited; neither was as adversarial toward his own society as Poe or Byron.[15] Eliot topped off

14. W. B. Yeats, introduction to *The Oxford Book of Modern Verse,* xxii.
15. T. S. Eliot, "American Literature," 236–37. Written in 1915 at Oxford, "Mr. Apollinax" updates Poe's Frogpondians as "Professor Channing-Cheetah" and his companions. In a radio talk of 1943, Eliot noted Poe's "bitter opposition to most of the literary men and movements in his country," as well as his role as "the craftsman," his concern with "artistic effect alone" (T. S. Eliot, "A Dream within a Dream," 243). "The romantic phase was an essential phase, not only in England but for the whole of Europe. After the death of Byron it may be said that romanticism became diffused. Two men, and perhaps two men only, inherited the spirit of English romanticism: Poe and Heine. I should add Baudelaire, but Baudelaire is already influenced by Poe. . . . In England the romantic cult was transformed by the enormous prestige of Tennyson; in America by Tennyson also and later by Whitman, the American Tennyson; . . ." (T. S. Eliot, review of *Israfel,* 219).

the review with a brilliant description of America's "starved environment": "Poe and Whitman, like bulbs in a glass bottle, could only exhaust what was in them." Though he eventually revised his judgment, the remark epitomizes his early, Jamesian critique of American literature, and informs Eliot scholarship to this day.[16]

"From Poe to Valéry," Eliot's well-known lecture of 1948, is incisive in its analysis of symbolism, but rather predictable in its discussion of Poe. Delivered at the Library of Congress in November, distributed in fifteen hundred copies as a New Year's gift from Eliot and his American publishers, and reprinted in the *Hudson Review* in 1949, the text saw wide circulation in the United States.[17] Both in addressing the influence of Poe on French poetry, and in his comments on Poe's American background, Eliot gave a polish to established opinion:

> It does not seem to me unfair to say that Poe has been regarded as a minor, or secondary, follower of the Romantic movement: a successor to the so-called "Gothic" novelists in his fiction, and a follower of Byron and Shelley in his verse. This however is to place him in the English tradition; and there certainly he does not belong. English readers sometimes account for that in Poe which is outside any English tradition, by saying that it is American; but this does not seem to me wholly true either, especially when we consider the other American writers of his own and an earlier generation. There is a certain flavour of provinciality about his work, in a sense in which Whitman is not in the least provincial: it is the provinciality of the person who is not at home where he belongs, but cannot get to anywhere else. Poe is a kind of displaced European; he is attracted to Paris, to Italy and to Spain, to places which he could endow with romantic gloom and grandeur. Although his ambit of movement hardly extended beyond the limits of Richmond and Boston longitudinally, and neither east nor west of these centres, he seems a wanderer with no fixed abode. There can be few authors of such eminence who have drawn so little from their own roots, who have been so isolated from any surroundings. (*TCTC*, 29)

Eliot's point is that Poe was exiled in mind without having gone anyplace. He several times hints at likenesses between himself and his subject, such

---

16. Eliot, "American Literature," 237. Cf. Hugh Kenner: "Though we can trace '*Ulalume*'s derivation from English romanticism, it has the air of a complete poetic method invented out of nothing and then exhausted, leaving no more for a successor to do" (Hugh Kenner, *The Invisible Poet: T. S. Eliot*, 137).

17. My source is Donald Gallup, *T. S. Eliot: A Bibliography*, 81.

as the course of movement from the South to the North, the attraction to dark European atmospheres, which we see in Eliot's gothic *Waste Land* passage, and the notion of an exiled "provinciality." F. O. Matthiessen had glossed this last predicament (in words Eliot probably had read) as "the excessive provincial consciousness of elements in literary tradition which Europeans would have taken for granted—and ignored." The lecture ends by stressing the importance of Poe when seen "through the eyes of Baudelaire, Mallarmé and most of all Valéry" (*TCTC*, 42)—thus confirming the wisdom of Edmund Wilson's *Axel's Castle* (1931) and honoring establishment precepts.[18]

Had it been reprinted or distributed in significant quantity prior to 1965, "American Literature and the American Language," with its concern for "strong local flavour" and "identity as well as difference" (*TCTC*, 54, 55), might have challenged the more doctrinaire formalists of the New Critical period. In this 1953 lecture, Eliot unexpectedly named Poe one of the "landmarks" of American literature, alongside Whitman and Mark Twain. Evidently, Whitman had contributed to the revolution in Eliot's thought. Whitman's essay on Poe in *Specimen Days* (1882), an occasional piece entitled "Edgar Poe's Significance," shows Poe to be a product of American culture:

> Almost without the first sign of moral principle, or of the concrete or its heroisms, or the simpler affections of the heart, Poe's verses illustrate an intense faculty for technical and abstract beauty, with the rhyming art to excess, an incorrigible propensity toward nocturnal themes, a demoniac undertone behind every page—and, by final judgement, probably belong among the electric lights of imaginative literature, brilliant and dazzling, but with no heat. There is an indescribable magnetism about the poet's life and reminiscences, as well as the poems. To one who could work out their subtle retracing and retrospect, the latter would make a close tally no doubt between the author's birth and antecedents, his childhood and youth, his physique, his so-call'd education, his studies and associates, the literary and social Baltimore, Richmond, Philadelphia and New York, of those times—not only the places and circumstances in themselves, but often, very often, in a strange spurning of, and reaction from them all. (*CPCP*, 873)

18. Matthiessen, *Achievement*, 42. Eliot would later decide that what "The Philosophy of Criticism" "suggested to the French poets was an aesthetic which might have come into being some other way, if Poe had never written or if Baudelaire had never read Poe" (T. S. Eliot, foreword to *Symbolisme from Poe to Mallarmé*, vii).

This is excellent criticism. It is true that here and throughout his essay, Whitman excludes Poe from an idealized America, the America of the preface to *Leaves of Grass*. But Whitman sees Poe's Americanness. He sees past the myth of Poe's romantic isolation, ignores his already conspicuous renown in France, and describes a "close tally" between Poe and his American environment.

Eliot adopts Whitman's viewpoint in "American Literature and the American Language," and in so doing modifies the "glass bottle" thesis of 1919 and 1948: "Perhaps all that one can say of Poe is that his was a type of imagination that created its own dream world; that anyone's dream world is conditioned by the world in which he lives; and that the real world behind Poe's fancy was the world of Baltimore and Richmond and Philadelphia that he knew" (*TCTC*, 55). Repeating Whitman's sequence of "Baltimore, Richmond, Philadelphia," Eliot, like Whitman, connects Poe's singular achievement to his life in American cities. Indeed, Eliot's entire approach to Poe and American literature changes in this important lecture, which I must put down for a moment in order to take up some related concerns. It was Whitman, the subject of the following pages, who led Eliot to his new critical perspective, though Ezra Pound should be acknowledged for having long been attentive to matters of American identity: "It can't be said that an alteration on Mr. Eliot's passport has altered the essential Americanness of his work," wrote Pound in 1938.[19] But Whitman had posed the essential question first: how could a "strange spurning" of America, an act of psychic exile, result in American poetry?

Eliot's self-revealing answer to this question lies in his long and byzantine reception of Whitman. Matriculating at Harvard College in 1906, Eliot no doubt discovered that Whitman was quoted abundantly. Only a decade or so earlier, faculty and students had combined to bring Whitman into prominence while the genteel tradition, the high, Anglophilic culture of James Russell Lowell, John Greenleaf Whittier, Oliver Wendell Holmes, and Henry Wadsworth Longfellow, was losing its cachet. Barrett Wendell, Eliot's freshman English teacher, had included an ambivalent chapter on Whitman in his popular study, *A Literary History of America*. For an aspiring poet, Wendell's (rather tortuous) closing comments would have been provoking: "The man who has done this is the only one who points out the stuff of

19. Ezra Pound, *Selected Prose*, 163.

which perhaps the new American literature of the future may in time be made." Professor William James had referred several times to Whitman in *The Varieties of Religious Experience,* a book from which Eliot took careful notes during his Harvard years. And on the same page as an *Advocate* review by Eliot, one finds Whitman called "the chief exponent of a peculiar age and social order"—an order that was progressivist, imperialist, and modern.[20]

Eliot's first substantial criticism of Whitman dates from 1926, when he compared Whitman to Tennyson. Whitman's role at Harvard, as the "chief exponent" of the new social order, is in the background:

> Between the ideas of the two men [Whitman and Tennyson], or, rather, between the relations of the ideas of each to his place and time, between the ways in which each held his ideas, there is a fundamental resemblance. Both were born laureates. Whitman, of course, fought hard against corruption, against Press servility, against slavery, against alcohol (and I dare say Tennyson would have done so under the same conditions); but essentially he was satisfied—too satisfied—with things as they are. . . .
>
> I do not mean to suggest that all discontent is divine, or that all self-righteousness is loathsome. On the contrary, both Tennyson and Whitman made satisfaction almost magnificent. It is not the best aspect of their verse. . . . Tennyson liked monarchs, and Whitman liked presidents. Both were conservative, rather than reactionary or revolutionary; that is to say, they believed explicitly in progress, and believed implicitly that progress consists in things remaining much as they are.[21]

The analysis turns on the assumption, familiar before World War II, that the reaction against the nineteenth-century faith in progress could claim the role of the avant-garde artistically and the rear guard culturally. Eliot insinuates his dislike both for the business of "laureates" (government work for superb propagandists with liberal political credentials), and for the

20. For cultural and historical analysis of Whitman's ascension at Harvard, see Kenneth Price, *Whitman and Tradition: The Poet in His Century,* 122–47. Eliot would cite Wendell's book at least twice, in "American Literature," 237, and "American Critics," 24. Barrett Wendell, *A Literary History of America,* 479. The review is credited to "W. C. G.," in all likelihood William Chase Greene, Eliot's classmate and later professor of Latin and Greek at Harvard; [William Chase Greene], review of *Walt Whitman,* 80.

21. T. S. Eliot, "Whitman and Tennyson," 426.

uniformity of the arts when conceived as progressive. In the context of such criticism, Tennyson and Whitman become interchangeable spokesmen for the liberal settlement, a single, transatlantic "suburban democracy."[22] Through the main channels of English and American culture, they had encouraged a stultifying conformity, with which the thinking individual must be discontent.

At the end of his review, Eliot remarks that Whitman's real strength owes nothing to his politics: "Beneath the declamations there is another tone, and behind all the illusions there is another vision. When Whitman speaks of lilacs or of the mocking-bird, his theories and beliefs drop away like a needless pretext."[23] This apparent afterthought suggests that Eliot, in some inward way, identified with Whitman—lilacs adorn the opening lines of *The Waste Land*, and an American songbird, evoking the hermit thrush of "When Lilacs Last in the Dooryard Bloom'd," is at the heart of what Eliot told Ford Madox Ford were the poem's only "*good* lines" (*WLF*, 129). Inseparable from his American subject matter, Whitman's "tone" and "vision" impart a spiritual recognition that abides "behind all the illusions" of the progressive banner. But Eliot is as yet reluctant to associate this spirituality with his native country, which, for his larger purposes, he rather indiscriminately politicizes.

Remembering back to his student days, Eliot commented in his 1928 introduction to Pound's *Selected Poems:* "I did not read Whitman until much later in life, and had to conquer an aversion to his form, as well as to much of his matter, in order to do so." Historically, this is surprising. One thinks of the Cantabrigians to whom Eliot remarked: "I have not read Proust." A week later, when a newcomer to this particular group asked Eliot about a recent translation of Proust, everyone was startled when he delivered a "weighty" tribute to it. Watching was a young William Empson, who concluded that Eliot "did not consider he had 'read' a book unless he had written copious notes. . . ." There can be little doubt that Eliot had at least noticed Whitman's poetry at Harvard. But if Eliot's unusual deployment of the word "read," by which he means "to know thoroughly" and not "to be

---

22. Ackroyd records that "in a circular which [Eliot] sent out to attract new subscribers in December [1924], he explained that the *Criterion* represented pure Toryism, which, in its espousal of 'reaction' and 'revolution' as opposed to old-fashioned 'suburban democracy,' would attract the younger generation" (Ackroyd, *T. S. Eliot,* 143).

23. Eliot, "Whitman and Tennyson," 426.

acquainted with," may be said to justify his remarks in the 1928 introduction, why the disdainful manner, with Eliot, perhaps echoing Matthew Arnold, needing as it were to outlast an aversion and conquer fate?[24]

Like other eminent poet-critics, Eliot at times shows less interest in fair play than in his own cultural authority; then again (as Oscar Wilde was fond of pointing out), audiences are seldom interested in fairness. The introduction to Pound proceeds from a modernist polemic, familiar to readers of the *Criterion,* that advanced international standards in art. Eliot sets forth three types of *vers libre:* his own, "that of Pound, and that of the disciples of Whitman." He continues: "I will not say that subsequently there have not appeared traces of reciprocal influence of several types upon one another, but I am here speaking of origins. . . . The form in which I began to write, in 1908 or 1909, was directly drawn from the study of Laforgue together with the later Elizabethan drama. . . ." In defining his style against that of third- and fourth-rate American imagists, and against such "provincials" as Amy Lowell, Carl Sandburg, and Edgar Lee Masters (against those, in sum, who threatened his and Pound's authority), Eliot pretermits forces behind his own movement. Laforgue had translated Whitman, and the poetic catalogs in "Prufrock" quite arguably reflect Whitman's influence on the French. Having studied Whitman for the development of his own *vers libre,* Laforgue would certainly have questioned Eliot's tendentious remark, "Whitman was a great prose writer" who spuriously "asserted that his great prose was a new form of verse." Moreover, Whitman himself provides numerous instances of the nineteenth-century international style.[25] As a strong-willed arbiter of taste, Eliot hides the issue's complexity—not only the question of Whitman's influence but the culturally specific background and prospect that his own (and Pound's) Americanness afforded—behind a wall of modernist agitprop.

In "Walt Whitman and Modern Poetry," a lecture of 1944, Eliot is less guarded toward Whitman than he was previously; the talk forgoes the more automatic prejudices of the Eliotic canon, and shows Eliot responding more

24. T. S. Eliot, introduction to *Ezra Pound: Selected Poems,* 8. William Empson, "The Style of the Master," 152–54. Cf. Matthew Arnold's "Resignation," in *The Poetical Works of Matthew Arnold,* 58–59, lines 215–18 and 247–48.

25. Eliot, introduction to *Ezra Pound,* 8. Jules Laforgue's translation is *Les Brins d'Herbes.* Eliot, introduction to *Ezra Pound,* 10. For Whitman's knowledge of European writers, see Roger Asselineau, "The European Roots of *Leaves of Grass.*"

disinterestedly to Whitman's genius. Unpublished until 1985, the lecture seeks to assess Whitman's originality:

> There are two kinds of poet: one we may call traditional (for lack of a better term)—and I mean by this the man who starts a tradition as much as the man who follows what others have started. This one finds a way of saying, which others can follow and adapt for saying what they themselves have to say. It is poets of this type who make the style and idiom of an age. The other kind (as great and greater) find a way of saying hardly adaptable to anything else except what they themselves have to say. Whitman is in this class.[26]

"Tradition" here blurs with convention; it has weakened (a fact for which Eliot apologizes) into "traditional." The greater poet may be the one who is not traditional in any obvious sense. When Eliot returns to his earlier comparison between Tennyson and Whitman, a change occurs that pertains to this reevaluation of tradition. He says that Whitman is "a greater poet than Tennyson: Tennyson is a great craftsman, but there is something more in Whitman's account of John Paul Jones's sea fight in *Song of Myself*—a greater depth and universality—than in Tennyson's 'Revenge,' or any of his military and patriotic poems."[27] One is not surprised that craftsmanship should yield precedence to "depth and universality"; but the fact that these latter qualities are summarized so vaguely, Eliot referring only to the "something more" of the heroic sea fight in *Song of Myself*, invites scrutiny.

Later in 1944, in an address to the Virgil Society entitled "What Is a Classic?" Eliot spoke of Virgil's unrivaled *"universality"* (*OPP*, 67), the same term he had applied to Whitman in "Walt Whitman and Modern Poetry." To compare the two lectures is to trace a lacuna in Eliot's poetics. Although Eliot could define Virgil's universality as the product of Roman cultural "maturity" in union with Virgil's individual "comprehensiveness" and "consciousness of history" (i.e. literary history), Whitman's universality remained undefined, unspecified as to intensity, and foreign to Eliot's model of European order. By Eliot's lights, Whitman could not "make the style and idiom of an age" because his rhythmic "singularity" had rendered him "unique in the whole history of literature." However, "the style and idiom

---

26. T. S. Eliot, "Walt Whitman and Modern Poetry," 1944 lecture transcribed by Donald Gallup in "Mr. Eliot at the Churchill Club," 98.
27. Ibid., 99.

of an age" do not ensure poetic greatness; Whitman's poetry may be greater than the merely traditional kind, and Eliot himself testifies to a universal power in Whitman's writing. Put another way, Eliot grapples here with the problem of sublimity, defined by Longinus as "the echo of greatness of spirit."[28]

A look at *Democratic Vistas,* written by Whitman shortly after the Civil War, clarifies Eliot's changing response to his American forerunner. In his discussion of the poet's role in America, Whitman argues, "the old undying elements remain. The task is, to successfully adjust them to new combinations, our own days" (*CPCP,* 968). He declares that America "must sternly promulgate her own new standard, yet old enough, and accepting the old, the perennial elements, and combining them into groups, unities, appropriate to the modern. . . ." (*CPCP,* 969). Whitman resembles Emerson in his call for a deep break from Europe and the development of an indigenous American character. But if Eliot, like Henry James, interpreted this call as an impediment to cultural maturity, Whitman's "universality" simply doesn't accord with Jamesian notions of America as culturally immature. Most important of all, Eliot follows Whitman in his desire to remake the past and not to imitate it, to re-create the old forms and not to rely on them. In drawing, as a poet, on his American perspective, Eliot contradicts his critical apologia for European culture.

It is not to deny their philosophical and religious differences to say that both Eliot and Whitman assimilate an American Protestant call for spiritual renewal, which translates into a poetic evangelism:[29]

> Allons! the inducements shall be greater,
> We will sail pathless and wild seas,

28. Ibid. For convenience, I use "Longinus" to designate the unknown author of the ancient Greek treatise *On the Sublime,* traditionally identified with Cassius Longinus.

29. In "Elias Hicks," a brief but loving biography from *November Boughs* (1888), Whitman describes his attending a "very fervid" meeting at which Hicks preached in 1829: "Then the words come from [Hicks's] lips, very emphatically and slowly pronounc'd, in a resonant, grave, melodious voice, *What is the chief end of man? I was told in my early youth, it was to glorify God, and seek and enjoy him forever*" (*CPCP,* 1,233; his emphasis). And Whitman subjoins an important note: "The true Christian religion (such was the teaching of Elias Hicks), consists neither in rites or Bibles or sermons or Sundays—but in noiseless secret ecstacy and unremitted aspiration, in purity. . . ." For Whitman's religious training, including his early exposure and deep attraction to Hicks, see Floyd Stovall, *The Foreground to "Leaves of Grass,"* 24–26, and Matthiessen, *American Renaissance,* 532–49.

> We will go where winds blow, waves dash, and the Yankee
> clipper speeds by under full sail.
> ("Song of the Open Road," *CPCP*, 303)

> Old men ought to be explorers
> Here and there does not matter
> We must be still and still moving
> Into another intensity
> For a further union, a deeper communion
> Through the dark cold and the empty desolation,
> The wave cry, the wind cry . . .
> (EC 202–8)

The Ulyssean pedigree of both passages is clear: Dante and Tennyson precede Whitman and Eliot, and Eliot may well have perused "Song of the Open Road." In observing the influence of Tennyson on the Americans, one finds, remarkably, that neither Eliot nor Whitman adopts Tennyson's elegiac tone. Vis-à-vis Whitman, Eliot cultivates a mode of spiritual self-inquiry in which the frontier has been internalized. By contrast, "Song of the Open Road" explores a frontier of personal knowledge and social intercourse that is topographically American. But both writers demand and achieve a powerful remaking of the heroic archetype. As a perpetual frontier, America had entered into Eliot's poetry and criticism, enhancing his emotional range and enriching his thought about the "new" work of literature.

I can return now to "American Literature and the American Language," the 1953 lecture in which Eliot's criticism of Poe and Whitman crystallized. Eliot begins the talk with autobiography. He identifies himself as a native of St. Louis, and the ensuing discussion of American literature conjoins personal and public references:

> Let me now suggest that a national literature comes to consciousness at the stage at which any young writer must be aware of several generations of writers behind him, in his own country and language, and amongst these generations several writers generally acknowledged to be of the great. The importance of this background for the young writer is incalculable. It is not necessary that this background should provide him with models for imitation. The young writer, certainly, should not be consciously bending his talent to conform to any supposed

> American or other tradition. The writers of the past, especially of the immediate past, in one's own place and language may be valuable to the young writer simply as something definite to rebel against. He will recognize the common ancestry: but he needn't necessarily *like* his relatives. For models to imitate, or for styles from which to learn, he may often more profitably go to writers of another country and another language, or of a remoter age. (*TCTC*, 56, his emphasis)

In the phrase "a national literature comes to consciousness," I hear an echo of "morning comes to consciousness" in "Preludes," so that an entire history of lessons learned and debts paid glints in the light of Eliot's self-making. His use of the term "ancestry," which recalls "Tradition and the Individual Talent," bears special weight given the number of poets in his own family tree, including the minor poet Christopher Pearce Cranch, the once-popular Rufus Dawes (whom Eliot called a "pest," and whom Poe "wiped the floor with" in a review), as well as Eliot's mother, Charlotte Eliot. Among his distant cousins, Eliot could name Whittier, J. R. Lowell, Herman Melville, and Nathaniel Hawthorne.[30]

What Eliot values most in the American tradition is its dynamic and open-ended character. He emphasizes the need to keep American poetry receptive to diverse and rival influences, and he argues that criticism cannot and should not formulate " 'what is American' based on the work of writers up to and including those now writing" (*TCTC*, 57). The upshot is that the identity of America must yield to, must accommodate, the particular creative drive of the individual poet. Though Eliot doesn't repudiate "Tradition and the Individual Talent," where tradition weighs heavily on the individual but where the past is, it must be remembered, "altered by the present," he in effect rewrites the essay as "America and the Individual Talent," where the message is more directly one of individual freedom. Recognizing that his poetry escaped the theoretical confines of Europe's "ideal order" (much as—an Eliotic point—all poetry eludes its criticism), he looked to America, the spiritual frontier, as a complement to that order.

I want at this point to suggest that contemporary criticism has stressed the question of Whitman's influence on Eliot to the exclusion of a more

---

30. On Dawes, see Eliot's review of *Israfel*, 219, and Eliot quoted in Robert Lowell, *Collected Prose*, 52. Eric Sigg provides a family tree of "T. S. Eliot's Literary Relatives" in his essay, "Eliot as a Product of America," 16–17.

rounded view of Eliot's significance in American poetry. In particular, I must break a lance with Harold Bloom. Other prominent critics of the post-Eliotic age tend either to banish Eliot, or to interpret him as a turn from the main path.[31] Bloom and his school include Eliot by painting him as the contumacious heir of Emerson and Whitman and by arguing that what is best in Eliot comes out of these writers. It is my concern that Bloom's narrow lineage precludes attention to Eliot's originality, as well as to the multivocal ferocity of American poets and leading critics like Bloom himself. For instance, Bloom writes, "Emerson fathered pragmatism; Poe fathered precisely nothing." Granting Poe a tie for "twelfth place" (with Sidney Lanier) in his ranking of nineteenth-century American poets, Bloom wants to bury Poe where no one will find him.[32] Hence, for the Bloomian critic, the dialectical interplay of Poe and Whitman vanishes from American poetry, and Poe's influence on Eliot (or Crane or Bishop) is adscititious.

Typical of the current emphasis is an essay written for one of Bloom's Chelsea House books, where Cleo McNelly Kearns compares "When Lilacs Last in the Dooryard Bloom'd" to *The Waste Land:* "Whitman's poem gives us not only the motifs and images of *The Waste Land . . .* but its very tone and pace, the steady andante which makes of both poems a walking meditation."[33] There is some real insight here, but the case is overstated; such criticism might lead a student to decide that Whitman and Eliot were simply pretty much alike. One may warm to the idea that *The Waste Land* is, in some respects, "a walking meditation." But in all fairness to Kearns, the work that started out as "He Do the Police in Different Voices" cannot in the final analysis be said to have a "steady" "tone and pace," while the Belladonna passage from "A Game of Chess" provides but one example of

31. To name some prominent and influential examples: Roy Harvey Pearce's *The Continuity of American Poetry* is respectful of Eliot, but places Eliot's "poetics of myth" as a "counter-current," a foil to the main line of American continuity; with less admiration, Joseph Riddel's "Decentering the Image" repudiates Eliot's "mythical method" as a nostalgic poetics of "mastery" or "totalization"; in *The Renewal of Literature: Emersonian Reflections,* Richard Poirier asserts that Eliot, because of his literary-cultural position, does not fit into the quintessential American tradition of Emerson; and Robert Bly, in *American Poetry: Wilderness and Domesticity,* begins with a chapter entitled, "A Wrong Turning in American Poetry," which is a programmatic goring of the modernism of Eliot, Pound, and Moore.

32. Harold Bloom, *Poetics of Influence,* 284, 281.

33. Cleo McNelly Kearns, "Realism, Politics, and Literary Persona in *The Waste Land,*" 150.

images and motifs that are a far cry from Whitman's—let alone bats and towers.[34]

When Eliot imitates Whitman, the effect is obvious, as in the ninth chorus from *The Rock* (1934):

> Out of the formless stone, when the artist united himself with stone,
> Spring always new forms of life, from the soul of man that is joined to
>   the soul of stone;
> Out of the meaningless practical shapes of all that is living or lifeless
> Joined with the artist's eye, new life, new form, new colour.
> Out of the sea of sound the life of music,
> Out of the slimy mud of words, out of the sleet and hail of verbal
>   imprecisions,
> Approximate thoughts and feelings, words that have taken the place
>   of thoughts and feelings,
> There spring the perfect order of speech, and the beauty of incantation.
>
> (Rock 9.16–24)

Toward the end of this passage, one notes a resemblance to the much greater poetry of "Burnt Norton":

> Words strain,
> Crack and sometimes break, under the burden,
> Under the tension, slip, slide, perish,

34. Sydney Musgrove's *T. S. Eliot and Walt Whitman* lies behind the popular Bloomian reading of Eliot (duly noted by Bloom; see his introduction to *"The Waste Land": Modern Critical Interpretations,* 2) and merits a response in this context. In an idiosyncratic but valuable essay that was ignored by the New Critical establishment (the New Zealand imprimatur didn't help), Musgrove was the first to supply a host of possible echoes of Whitman in Eliot; some are quite intriguing, some are in need of space suits. Seeing Eliot's relation to Whitman as a series of oppositions, Musgrove wrote: "Time against eternity; present life against omnipresent death; the offered hand against the avoided face; the humanist against the theologian; these are the contests in which the elder and the younger American are ranged in hostility" (Sydney Musgrove, *T. S. Eliot and Walt Whitman,* 80). This is to take too black-and-white a view: Eliot and Whitman are not "ranged in hostility," a phrase that would be more at home in military history. As a poet, Eliot was less a theologian than a quester; capable of being in uncertainties, he shared, with Whitman, Keats's "negative capability." When his friend and confidant P. E. More inquired if his conversion to Anglo-Catholicism would change his poetry, Eliot reportedly exclaimed: "No; in that I am absolutely unconverted!" (P. E. More, review of *Selected Essays,* 28). Even in *Four Quartets,* Eliot's faith is exploratory, and (as I shall continue to argue in this book) relies very much on an American experience of the frontier in order to do that exploring.

Decay with imprecision, will not stay in place,
Will not stay still.

(BN 149–53)

Eliot, *qua* Eliot, is more condensed than Whitman. He has a more refined dramatic sense. He is a product of very different times. If, in achieving his unique voice and style, Eliot distances himself from the styles of other masters, then I cannot see the point of calling him any man's secondary.

In reading Whitman, Eliot could not share Whitman's faith in the imagination as a vehicle for social reform; he rejected as well Whitman's imperialistic vision of the United States.[35] Not believing in American "prophets en masse," he held the simple separate person in lower esteem, and he frowned on the supposed equality of body and soul. But these differences were themselves contingent upon a more fundamental rapport created by the American phenomena that link the two writers, such as the meanings, rhythms, and sounds that the United States brings to the English language, the protean quality of American cities, the plant and animal life of the New World, the vast geography of the country and its shorelines, the view of Europe from America (and vice versa), an understanding of the nation's origins and an attachment to its myths and history (especially the Civil War), and a preoccupation with such realities as individualism and the frontier.

What seems very important, but has been generally overlooked, is that Eliot's intense dialogue with Poe, Whitman, and other American writers helped him forge his ironic and ventriloquizing style. Of course, there were other impetuses than local ones for the early Eliot, such as the discovery of Laforgue, but Eliot's consciousness of literary history in particular is avant-garde and American: the social upheavals that confronted his family and university, together with the sharp acceleration of urban life and the moral bankruptcy of American nationalism, enabled Eliot to realize that a nineteenth-century sensibility would no longer suffice for a modern poetic.

35. For Eliot's deflating view of U.S. imperialism and "Yankee wardogs," see "The Fall of Admiral Barry" (*LTSE*, 587). Though Mrs. Eliot doesn't identify the author of "The Fall of Admiral Barry" in her edition of her husband's letters, Donald Gallup, who did the research on the ballad for Mrs. Eliot, finds "justification for saying that the verses are Eliot's" (Donald Gallup, conversation with author, September 15, 1993). Marie Borroff has since pointed out to me that Eliot's chief source was Tennyson's "The Revenge," a work in Tennyson's laureate vein, which Eliot apparently parodied for the amusement of his fellow Yankee, Pound.

It was thus through his Americanness that Eliot arrived in England ready to debate the Georgian literary establishment. Though one cannot and should not reduce Eliot's poems to acts of dialogue with other poets, Eliot's acutely self-conscious lyricism shows his keen awareness of American voices that, in intruding upon the act of writing, challenged his critical appraisal of his "ancestry," and problematized his more guarded moments of self-definition.

2 | **Prufrock's Guilty Pleasures**

ELIOT DESCENDED FROM THE original Puritan settlers of the Massachusetts Bay Colony, who believed that the Bible alone held the means of organizing a successful polity.[1] His mother's ancestor Isaac Stearns arrived from England in 1630 and helped found the city of Salem. Eliot's first patrilineal ancestor in New England, Andrew Eliot, emigrated from East Coker, Somerset, to the Bay Colony in about 1667. A "cordwainer" or shoemaker by profession, Andrew was several times chosen selectman of Salem and finally became town clerk. In 1692, he sat in judgment of the Salem witches; later in life he is said to have suffered great agony over his part in the hangings.[2]

As a member of the Bay Colony, Andrew Eliot hewed to an idea that was the foundation both of church government and of social unity, namely, the public covenant between God and his people.[3] Distinct from the covenant of grace, which signaled a private compact between God and the sainted individual, the public covenant established the Bay Colony's relations with Jehovah on the basis of its pledge to build a city of God: if the colonists sank into the mire of worldliness and corruption, the covenant would be revoked. Formally outlined by John Winthrop in 1630, in his lay sermon "A Modell of

---

1. Not that their leaders were narrow in their learning: they brought to New England a rich tradition, in theology, psychology, logic, and rhetoric, which, according to Perry Miller, "incorporated the learning of Humanism and the erudition of Renaissance Protestantism" (Perry Miller, *The New England Mind: From Colony to Province*, 14).

2. My source is Matthiessen, *Achievement*, xix.

3. Miller, *New England Mind*, 21–22.

Christian Charity," the covenant represented a unique "bond of marriage" between God and New England, and it engendered responsibilities that fell heavily on every individual, rich and poor alike. It especially succeeded in ensuring dedication to communal decisions, such as declarations of war.

The public covenant inspired the invention of an American sermonical form, which Perry Miller called "the jeremiad," and which he described as having crystallized in a series of sermons delivered by second- and third-generation New England Puritans. In weighing the connotations of Samuel Danforth's "Errand into the Wilderness," Miller perceived in Danforth's words a sundering of the colonists from their original mission, and of their rhetoric from their emerging history. According to Miller, Danforth's 1670 sermon functioned as a ritual admission of guilt and loss of moral purpose during a mercantile "process of Americanization."[4] The term "jeremiad" referred to the clergy's formulaic tongue-lashings of their flock, whose members were endangering the covenant by developing a commercial society.

In *The American Jeremiad*, Sacvan Bercovitch acknowledged the permanence of Miller's work but argued that Miller had failed to recognize how the preachers adopted the jeremiad—as America expanded in unlooked-for ways—in the service of reinforcing community. Bercovitch defined the American jeremiad as "a ritual designed to join social criticism to spiritual renewal, public to private identity, the shifting 'signs of the times' to certain traditional metaphors, themes, and symbols."[5] Where Miller regarded the jeremiad in terms of the heavy sense of dereliction that haunted the children and grandchildren of the visionary first settlers, Bercovitch saw an effort to recoup a feeling of collective identity and purpose. I will be building on Bercovitch's thesis that, from Danforth on, the call to unite private and public identities on behalf of an American ideal is a key element of the American Puritan sermonical tradition. Yet, with an eye toward the later Eliot, I want to preserve the integrity and personal significance of the covenant of grace, which exists apart from structural effects that Bercovitch isolates.

One is struck by the number of ministers that descend from Andrew Eliot: a later Andrew Eliot, Congregationalist pastor at Boston's New North

4. Perry Miller, *Errand into the Wilderness*, 8–9.
5. Sacvan Bercovitch, *The American Jeremiad*, xi.

Church during the revolutionary period and T. S. Eliot's great-great-great-grandfather; the poet's grandfather, William Greenleaf Eliot, who moved west in 1834 to establish a Unitarian church in St. Louis; his uncle, Thomas Lamb Eliot, who founded the Unitarian ministry in Portland, Oregon; his first cousin, Thomas Lamb Eliot Jr.; and another first cousin, Frederick May Eliot, who attended Harvard with T. S. Eliot and became the premier American Unitarian spokesman of the twentieth century. With similar ties on her side of the family, Charlotte Champe Stearns Eliot, the poet's mother, extended this clerical heritage in her poetry and in a biography of her father-in-law, *William Greenleaf Eliot,* which is dedicated to her children, "lest they forget." If Margaret Fuller never saw much in William Eliot, Emerson, visiting St. Louis in the 1840s, praised his sermons.[6] T. S. Eliot's own remarks about his grandfather are often quoted, but they will bear repetition:

> I never knew my grandfather: he died a year before my birth. But I was brought up to be very much aware of him: so much so, that as a child I thought of him as still the head of the family—a ruler for whom *in absentia* my grandmother stood as vicegerent. The standard of conduct was that which my grandfather had set; our moral judgments, our decisions between duty and self-indulgence, were taken as if, like Moses, he had brought down the tables of the Law, any deviation from which would be sinful. Not the least of these laws . . . was the law of Public Service. . . . (*TCTC*, 44)

Echoing the typological language of American Puritan chroniclers like William Bradford and Cotton Mather, Eliot describes his grandfather as a Moses bringing the Law of God to the wilderness—and St. Louis practically was the wilderness in 1834. A tinge of irony does not belie the speaker's seriousness; rather, it reflects his complex sense of history. For T. S. Eliot, William Eliot personified the Puritan errand, an errand that had achieved very mixed results.

T. S. Eliot entered Harvard College in 1906 at the age of seventeen; he was five years away from "The Love Song of J. Alfred Prufrock." In 1908, he reviewed Van Wyck Brooks's lyrical but penetrating account of a sinking culture, *The Wine of the Puritans.* Brooks had himself attended

---

6. Charlotte Eliot, *William Greenleaf Eliot,* v (in return, T. S. Eliot would dedicate *For Lancelot Andrewes* to her). William Deiss, "William Greenleaf Eliot: The Formative Years (1811–1834)," 15. Ralph Waldo Emerson, *The Letters of Ralph Waldo Emerson,* 4:338.

Harvard, where he and Eliot were on friendly terms, and his book provides a record both of the social shifts that awaited the new generation, and of the consequent debates. For Brooks, the Puritan legacy in the twentieth century was not even in crisis—it was merely superannuated: "The New England idea, adequate for a small province, naturally became inadequate for the expression of a great nation. Adapted as this idea was to the needs of a frugal, intellectual people whose development was strictly intensive rather than extensive, it was unable to meet the needs of great prosperity, imperialism and cosmopolitanism."[7] The young Brooks—prior to his nervous breakdown and ensuing change of values—regarded old New England with the poise of an anthropologist. Identifying with Brooks's cultural assessment, Eliot remarked:

> This is a book which probably will chiefly interest one class of Americans (a class, however, of some importance): the Americans retained to their native country by business relations or socialities or by a sense of duty—the last reason implying a real sacrifice—while their hearts are always in Europe. To these, double-dealers with themselves, people of divided allegiance except in times of emotional crisis, Mr. Brooks' treatise will come as a definition of their discontent. But he should find a larger audience than this class alone. The reasons for the failure of American life (at present)—social, political, in education and in art, are surgically exposed; with an unusual acuteness of distinction and refinement of taste; and the more sensitive of us may find ourselves shivering under the operation. For the book is a confession of national weaknesses; if one take it rightly, a wholesome revelation.[8]

The review mingles two types of expression, an elegant aestheticism characterized by the words "unusual distinction and refinement of taste," and a Calvinistic concern with atonement and sanctification that underlies such metaphors as "surgically exposed," "shivering under the operation," and the homiletic "wholesome revelation." In the first register, Eliot wears the connoisseur's sensibility that became one major response of patrician sons to their political disenfranchisement; in the second register, that of the

7. See Eliot's letter to Brooks (August 9, 1920), in *LTSE*, 397. Van Wyck Brooks, *The Wine of the Puritans*, 5.
8. Eliot, review of *The Wine of the Puritans*, 80; quoted in Eric Sigg, *The American T. S. Eliot: A Study of the Early Writings*, 149.

American Puritan sermonical tradition, he activates the pastoral conscience that undergirded his family's power and importance in the eighteenth and nineteenth centuries. Like a Puritan preacher, Eliot admonishes his own people: his stinging remark about education aims at Harvard University and its president, Charles William Eliot, his third cousin twice removed and yet another descendent of the original Andrew.[9] Especially significant for the author of "Prufrock," however, is the review's dramatic sense of "divided allegiance," between "duty," on one side of the Atlantic Ocean, and Europe, with its associations of poetry and art, on the other.

My purpose in this chapter is to connect "The Love Song of J. Alfred Prufrock" to the tradition surveyed by Miller and Bercovitch, a tradition that endured for centuries in the homes of clergymen, and that furnishes a common bond between Eliot and Emerson. It might seem more appropriate to link Eliot to English preachers: one thinks of his interest in Donne, Hugh Latimer, and Lancelot Andrewes. Here, however, as is very often the case with Eliot, American subtexts accompany English topics. In a 1919 review, he drew attention to the sermon as "a form of literary art," and by way of Donne pondered the supreme difficulties posed by the sermon for the artistic ego;[10] the same year, he asked his mother for sermons by Andrew Eliot and Theodore Parker (*LTSE*, 274). Though satirical, "Mr. Eliot's Sunday Morning Service," written in 1918, reveals a concern with sermonizing, while the ambiguity of "Mr. Eliot" suggests an encounter with ancestral preachers.[11] And with "Gerontion" and *The Waste Land*, published in 1920 and 1922, respectively, Eliot turned visibly to his roots in the sermon: the theme of errand, the jeremiad, the Augustinian covenant of grace.[12]

In "Prufrock" he rebels against the family pulpit. I will discuss how Eliot confronts his clerical inheritance, both through his irreverent use of sermonical language in the poem, and through a *bellum intestinum* that

9. For T. S. Eliot's critique of the educational policies and liberal reforms of Charles William Eliot, see Herbert Howarth's invaluable *Notes on Some Figures behind T. S. Eliot*, 86–89.

10. T. S. Eliot, "The Preacher as Artist."

11. I am indebted to Sigg, *American T. S. Eliot*, 252 n.

12. Miller described *The Waste Land* as "pos[ing] all the religious questions anew . . . in [a] tremendous revival sermon" (Perry Miller, *Nature's Nation*, 282). In a thoughtful article, Robert Abboud distinguishes between the American and the English jeremiad, and defines "Gerontion" and *The Waste Land* as returning "to a more traditional, European-type jeremiad," although Eliot is responding to "a long tradition of American jeremiads" (Robert Abboud, "Jeremiah's Mad Again").

marks his coming of age as a poet: his resistance to the sermonical writings of his mother. For whatever reasons—canonical tastes, international biases, or perhaps old-fashioned snobbery—modernist critics have tended to ignore Charlotte Eliot. As if to compensate for this critical neglect, several of T. S. Eliot's biographers have claimed a literary significance for the Eliots' remarkable mother-son relationship.[13] Well-educated by nineteenth-century standards, devoutly Unitarian, liberally Republican, and a versifier who occasionally verged on poetry, Charlotte Eliot has emerged as a considerable influence on her son's artistic development.

The composition of "Prufrock" dates from 1910, when Eliot was pursuing his master's degree at Harvard. He finished the poem the next year in Europe. Among other themes, a debate between duty and love of European culture, much like the conflict expounded in the review of Brooks, reverberates in the poem's opening lines:

> Let us go then, you and I,
> . . . .
> Let us go, through certain half-deserted streets,
> The muttering retreats
> Of restless nights in one-night cheap hotels
> And sawdust restaurants with oyster-shells:
> Streets that follow like a tedious argument
> Of insidious intent
> To lead you to an overwhelming question . . .
>
>   ("Prufrock" 1, 4–10)

This opening invites comparison with a work by Charlotte Eliot, a poem in three sections totaling almost two hundred lines, called "The Wednesday Club." Her son was about twelve when Charlotte wrote "The Wednesday Club," and its progressivist message resembles that of his Smith Academy graduation poem, written when he was sixteen.[14] I have no proof that T. S. Eliot knew the poem, but it is likely that Charlotte would have shown this

---

13. See Ackroyd, *T. S. Eliot*, 19–20; Lyndall Gordon, *Eliot's Early Years*, 4–6; and Herbert Howarth, *Notes*, 22–35, and "Charlotte Champe Stearns Eliot."

14. The graduation poem is untitled. In the thirteenth section Eliot apostrophizes Smith Academy: "And let thy motto be, proud and serene, / Still as the years pass by, the word 'Progress!' " ("[At Graduation 1905]," *PWEY*, 17). The poem, which begins with a conceit of "colonists embarking," represents the late-Puritan heritage and progressivist ethos that Eliot would soon resist.

ambitious work to her son, whom she treated as an intellectual peer, and whose literary inclinations were obvious to the family from an early age. The Wednesday Club was a women's organization and an instrument of reform:

> Though culture may be our corner stone,
> We cannot exist for culture alone
> In scholarly retreat.
>
> For lo! grave problems press.
> The pleadings of distress
> Will follow the mind's sublimest flight,
> A voice from the depths disturb the height,
> When wrongs demand redress.
> The Wednesday Club in its action leads,
> Crowning progressive thought with deeds,
> It works for righteousness.[15]

Charlotte Eliot beats the drum of "progressive thought": the enemy in her poem is "retreat," the antithesis of progress. For T. S. Eliot in 1910, his mother's progressivism runs counter to poetry and contrary to wisdom and truth. The "muttering retreats" that allure him connote a domain of poetic intensity, an embrace of "culture alone" where culture is high and European. I associate "retreats" with poetry because the urban setting of "Prufrock" evokes Eliot's study of French models. As he would recall: "I think that from Baudelaire I learned first . . . the poetical possibilities . . . of the more sordid aspects of the modern metropolis, of the possibility of fusion between the sordidly realistic and the phantasmagoric. . . . I learned that the sort of material that I had, . . . in an industrial city in America, could be material for poetry" (*TCTC*, 126). In assimilating the urbanism of Baudelaire and Laforgue, Eliot developed a European style and abandoned his mother's American social consciousness. "The Love Song of J. Alfred Prufrock" records his altered social and emotional responses to his native surroundings, as well as an accompanying shift from moral to aesthetic concerns.[16]

---

15. Charlotte Eliot, "The Wednesday Club." Howarth quotes from the poem in *Notes*, 24. Though there is no date on the typescript, the work dates itself: "The twentieth century dawns . . ."

16. As I've suggested in Chapter 1, Eliot's reading of Poe abetted and complicated this process.

Where in "Prufrock" "streets" "follow [you] like a tedious argument,"
in "The Wednesday Club" "pleadings" of conscience "follow the mind's
sublimest flight." Charlotte's "pleadings" constitute a call for self-sacrifice
that rings throughout the religious, literary, and political writings of late-
Puritan America—a call vigorously seconded by "The Wednesday Club."[17]
Speaking of "we," she assumes that the solitary mind in its "sublimest flight"
will respond to duty's command. By contrast, the fact that Prufrock addresses "you and I" reflects authorial self-division. Like a guilty conscience,
the "argument of insidious intent" has the effect of dividing the speaker, of
separating "us" into "you" and "I."

Eliot's description of Laforguian irony as "a *dédoublement* of the personality" is often cited by critics of "Prufrock" to explain the poem's motif
of self-division.[18] In his 1926 Clark Lectures, Eliot made some clarifying
remarks about the French poet in whom he recognized "a temperament
akin to" his own (*TCTC*, 126): "For Laforgue, life was *consciously* divided
into thought and feeling. . . . They did not fit. Hence the metaphysicality of
Laforgue reaches in two directions: the intellectualising of the feeling and
the emotionalising of the idea. Where they meet, they come into conflict,
and Laforgue's irony, an irony always employed against himself, ensues"
(*VMP*, 212–13, Eliot's emphasis). Like Laforgue, the Eliot of "Prufrock"
encountered a resounding clash between his thought and his feeling. The
failure of inherited systems of thought, especially in the areas of morality
and religion, to arouse the required emotions in him, compounded the
lack of accommodation in those inherited systems for the emotions and
feelings that he did experience, no doubt intensely. The result was Eliot's
early interest in Laforguian *dédoublement*. Self-division became his subject.

17. "These are the days when women must be wise / And crown their effort with self-
sacrifice" (Charlotte Eliot, "The Wednesday Club").

18. T. S. Eliot, "A Commentary" (April 1933), 469. I would question the interpretation
of *dédoublement* given by the learned Eliot scholar, A. D. Moody, insofar as he suggests
that Prufrock succumbs to, while Eliot overcomes, this psychic split: "By a *dédoublement*
of personality . . . the poet assumes a double presence, being at once the actor and the
consciousness of his action. Moreover, as his consciousness develops in the poem, it alters
from detached observer to an active, directing will. Thus he does not yield to his fate, as
Prufrock does, but deliberately orders his feeling according to his vision. This is a love song in
which the love and the poetry become a form of moral life" (A. David Moody, *Thomas Stearns
Eliot, Poet*, 38). Moody finds that Eliot is both the actor, Prufrock, and the consciousness
of his action; as the poet's apperception expresses itself or achieves form, it too becomes an
actor, with the result that, from the author's standpoint, the initial *dédoublement* is healed
by the creative will. I would suggest that, from the opening line to the final moment of
drowning, Eliot's own self-division is the occasion of Prufrock's monologue.

Resuming the comparison of "Prufrock" and "The Wednesday Club,"
I would note that, after the parallels "retreat"/"retreats" and "follow"/
"follow," there is another close likeness between the poems in the words
"leads" and "lead." Where the Wednesday Club "leads" in its "action," the
"argument" of "Prufrock" is said to "lead" to an unspecified "overwhelming question." Though Prufrock's "argument" and his "question" remain
as vague as their setting, a clue for tracking his movement of thought
is provided by the systematically inverse parallels with "The Wednesday
Club." Charlotte Eliot in effect admonishes: "Do not retreat, follow your
conscience, we shall lead together in our action." Prufrock may be said to
mutter: "Let us retreat, a tedious argument will follow automatically, and
it will lead to self-division."

An early Eliot manuscript throws considerable light on "the overwhelming question" and the origins of "The Love Song of J. Alfred Prufrock." It
is an untitled fragment of twenty-two lines beginning "Of those ideas in
his head," which survives on a small sheet of white stationery inserted into
Eliot's Gloucester notebook, between leaf 51, "Morning at the Window,"
and leaf 52, "The Little Passion From 'An Agony in the Garret.'"[19] The
narrator of this curious poem describes the ordeal of a deranged *flâneur*
who hallucinates his way through the streets of an unnamed city. Though
the narrator is skeptical about "those ideas" in the other man's head, he
is implicated in the other's urban wanderings; the two share in the febrile
experience that the poem depicts.

The handwriting of the manuscript is the elongated and spiky "Paris
hand" of 1910–1911 (Eliot changed his handwriting dramatically during
his year abroad),[20] whereas "The Little Passion From 'An Agony in the

19. T. S. Eliot, "The Little Passion From 'An Agony in the Garret'" (*IMH*, 57). In his
masterly edition of Eliot's *Inventions of the March Hare: Poems, 1909–1917*, Christopher
Ricks uses this title for both poems; but as he notes, this second poem (ii) is untitled, "in
pencil on a separate sheet laid in" (*IMH*, 58). He does not date either poem.

After the Berg Collection of the New York Public Library acquired Eliot's early manuscripts from the heir of John Quinn, the New York lawyer and patron of the arts, a curator
transferred the poem into the notebook from a miscellany of twenty-nine "loose leaves." I
infer that the library transferred "Of those ideas in his head" into the notebook because "The
Little Passion from 'An Agony in the Garret'" is a revision of its middle strophes. For the
history of the notebook and the "loose leaves," see Donald Gallup, "The 'Lost' Manuscripts
of T. S. Eliot"; and *IMH*, xi–xviii. I follow Ricks in his reading: "Of those ideas in his head";
Gallup has "Of these ideas. . . ."

20. See Gordon, *Eliot's Early Years*, 43; and John T. Mayer, *T. S. Eliot's Silent Voices*, 41.

Garret,' " like "Morning at the Window" (composed in England in 1914), is drafted in the rounded, more fluid, post-Paris hand. Citing as support the datable handwriting, I want to propose that "Of those ideas in his head" belongs to the early draft material of "The Love Song of J. Alfred Prufrock." It is likely that the parallels between Eliot's and his mother's uses of "retreat," "follow," and "lead" first occurred here: the words are closely arranged and, with one repetition, in the same order as in "The Wednesday Club" and "The Love Song of J. Alfred Prufrock." Yet my main interest in this draft stems from a point of difference: in it the city wanderings lead to an "inevitable cross / Whereon our souls are spread, and bleed" (*IMH,* 57), and not an "overwhelming question." I interpret this "cross" as evidence that, consciously or unconsciously, Eliot in "Prufrock" was responding to his mother's argument for self-sacrifice, an argument for surrendering one's private desires on behalf of a great Christian ideal. Of course, an argument for self-sacrifice need not be understood in terms of crucifixion, but, like his mother, Eliot makes prominent use of the sacrificial themes of crucifixion and martyrdom in his writing.

The "overwhelming question" belongs to a work that is everywhere porous to ambiguity. Arising twice (lines 10 and 93), it accrues an aura of sublime mystery, despite Prufrock's inconsequence. Comparison of the poem with "Of those ideas in his head" and "The Wednesday Club" tells us something of what Eliot meant by his "question," however, and thus gives entry to the American background of the poem. Whatever its larger import, the "overwhelming question" subsumes a crisis of conscience and identity. It may be said to signify the pivotal debate on which the poem's opening hinges. When he wrote "Prufrock," the poet T. S. Eliot, in some sense the Prufrockian "I," registered his resistance to the sacrifice of European poetry and culture on which his identity as an American Eliot, conversely the Prufrockian "you," was contingent. Put another way, he turned his back on a family obligation, voiced by "The Wednesday Club," to unite his private and public identities.

A prophetic sense of American history, a national mission, imbues American Puritanism. Clergymen's households have been especially receptive to this missionary heritage and, as I have been arguing, T. S. Eliot's family was no exception. Rebelling against his heritage, Eliot takes wry aim at all things churchly in "The Love Song of J. Alfred Prufrock." The allusion to

John the Baptist, set within a sequence of comic rhymes, illustrates the poet's irreverent approach to this category of symbols and idioms:

> Should I, after tea and cakes and ices,
> Have the strength to force the moment to its crisis?
> But though I have wept and fasted, wept and prayed,
> Though I have seen my head (grown slightly bald) brought in upon a
>   platter,
> I am no prophet—and here's no great matter;
> I have seen the moment of my greatness flicker,
> And I have seen the eternal Footman hold my coat, and snicker,
> And in short, I was afraid.
>
> ("Prufrock" 79–86)

Commentators have cited Laforgue's *Salomé,* from the *Moralités légendaires,* as a source for Prufrock's "head . . . brought in upon a platter." In his elaborate portrayal of Salome, Laforgue burlesques the femme fatale of nineteenth-century European painting and literature, including other depictions of Salome herself.[21] Iaokanann, an updated John the Baptist, takes her virginity and must pay with his head. Besides the traditional motif of decapitation, Eliot seems to have adopted Laforgue's idea of a modernized treatment of the biblical tale.

The religious and literary culture of New England provides a context for Prufrock's allusion to John the Baptist that has not been considered by critics. According to Bercovitch, the "figural use of John the Baptist is a characteristic of the New England pulpit, and part of the Puritan legacy to American rhetoric." Bercovitch cites Danforth, Thomas Hooker, Edward Johnson, Increase Mather, and Jonathan Edwards as examples of Puritan writers who interpreted John as a typological forerunner of their own mission to prepare the way for Christ in the American wilderness. By the nineteenth century, the figure of John the Baptist prophesying to Americans had become a familiar sight to readers in New England. Nationalized versions of the prophet appeared in the prose of Emerson and Horace Bushnell.[22] Additional research shows that poets William Cullen Bryant, John Greenleaf Whittier, and James Russell Lowell treated John as a symbol

---

21. See Mario Praz, *The Romantic Agony,* 291–303.
22. Bercovitch, *American Jeremiad,* 14 (quote), 11–16.

of either national or Puritan mission in "The Prairies," "The Preacher," and "An Interview with Miles Standish," respectively.

Charlotte Eliot also wrote in this tradition. Among the miscellaneous poems that survive in a scrapbook in Harvard's Eliot Collection is one entitled "God's Kingdom Is at Hand. Repent!" Published in the *Christian Register,* a Unitarian weekly, the poem says a good deal about the clerical ethos of the Eliot family:

> His voice was heard in wild Judaea,—
>   A voice of gladness and lament.
> He cried in accents strong and clear:
>   "God's kingdom is at hand. Repent!"
>
> That voice still echoing remains.
>   We listen, startled and attent;
> We grasp our treasures, count our gains:
>   "God's kingdom is at hand. Repent!"[23]

Charlotte's poem helps confirm the ubiquity of John the Baptist as a symbol of the prophetic and missionary ideals of late-Puritan culture; Eliot's background was such that he would have known this symbol.

From Eliot's perspective the figure of John the Baptist prophesying was very probably a cliché, a tenuous link to Puritan traditions that were becoming part of the dead past. George Santayana, who taught Eliot at Harvard, had enjoyed a sally at the expense of Puritan cultural and literary traditions by having a fictional undergraduate describe Whitman as "the voice of nature crying in the wilderness of convention" (cf. Matt. 3:3).[24] Applying Laforgue's example, Eliot outdid his teacher in the sheer force of his iconoclasm: the *Moralités légendaires* had presented the Baptist in an aspect ripe with expressive possibilities for a disaffected late-Puritan writer circa 1910. In "The Love Song of J. Alfred Prufrock" the prophet no longer prophesies in the American wilderness; instead he is silenced and somewhat comically disfigured. With the image of Prufrock's "head . . .

23. Charlotte Eliot, "God's Kingdom Is at Hand. Repent!" stanzas 1 and 3. The rhyme of "Judaea" and "clear" demonstrates that Charlotte's own accents were "strong and clear" and of New England; young Tom Eliot spoke with a Missouri drawl.

24. George Santayana, *George Santayana's America*, 99; originally published in "Walt Whitman: A Dialogue," in the *Harvard Monthly* of May 1890.

brought in upon a platter," Eliot disrupted a long tradition of American Puritan iconography, and implicitly repudiated a legacy of mission and prophetic calling that survived within his immediate family.

A second element in the passage, which immediately precedes the reference to John the Baptist, elucidates the depth of the poem's engagement with American Puritanism. Prufrock's self-portrait of weeping, prayer, and fasting (line 81) recalls the ritual day of humiliation that Puritan New England had formerly observed in response to social disaster. The Fast Day, the last vestige of the day of humiliation, was not officially abolished in Massachusetts until 1894. A book published in Boston in 1895, W. Love's *The Fast and Thanksgiving Days of New England,* underscores Eliot's connection to the Puritan tradition of fasts by citing the Reverend Andrew Eliot's "A Sermon Preached on the Publick Fast."[25] Like the allusion to John the Baptist, Prufrock's fasting bespeaks an intimate knowledge of the sermonical traditions of New England, and registers the breakdown of those traditions.

Much of the poem's skewed sermonizing is directed by the author at his own heritage. In the following passage, Prufrock's parody of the biblical "Preacher" in Ecclesiastes[26] evokes both a missing narrative of history and its homiletic expression, an attempt to reclaim a sense of "purpose under heaven" (Eccles. 3:1). Freed from history, wholly subjective, time has no end for a man with no mission:

> And indeed there will be time
> For the yellow smoke that slides along the street
> Rubbing its back upon the window-panes;
> There will be time, there will be time
> To prepare a face to meet the faces that you meet;
> There will be time to murder and create,
> And time for all the works and days of hands
> That lift and drop a question on your plate;
> Time for you and time for me,
> And time yet for a hundred indecisions,
> And for a hundred visions and revisions,
> Before the taking of a toast and tea.
>
> ("Prufrock" 23–34)

25. W. DeLoss Love Jr., *The Fast and Thanksgiving Days of New England,* 534.
26. Kenner observes the biblical echo in *Invisible Poet,* 12.

A mock preacher celebrating a Eucharist of "toast and tea,"[27] Prufrock lampoons the biblical idiom with sonorous but empty phrases of murder and creation. Eliot is suggesting that the American Puritan errand, the legacy of theocratic preachers, has failed to find present-day continuators: "all the works and days of hands / That lift and drop a question on your plate" implies a momentous inheritance of others' time and labor that, in the trivial setting of genteel society, can no longer inspire a spirit of self-sacrifice. The situation has its devilish side for the poet, who found his epigraph in Dante's *Inferno*. In the persona of Prufrock, Eliot cannot in good conscience accept the solace of aesthetic pleasure: to escape, self-indulgently, into the subjective time of the poem, the vehicle of his wordplay and imagery, is to insinuate the loss of a redemptive history that it is his duty to fulfill.

A brief comparison with some English poets helps set off Prufrock's connection to New England. It may surely be said that Tennyson admitted guilt, that he felt uneasy about the isolation of the poet from his community and about his absorption in aesthetics, but "all the works of days and hands / That lift and drop a question on your plate" expresses (leaving matters of imagery aside) something distinctly un-Tennysonian: it collapses private into public identity through a ritualized act of ingestion—the figure of the Eucharist persisting in the background. In Tennyson, as is the case with Browning, Arnold, and Swinburne, the poet may laud or criticize his country, but his perspective and England's are not identical. In "The Love Song of J. Alfred Prufrock" (and throughout Eliot's oeuvre), there is a pressure, sermonical in origin, to unify private identity and public history. By inventing a persona, Eliot dramatizes this relation of private and public, and ensures that Prufrock confront the structures of thought and feeling prescribed by the national mission.

A key difference between English and American poetry emerges in the Divinity School Address, where Emerson remarks: "None assayeth the stern ambition to be the Self of the nation, and of nature, but each would be an easy secondary to some Christian scheme, or sectarian connection, or some eminent man" (*Works*, 1:145). On the union of nature and humanity, Coleridge had written, "[Nature] is not only coherent but identical, and one and the same with our own self-consciousness." On the subject of originality,

27. Compare "White flannel ceremonial / With cakes and tea" in "Goldfish (Essence of Summer Magazines)" (*IMH*, 28). Eliot would remark that his parents took part in the monthly Unitarian communion but did not see to it that he did so (T. S. Eliot to William Force Stead, February 2, 1927).

Wordsworth, crowning the eighteenth-century reception of Longinus, had argued, "Every author, as far as he is great and at the same time *original,* has the task of *creating* the taste by which he is to be enjoyed. . . ."[28] Emerson built on Coleridge in extending the union of self and nature to include the nation, and resembled Wordsworth in arguing the greatness and originality of his cause.

Emerson told his audience at Harvard that the self should strive to become the embodiment of a nation where humanity would realize the full potential of nature. He had found a way of reclaiming the old American Puritan sense of duty in terms that were consonant with the age of Wordsworth and Coleridge. The point becomes clearer when we observe the resemblance of Emerson's threefold union to Trinitarianism, with nature as a version of God, the self as Divine Son, and the nation as Holy Spirit. The Harvard address invites this comparison, with Emerson urging his hearers: "Yourself a newborn bard of the Holy Ghost,—cast behind you all conformity, and acquaint men at first hand with Deity" (*Works,* 1:146). The means of contact between self and community, as between prophet and nation, would be spirit.

Though Emerson was in fact ringing the death knell of Puritanism in America, he was also seeking to transform, so as to renew, the spiritual intensity of his Puritan ancestors.[29] Governor Winthrop's vision of a "city upon a hill" survives in the Divinity School Address as a spiritual inheritance. Whether or not we read Emerson as a social progressive, his impulse to unite the self with an idealized America is quite strong. However mechanically, however pathetically, this impulse survives in the Eliot of "Prufrock," and connects him to Emerson and the American Puritan sermonical tradition.

Neither Tennyson nor Browning respond to this kind of social pressure in their uses of the dramatic monologue. To be sure, they are often preoccupied with conflicts between the aesthetic and the ethical; but they perfect their art in better conscience. Eliot, to use a Prufrockian word, "malingers" with

28. Samuel Taylor Coleridge, *Collected Works of Samuel Taylor Coleridge,* 71:260. William Wordsworth, *Wordsworth's Literary Criticism,* 210.

29. Compare the recent Emerson biography, by Robert D. Richardson Jr., who says that Emerson, in an unpublished 1842 lecture, "traced the New England character back to Puritan times, remarking . . . that the religious aspirations of the seventeenth century are 'the most creative energy in our experience'" (Robert D. Richardson Jr., *Emerson: The Mind on Fire,* 385).

the aesthetic. Tennyson gives us song after song in *Maud,* form after form. English history waits patiently before entering at the end of his poem. Prufrock's litany of time is an expression of nervousness that betrays anxiety and guilt about the elision of redemptive history. In large measure, Prufrock is Eliot trying to abandon the mission of his ancestors. His "plate," like the "platter" on which his head appears, was fired in Boston.

In a letter written in 1914 to his cousin Eleanor Hinkley, Eliot returns to the theme of his family's missionary heritage. Scripting various "brilliants" for his cousin's amusement, he describes a "Thanksgiving Day sermon": " 'And what are we, the young men of America, doing to help build the city of God?' . . . (Silence, followed by heavy breathing)" (*LTSE,* 73). The sense of bathos, of an overwhelming task that dwarfs the would-be heroes, recalls the terminal inadequacy of Prufrock. Like the letter to Eleanor Hinkley, "The Love Song of J. Alfred Prufrock" represents Eliot's reaction against a legacy at once too demanding and too futile to be renewed.

When one considers the depth of Eliot's rebellion against his familial inheritance, it is unsurprising that he felt stymied as a poet during the years immediately following "Prufrock": he had little idea how to develop because he had so utterly rejected his history and its resources. After a number of false starts, his career as a poet would resume in a more rigorous and thorough renunciation of New England and America. He would proceed from reaction to reaction.

3 | Sweeney and the Individual Talent

WHEN HE WROTE "COUSIN NANCY" in 1915, Eliot was studying philosophy at Oxford and resisting his family's expectations that he return permanently to Boston. Pound, whom he had met in September 1914, argued that life in America was inimical to literary effort and urged him to stay in Europe and write. "Cousin Nancy" comments on this moment of choice, on which the history of modernism turns with the fine if illusory force of retrospect: the barrenness of New England's hills foreshadows the drought and sterility of *The Waste Land,* and further down the modernist highway one can catch a glimpse of Robert Lowell's *Life Studies.*[1] An important clue to Eliot's intentions in the poem is the cognomen of "Ellicott," which combines the poet's own name with that of Endicott, well known to chroniclers of New England. Readers of Hawthorne will also remember this historic Yankee name, and I would like to begin this chapter by comparing "Cousin Nancy" to Hawthorne's "Endicott and the Red Cross," which was originally published in 1838.[2]

Like "Cousin Nancy," "Endicott and the Red Cross" describes rebellion: all the figures whom Hawthorne sketches are recusants of one sort or another. Along with John Endicott, who tears the Red Cross from a British ensign at the story's end, we meet "an Episcopalian and suspected Catholic" whose neck reposes in the Salem pillory; a royalist whose legs occupy the

1. See Daniel Hoffman, "Poetry," 483.
2. In "American Literature," Eliot would cite the tale as an example of Hawthorne's "genius for titles."

adjacent stocks; "a wanton gospeller" later described by Endicott as "that accursed rhapsodist"; an Anne Hutchinson character with "a cleft stick on her tongue"; a type of Hester Prynne wearing an ingeniously woven "A"; and a sympathetically drawn Roger Williams. There is also the general populace:

> Among the crowd were several, whose punishment would be life-long; some, whose ears had been cropt, like those of puppy-dogs; others, whose cheeks had been branded with the initials of their misdemeanors; one, with his nostrils slit and seared; and another, with a halter about his neck, which he was forbidden ever to take off, or to conceal beneath his garments. Methinks he must have been grievously tempted to affix the other end of the rope to some convenient beam or bough.[3]

Hawthorne notes that if the early Puritans were more obsessed with sin than their present-day descendants, the two generations are, nonetheless, equally "vicious." Having thus intimated the past's relevance, he focuses on the origins of a perversely durable culture of rebellion. The tale concludes dryly: "And forever honored be the name Endicott! We look back through the ages, and recognize in the rending of the Red Cross from New England's banner the first omen of that deliverance which our fathers consummated after the bones of the stern Puritan had lain more than a century in the dust."[4] Endicott's act was ominous, indeed, of more of the same behavior and more of the same dust, though by 1838 the old Congregationalism had faded noiselessly from the streets of Salem, and the purpose or final cause of Endicott's rebellion was grist for Hawthorne's ironic mill.

By way of "Endicott and the Red Cross," the name "Ellicott" implicates Eliot in a conventional pattern of dissent. Nancy is a mock-heroine with enough strength to rile her aunts. Behind the polite satire, there lies Eliot's own dread of Boston, where he would appear rebelliously engaged in "modern" activities, only to suffer artistic inanition. I suspect the end of Meredith's "Lucifer in Starlight" (1883) symbolized this hopeless state for him:[5]

3. Nathaniel Hawthorne, *The Centenary Edition of the Works of Nathaniel Hawthorne,* 9:435.
4. Ibid., 9:441.
5. Grover Smith records the echo of Meredith in his authoritative study of Eliot's sources, *T. S. Eliot's Poetry and Plays,* 32.

> Soaring through wider zones that pricked his scars
> With memory of the old revolt from Awe,
> He reached a middle height, and at the stars,
> Which are the brain of heaven, he looked, and sank.
> Around the ancient track marched, rank on rank,
> The army of unalterable law.[6]

As morning star and evening star, Meredith's Lucifer has become a cog in the cosmic orrery: it is with this very late echo of *Paradise Lost* that Eliot portrayed the spiritual exhaustion of New England. To rebel in earnest, one would have to escape.

Eliot's characterization of Emerson as a "guardian of the faith," a knight of the Boston Brahmins, is an irony that bears on the autobiographical component of "Cousin Nancy." In striking ways, Emerson's life resembles Eliot's. Like Emerson, Eliot came from old New England stock. Emerson was the son of a Unitarian minister; Eliot was the grandson of a Unitarian minister. Both writers were deeply influenced by pious and intelligent women in their family: Emerson by his mother and aunt, Eliot by his mother and grown-up sisters. Both rebelled from a Unitarianism that seemed emotionally desiccating, and found succor in *The Bhagavad-Gita*. As F. O. Matthiessen observed, both "felt a deep kinship with the long buried modes of thought and feeling of the seventeenth century." More recently, Ronald Bush has commented on Eliot's biographical likeness to Emerson and on their spiritual agon. Though I am indebted to Bush's general perception of Emerson's importance in Eliot's development, I question his argument that Eliot's "closest encounter" with Emerson occurred through the medium of the "familiar compound ghost" of D. H. Lawrence.[7] In my view, the encounter was more direct—one may fairly point out that Emerson is called by his own name in two of Eliot's poems, "Cousin Nancy" and "Sweeney Erect."

If Emerson was an uncanny presence for Eliot, Eliot knew that Emerson was himself caught in the machinations of fate. One of the great nonconformists of Western culture, Emerson prophesied his own destiny in his mordant comment about Christ, "churches are not built on his principles, but on his tropes" (*Works*, 1:129). Emerson's principles have

6. George Meredith, *The Poems of George Meredith*, 1:285.
7. Matthiessen, *Achievement*, 8. Ronald Bush, "T. S. Eliot: Singing the Emerson Blues."

been succeeded, says Eliot, by his tropes—the "unalterable law" of Boston. The "glazen shelves" from which Emerson and Arnold keep watch—their names printed on handsome bindings—insinuate that Emerson's eyes, the windows of his vision, have "glazed" over; in the service of Boston society, Emerson, the living intellect that survives in his books and touches his readers, no longer sees face-to-face, but through a glass darkly.[8]

As "Cousin Nancy" would suggest, Emerson had been assimilated into the liberal, late-Puritan mainstream, the milieu of Eliot's social class, well before the turn of the century. Though Eliot did not study Emerson closely until 1917, when he lectured on Emerson's poetry for a University of London extension class, the Concord Sage played a leading role in a family tradition of poetry and liberal theology. Charlotte Eliot drew from Emerson in her poems, and while at the Harvard Divinity School in the 1830s, William Greenleaf Eliot, the poet's grandfather, entered into the early Transcendentalist coterie of Margaret Fuller and William Henry Channing.[9] From Eliot's perspective, the differences between Emerson and William Ellery Channing, whose 1819 sermon on "Unitarian Christianity" gave the classic definition of the Unitarian faith in America, were virtually eclipsed by the historical convergence of these figures in his immediate family culture. It may be said, from the standpoint of intellectual history, that Channing's rationalism and Emerson's skeptical and antirationalist temperament cannot be reconciled; but Eliot's experience shows they were reconciled, or at least mixed together, by late-Puritan society.

This cultural mélange becomes visible in Eliot's introduction to Charlotte Eliot's *Savonarola,* published in 1926. In the context of saying, "a work of historical fiction is much more a document on its own time than on the time portrayed," the son describes the mother's protagonist as "a disciple" of Emerson and W. E. Channing.[10] Understanding *Savonarola* to be a product of his native culture, Eliot reported the facts as he knew them. Emerson had

8. Matthew Arnold's appearance in Eliot's poem may reflect the enthusiastic response given by American Unitarians to *St. Paul and Protestantism;* see John Henry Raleigh, *Matthew Arnold and American Culture,* 54. By 1895 a cult of Arnold, "The Apostle of Culture," flourished among the literary journals of the Northeast, but only a decade later the Arnoldians were regarded as "anachronistic" (ibid., 131–40).

9. Eliot taught Emerson's poetry in a course entitled "Modern English Literature"; see Ronald Schuchard, "T. S. Eliot as an Extension Lecturer," part 2, 294. Deiss, "William Greenleaf Eliot," 14–16.

10. T. S. Eliot, introduction to *Savonarola,* vii, x.

rebelled furiously against the establishment that W. E. Channing helped build, only to find himself in Channing's bosom company a generation later.

Two years after he wrote "Cousin Nancy," Eliot composed "Eeldrop and Appleplex," a short dialogue in which he scrutinized the fate of individualism:

> "But at least," said Appleplex, "we are . . ."
> "Individualists. No!! nor anti-intellectualists. These also are labels. The 'individualist' is a member of a mob as fully as any other man: and the mob of individualists is the most unpleasing, because it has the least character."[11]

No doubt America was on Eliot's mind. The American phenomenon of "individualism" was first described as a democratic and leveling mode of self-withdrawal by Tocqueville (who coined the term in French) during the years of the Jackson administration. Emerson elevated individualism into self-reliance and radical social consciousness, but was soon assimilated both by late-Puritan liberal theology and by the champions of free enterprise, despite pockets of intellectual resistance. In *America's Coming-of-Age* (1915), Van Wyck Brooks held that, lacking the power to influence practical affairs, Emerson had merely lent a spiritual veneer to American materialism. A contemporary apologist for Emerson, David Bromwich locates Emerson's legacy in the avant-garde and contends, "Since Emerson, the project of literary radicalism has never been isolable from an ambition to reform our social arrangements." Bromwich's record of a discontinuous history of avant-garde struggle is moving and intelligent, but it simply misses the gist of Eliot's critique of Emerson by, first, interpreting "Tradition and the Individual Talent" as a manifesto for the individual talent of avant-garde critics (a shrewd but limited reading) and, second, by relegating Eliot's un-Emersonian social perspective to "the Eliotic-Trotskyist sermon against mass culture," that is, to the intellectual legacy of the "Eliotic-Trotskyist group around *Partisan Review*" in the 1930s and 1940s; this is a little too convenient, reductive both of Eliot and of the *Partisan Review*, whose editors, William Phillips and Philip Rahv, according to Harvey Teres, effected an "unprecedented degree of autonomy, tolerance, and rigor" in leftist American literary criticism. If Harold Bloom is right, that "Emerson

---

11. T. S. Eliot, "Eeldrop and Appleplex," part 1, 10–11.

is the mind of our climate,"[12] then we need to be more direct in addressing Eliot's response to Emerson, which offers a close examination of Bromwich's inescapable terms: literature and reform.

My cynosure in this chapter will be Eliot's "Sweeney," a character thought to be based on a Boston Irishman named O'Donnell, who instructed Eliot in the pugilistic arts.[13] The so-called "Sweeney poems" comprise "Mr. Eliot's Sunday Morning Service" and "Sweeney Among the Nightingales," which saw the light of print in September 1918, followed by "Sweeney Erect," which Eliot probably completed by May 1919.[14] In between these dates World War I ended, in November 1918. The three Sweeney poems exhibit a catena of interests, from late-Puritan liberal theology to the fate of the individual to the Americanization of the West. Throughout, Eliot develops a range of moral responses to the modern world: the Sweeney poems are in fact poems with morals.

"Mr. Eliot's Sunday Morning Service" begins with some very heavy language. It was probably Laforgue who suggested this particular effect to Eliot, the use of scientific terms and neologisms as the expression of an intellect out of balance with the emotions. In "The Metaphysical Poets," a 1921 essay, Eliot would devote several paragraphs in defense of such "difficult" poetry, which he explained, with some justification, by reference to a metaphysical conceit (*SE*, 248–49). Glossing the heterogeneous ideas of Eliot's opening stanzas, one might say that the extremely prolific "sutlers," the "bees" who appear later in the poem, have a parallel relation to the Word, which in turn represents the abundant fertilization of τὸ ἓν or the One, the indefinable unity that transcends Being in Neoplatonic cosmology. Aside from completing a wittily turned formal scheme, "Origen" bears a cluster of meanings. The philosopher Origen was, like Plotinus, a student of Ammonius Saccas of Alexandria, considered by many to be the founder of Neoplatonism. As an exegete, Origen is renowned for his enormous output of written works—some six thousand books and endless biblical

12. On the Jacksonian ideology of individualism and the Emersonian legacy of liberal dissent, see Sacvan Bercovitch, *The Rites of Assent: Transformations in the Symbolic Construction of America*, 307–52. David Bromwich, *A Choice of Inheritance: Self and Community from Edmund Burke to Robert Frost*, 152, 157. Harvey Teres, "Remaking Marxist Criticism: *Partisan Review*'s Eliotic Leftism, 1934–1936," 69. Bloom, *Poetics*, 309.

13. See Conrad Aiken, "King Bolo and Others," 21.

14. For the critical history of the Sweeney poems, see Nigel Alderman, " 'Where Are the Eagles and the Trumpets?' The Strange Case of Eliot's Missing Quatrains."

commentaries. In the third century it was his patristic achievement to fuse Christian theology and Neoplatonism. In particular, he connected the Greek Logos to the promised Messiah of Jewish prophetic writings.

Eliot may have had the Neoplatonism of Emerson in mind when he wrote "Mr. Eliot's Sunday Morning Service," for Origen is a type of "the Word," much like the Emersonian poet.[15] At "the mensual turn of time," he devised his syncretic philosophy and effected a logorrheic act of creation: by repeating the line, "In the beginning was the Word," Eliot stresses Origen's role as a type of Logos. A pun on "Origen" arguably points to Emerson's famous query: "Why should not we also enjoy an original relation to the universe?" (*Works*, 1:3). This suggestion may sound far-fetched, but Origen's actual failure to be an origin or Logos is a provoking aspect of the poem. The adjective "enervate" alludes to a youthful error by the theologian, the result of an overly literal reading of Matthew 19:12: "There be eunuchs, which have made themselves eunuchs for the kingdom of God's sake." Self-castrated in his zeal for the kingdom of God, Origen would ironically suggest that "an original relation," an existence outside the fallen realm of bodily generation, is beyond the reach of theologians. The poem would thus imply an unbridgeable divide between the human and the divine, a divide that Emerson could not accept.

A quattrocento rendering of the Trinity offers a sharp contrast to Origen's Neoplatonic cosmology, as Eliot's Umbrian painting replaces τὸ ἕν with the Father, and the Word with the Baptized God (the "sapient sutlers of the Lord" give way to the Paraclete). Freed from the wordiness of Origen, Emerson, and "Mr. Eliot" himself, the anonymous Umbrian painter brings forth water from the rock.[16] The "water pale and thin," the entire design and finish of the wall painting, testify to a miracle, not of religion, but of art.[17]

15. Emerson writes: "What a little of all we know is said! What drops of all the sea of our science are baled up! and by what accident it is that these are exposed, when so many secrets sleep in nature! Hence the necessity of speech and song; hence these throbs and heart-beatings in the orator, at the door of the assembly, to the end namely that thought may be ejaculated as Logos, or Word" (*Works*, 3:40).

16. In 1917, Eliot jotted down his impressions of Emerson for his mother: "I am busy reading Emerson. He strikes me as very wordy. He has something to say often, but he spreads it out and uses very general terms; it seems more oratory than literature" (*LTSE*, 196). The preference for compactness and exactitude of presentation is typical of Eliot.

17. Remarkably, Eliot places art on equal ground with religion in his 1917 review of William Temple's *Mens Creatrix*. ("*Mens*" may be translated as "mind" or "intellect," and it

After this formal ecphrasis, the poet turns his attention to a church scene. Eliot had repeatedly expressed his distaste for Puritan sexual mores in his writings of this period (a review of Amy Lowell furnishing one such opportunity),[18] and it may be remarked that both "enervate Origen" and the poem's churchgoers betray the folly of unmitigated sexual repression:

> The sable presbyters approach
> The avenue of penitence;
> The young are red and pustular
> Clutching piaculative pence.
> ("Mr. Eliot's" 17–20)

Outside the church, "the bees / With hairy bellies" go about their business of "staminate and pistillate," blissfully exempt from the physical and intellectual symptoms of Puritan sexuality, though the poet indulges in some mock censorship by referring to the "Blest office of the epicene," as though the bees, those "sapient sutlers," were doing their sex-denying part for the kingdom of heaven.

At the end of the poem we suffer a last emanation downward, and Sweeney appears:

> Sweeney shifts from ham to ham
> Stirring the water in his bath.
> The masters of the subtle schools
> Are controversial, polymath.
> ("Mr. Eliot's" 25–28)

---

provides a clue for deciphering Eliot's neologism, "mensual.") The review tactfully demurs from Temple's Anglican polemic: "To agree with the author we must not only concede that 'Intellect and Imagination . . . would reach their culmination in the apprehension and contemplation of the supreme principle of the universe adequately embodied and incarnate,' but that this culmination is found in Christianity. And might it not be maintained that religion, however poor our lives would be without it, is only one form of satisfaction among others, rather than the culminating satisfaction of all satisfactions?" (T. S. Eliot, review of *Mens Creatrix*, 542–43). Surely by "other forms of satisfaction" Eliot is referring to art, philosophy, and other humanistic pursuits.

18. Eliot writes: "And I observe that although Puritanism is 'virulent poison' [he is quoting Amy Lowell's *Tendencies in Modern Poetry*], Miss Lowell exclaims: 'How many excellent books of the past age are neglected because of this overinsistence on sex! . . . The plays of Congreve would be as well known as those of Sheridan were it not for this. It is slow suicide for an author to commit this blunder'" (T. S. Eliot, "Disjecta Membra," 55). Eliot abstains from further comment.

"The masters of the subtle schools" are no more able to resolve meta-physical questions than Sweeney. Eliot's point is not one of simple anti-intellectualism; more accurately, he is a witty renegade aiming his "sermon" at the intellectual pulpits of St. Louis and Boston. His moral is that human knowledge can never escape the fallen state of the body; Eliot thus repudiates the Pelagianism and optimistic rationalism that W. E. Channing preached in such sermons as "Likeness to God."[19] The physical world (which includes Sweeney himself, pictured literally displacing water), nature, the "gesso ground" of the painting, the poet's dense, punning language (which is conspicuously a flawed language, a perversion of the Word), and Origen, stand irremediably juxtaposed to the divine, which is symbolized by the purely mental sphere of τὸ ἕν. The facts of the human body's physical condition, reflected in the imperfect nature of language itself, contest the divinization of the human word that characterizes Emerson in "The Poet."

Eliot's concern with fallibility signals a transition from aesthetics to ethics that occurs in "Mr. Eliot's Sunday Morning Service" and all the Sweeney poems. His belief that language and religion are in practice bound to the natural world, which is itself axiologically neutral, issues from a moral critique of Emerson and American Unitarianism. "All first-rate poetry is occupied with morality," declared Eliot in 1921, a statement in which Pound, who was beginning his Paris phase, saw Eliot coveting "the mantle of Matthew Arnold."[20] There is some justice in Pound's droll snobbery; but it is fair to say that, on the all-important subject of good and evil, Eliot was responding to his American forerunners.

In the spring of 1919, Eliot applauded an essay by an American professor, John Erskine, who had written:

19. Another possible target of Eliot's satire is the Reverend Theodore Parker, a nineteenth-century Unitarian turned Transcendentalist, who held to a doctrine of unmediated communion with an Absolute Being and believed that such communion would lead to the correction of social wrongs. Eliot requested Parker's sermons in a 1919 letter to his mother (*LTSE*, 274).

20. T. S. Eliot, "The Lesson of Baudelaire," 4. Eliot circa *The Sacred Wood* (1920) is sometimes perceived as focusing on poetry to the exclusion of large moral questions. This brief essay effectively nullifies such a view (as should a close reading of *The Sacred Wood*)—despite the fact that Eliot's own "Preface to the 1928 Edition" of *The Sacred Wood* would tend to support it. Pound begins "Historical Survey," a 1921 *Little Review* piece, with an epigraph: "The mantle of Matthew Arnold has descended." He then refers to Eliot as the "Dean of English criticism" (Ezra Pound, "Historical Survey," 39).

[Hawthorne] was no mystic. . . . He was a philosophical experimenter, in whose method was no room for optimism or for prepossessions of any kind. . . . He was really the questioner, the detached observer, that other Transcendentalists thought they were. . . .

If to be . . . interested in the soul is to be a psychologist, then Hawthorne was one. . . . But if the term denotes attention to motives and to fine mental processes, to the anatomy . . . of the character, then Hawthorne was no such psychologist as, let us say, Henry James. He studied no subtle character, nor any character subtly. He was a moralist rather than a psychologist.

This drew the following comment from Eliot:

Neither Emerson nor any of the others [i.e. other Transcendentalists] was a real observer of the moral life. Hawthorne was, and was a realist. He had, also, what no one else in Boston had—the firmness, the true coldness, the hard coldness of the genuine artist. In consequence, the observation of the moral life in *The Scarlet Letter,* in *The House of the Seven Gables,* and even in some of the tales and sketches, has solidity, has permanence, the permanence of art. It will always be of use; the essays of Emerson are already an encumbrance.[21]

Reacting against a deficient moral perspective in Emerson, Eliot lauds Hawthorne's dispassionate power to judge good from evil.[22] He asserts that "the moral life" can be studied objectively, apart from what Erskine calls "prepossessions." Although the review suffers from its authoritarian tone, the critic who abstracts Eliot's response to Emerson from the sphere of ethics is likely to miss the point. The real gravamen of Eliot's case against Emerson lies in Eliot's moral criticism. Emerson's essays were "an encumbrance" because their subjective morality was not adoptable beyond Emerson's local interests.

While engaged in writing "Mr. Eliot's Sunday Morning Service" and "Sweeney Among the Nightingales," Eliot published a review of Edward Fawcett's *The World as Imagination,* a work of idealistic philosophy. Though

21. Eliot, "American Literature," 237.

22. Cf.: "Baudelaire was aware of what most mattered: the problem of good and evil. What gives French seventeenth-century literature its solidity is the fact that it had Morals, that it had a coherent point of view" (Eliot, "Lesson of Baudelaire," 4). For Eliot's relation to Hawthorne, see Ronald Bush, "Nathaniel Hawthorne and T. S. Eliot's American Connection."

the notice was generally favorable, Eliot seized on an Emersonian ingredient in Fawcett's work and criticized it:

> [Fawcett's] absolutist tendency is most apparent in connection with the problem of evil. Evils are real; and some space is devoted to a protest against explaining them away. But evil belongs only to the time-process; "there can be no evil in the cosmic imagination considered apart from the creative episodes." Evil is born with a "change," aptly described as the "Fall." "The victimiser and the victims are the same reality . . . this is tremendous truth." Tremendous, but yet a household word. It is our old acquaintance, the Red Slayer, *la plaie et le couteau!*[23]

One wonders how literally the word "household" should be taken, for Eliot's was a very literary, very Emersonian childhood. Citing "Brahma" and Baudelaire's allusion to "Brahma" in "L'Héautontimorouménos," he girds at Emerson's doctrine of compensation. I infer that the carnage in Europe inspired his scorn for the idea that the slayer and the slain are "the same reality." By exposing the stubbornness of evil as a fact that resists moral algebra, the contest with Germany provided grounds for Emerson's demotion.

Nonetheless, the Emersonian in Eliot could not wholly be checked. In an early manuscript from *The Waste Land* drafts, Eliot sounds the very note for which he chides Fawcett:

> I am the Resurrection and the Life
> I am the things that stay, and those that flow.
> I am the husband and the wife
> And the victim and the sacrificial knife
> I am the fire, and the butter also.
>
> (*WLF,* 111)

One may read this pastiche of Emerson, the Gospel of John (11:25), and *The Bhagavad-Gita* as unmitigated irony. But the idealist perspective that I find here is not alien to *The Waste Land,* though Eliot in that poem balances a vast subjectivity with a profound awareness of the physical and psychological limitations of the self, and with a historical imagination that succeeds in conveying a very broad emotional range.

23. T. S. Eliot, review of *The World as Imagination,* 572.

"Sweeney Among the Nightingales" shows Eliot seeking to distinguish the natural world from the literary and religious framework by which we interpret it; by a kind of negative argument or *occultatio,* the poet depicts civilization as a fragile but necessary means of coordinating nature and human nature. Although the plot of the *Agamemnon* informs the vaguely adulterous and murderous drama of Sweeney in the café (the Greek epigraph suggests this connection), Eliot doesn't cite Aeschylus in order to affirm the durability of tradition. Rather, he writes as an artist uncertain about the power of the arts, and hence the culture, to shape and interpret and absorb contemporary events. As he remarked in 1918, "What we want is to disturb and alarm the public: to upset its reliance upon Shakespeare . . . to point out that at any moment the relation of a modern Englishman to Shakespeare may be discovered to be that of a modern Greek to Aeschylus."[24] Thus intending to shock his readers, Eliot experiments with the removal of cultural props, not their application.

In Attic tragedy, an order of civilized rule aims to integrate socially primitive experience by sanctifying the profane in the cultural memory. An important site for this integration of the sacred and the profane is the grove at Colonus, alluded to (a bit too obliquely) by Eliot at the end of his poem:[25]

> The nightingales are singing near
> The Convent of the Sacred Heart,
>
> And sang within the bloody wood
> When Agamemnon cried aloud
> And let their liquid siftings fall
> To stain the stiff dishonoured shroud.
>   ("Nightingales" 35–40)

The grove at Colonus was sacred to the Eumenides or Furies, the wrathful goddesses who were finally placated by Athena, protector of Orestes (Agamemnon's son and avenger), when she promised they would be honored in her land. This act of propitiation by Athens and its tutelary goddess,

24. T. S. Eliot, "Observations," 69.
25. Years after he wrote "Sweeney Among the Nightingales," Eliot explained: "the wood I had in mind was the grove of the furies at Colonus; I called it 'bloody' because of the blood of Agamemnon at Argos" (T. S. Eliot, letter to the editor, 1958).

which established the Areopagus, connects the *Oresteia* to *Oedipus at Colonus.*

Eliot's allusive details evoke Colonus, but his poem doesn't conclude with an act of sanctification, a structured assimilation of the inhuman powers of fate and necessity that Oedipus came to represent in his own person. Such an act would require, at the very least, a readable set of symbols—a metaphoric glass through which to see nature and human nature. Instead of providing such a glass, the poet cancels precisely those literary and religious conventions that would have brought order and meaning to his work. Nature, symbolized by nightingales that should allude to Attic and English poetry, is entirely indifferent to humankind: birds mean birdsong as well as "liquid siftings," the un-Keatsian guano. As the one who "guards the hornèd gate," Sweeney calls into question the custodianship and use of classical culture. The "Convent of the Sacred Heart" sinks neutrally into the background, as if calling into doubt the religious bond between suffering and truth—the basis for Attic and Christian theodicy. "Sweeney Among the Nightingales" was a bomb in the lap of the wartime literati, who alone were trained to comprehend the poet's ironic use of the same allusive framework—classical and romantic—that he pulverizes in keeping with the spirit of the age.

As early as the 1860s, Matthew Arnold was asking: "What influence may help us to prevent the English people from becoming, with the growth of democracy, *Americanised?*" During his London years, Pound defended the potential of American culture, but Eliot was more in line with Arnold. In 1916, reviewing a book of essays by Stephen Leacock, he comments: "[Leacock] sees in the chaos of American life only an advanced stage of a disease which menaces Europe; the philosophy of comfort without ideals, the cheap and easy utilitarianism of popular education and the dead level."[26] Eliot welcomed this low estimate of American life; John Dewey, by contrast, would argue in *The Public and Its Problems* (1927) that democracy entailed high standards of personal conduct. But Eliot shared with Dewey, who himself feared a general disintegration of family, church, and neighborhood, a sense that American democracy was in crisis.

In his 1928 preface to E. A. Mowrer's *This American World,* Eliot revived the metaphor of disease:

26. Matthew Arnold, *Prose Works,* 2:16. T. S. Eliot, "Mr. Leacock Serious," 405.

[Mowrer] inquires into the origin, as well as the nature, of Americanism; traces it back to Europe; and finds that what are supposed to be the specifically American qualities and vices, are merely the European qualities and vices given a new growth in a different soil. Europe, therefore, in accepting American contributions the danger of which Mr. Mowrer certainly does not palliate, has contracted a malady the germs of which were bred in her own system. Americanization, in short, would probably have happened anyway; America itself has merely accelerated the process.

This is an idea which must have occurred to many thoughtful minds. . . . [27]

The passage, notwithstanding its mannered adverbs and mock-pedantic style, clarifies the metaphor of cultural illness that Eliot had used to much effect in his poetry. When he wrote the Sweeney poems, disease was literally a great public concern. Alongside the war, another disaster in contemporary headlines was the Spanish influenza of 1918–1919, the worst epidemic of the century, claiming about twenty million lives. In "Sweeney Among the Nightingales," one may detect references to the plague in the "person in the Spanish cape" and in the line "Death and the Raven drift above"—the shadow of death was hanging over all. A good example of Eliot's "difficult" metaphysical sensibility, the likening of biological to cultural sickness broadens the paradigmatic shift in Eliot's poetry, already underway in "Mr. Eliot's Sunday Morning Service," from a psychological to a physiological understanding of human existence.

Having seconded Arnold's fears about Americanization, Eliot needed to explain his own peculiar position as an American poet-critic and, presumably, a representative of American culture. Thus, one isn't surprised to find him, in his 1917 review of Harriet Monroe's anthology of American poetry, saving a place for American contributions to the arts: "The resultant impression [of the anthology] is a very chaotic world indeed; a world prevailingly Yanqui, but all the more interesting for that." He goes on to layer his position: "One thinks of Henry James asking his way of an Italian mill-hand in the streets of Salem."[28] Appropriately for this period, Eliot shows an enthusiasm for interesting chaos. But if the mill-hand embodies democracy,

27. T. S. Eliot, preface to *This American World*, xi.
28. T. S. Eliot, "Reflections on Contemporary Poetry" (November 1917), 151.

labor, and an ambiguous power of change, the American melting pot clearly threatened traditions that Eliot, as much as James, prized above all others. Unlike James a decade earlier, the Eliot of 1917 did not return to America. It returned to him.

Sweeney, the Irish invader, was Eliot's unreliable envoy in a world of rapid Americanization. While adapting to England, Eliot took up a question asked by "the visionary tourist," James: "Do certain impressions [of America] represent the absolute extinction of old sensibilities, or do they represent only new forms of them?"[29] Whitman had earlier seen America's capacity for renewal of "the old, the perennial elements"; although James's talk of "sensibilities" shows a bias toward high culture, he was very probably aware of Whitman. Eliot's Sweeney poems alternate between Jamesian loyalty to the old order and Whitman's more Emersonian call for heroic renewal. In "Sweeney Among the Nightingales," Eliot contrasted Agamemnon and Sweeney so as to inform whatever audience still possessed "old sensibilities" that their future was in peril; the potential for civilization, barely extant among the overturned props of the cultural stage, gives the poem the intense seriousness that Eliot claimed for it (*LTSE*, 363). After the war, Eliot connected an "absolute extinction of old sensibilities" to his impressions of an Americanized world; written during or close to President Wilson's visit to England in early 1919, when wild crowds greeted Wilson as the hero who would save civilization, "Sweeney Erect" severely but wittily rebukes Europeans and Americans who were optimistic about the days ahead.

The cultural landscape was changing quickly. As part of his response, Eliot devoted a stanza of "Sweeney Erect" to Emerson:

> (The lengthened shadow of a man
>   Is history, said Emerson
> Who had not seen the silhouette
>   Of Sweeney straddled in the sun.)
>   ("Sweeney Erect" 25–28)

The image of "Sweeney straddled in the sun" evokes the *Colossus* of Rhodes, the giant statue of a sea-straddling Apollo built at the entrance of the harbor

29. Jonathan Morse compares Sweeney to the Irishman of Thomas Nast's cartoons, and surveys anti-Irish sentiment in Thoreau and Thoreau's Massachusetts; see Jonathan Morse, "Sweeney, the Sties of the Irish, and *The Waste Land*." Henry James, *The American Scene*, 477; Eliot perused *The American Scene* in 1918 and praised it highly.

at Rhodes, easternmost of the Aegean islands, in about 300 B.C. The poem begins with an Aegean setting, and a reference to the *Colossus* would be well in keeping with Eliot's interplay of historical perspectives.

By putting Sweeney where the *Colossus* had stood, as the symbol of an age, Eliot doesn't dismiss Emerson's "great man" theory of history— more interestingly, he uses it to comment on the dawn of the postwar era.[30] Emerson had written: "An institution is the lengthened shadow of one man; as, Monachism, of the Hermit Anthony; the Reformation, of Luther; Quakerism, of Fox; Methodism, of Wesley; Abolition, of Clarkson. Scipio, Milton called 'the height of Rome'; and all history resolves itself very easily into the biography of a few stout and earnest persons" (*Works*, 2:61). The "silhouette / Of Sweeney straddled in the sun" asks us to consider what "Sweeneyism" might be. And while the hero of "Sweeney Among the Nightingales" was an ambiguous figure, with an air of human mystery about him, in "Sweeney Erect" he is a creature of biology. The poem abounds in sinew and reflex, with Eliot wielding a physiological poetic—morning "stirs" the organism and thereby produces vapor:

> Morning stirs the feet and hands
> (Nausicaa and Polypheme).
> Gesture of orang-outang
> Rises from the sheets in steam.
> ("Sweeney Erect" 9–12)

In the opening stanzas, with their references to "the unstilled Cyclades" and "the perjured sails" of Theseus, the poet rips the mask of civility from a classical world that he commands another to "paint" and "display." The reference to "Nausicaa and Polypheme," to the noble friend and ignoble foe of Odysseus, extends this brutal classicism by letting the monster get the girl. Stripped bare of classical facades, denuded of "the old sensibilities" (or of "perennial elements"), the modern is antithetical to the heroic; the "lengthened shadow" of Sweeney means no history at all.

While "Sweeney Among the Nightingales" is more a warning than a polemic, "Sweeney Erect" advances an argument, in opposition to Emerson,

---

30. James Longenbach makes a kindred observation in his reading of the passage but then proceeds to different interests and emphases. See James Longenbach, "*Ara Vos Prec*: Satire and Suffering," 56.

that civil and spiritual order must come to the individual from outside the self; otherwise, the individual will disappear into the mass of human physiology.[31] Caricaturing what Emerson called "the aboriginal Self, on which a universal reliance may be grounded" (*Works*, 2:63), Eliot says that self-reliance is an insufficient basis for the self's spiritual and social needs. The "house" of the poem is a disorderly house, a brothel, in which the characters follow the meanest terms of Hobbesian self-interest. Sweeney, Mrs. Turner, and the others have no lasting basis for community, and the poem ends accordingly, as Doris brings a quick, physical cure, "sal volatile / And a glass of brandy neat," to quiet down a fellow prostitute, who is hopelessly lacking in English reserve.

Eliot would have agreed with Sacvan Bercovitch, where Bercovitch interprets Emersonian individualism as "a dream vision of laissez-faire." Eliot's critique of Emerson belongs to an American reevaluation, extending in diverse forms from Irving Babbitt, Eliot's teacher at Harvard, who championed "perfecting the individual" on terms different from Emerson's, to H. Richard and Reinhold Niebuhr, who questioned the assumptions behind the dream vision. In part because Eliot wanted to outmaneuver Emerson, to be the true radical, the Sweeney poems are less a plea for tradition, and more a dissolving of what Edmund Burke called "the pleasing illusions . . . which harmonize . . . the different shades of life"; Eliot had in fact compared Burke to the American humanist P. E. More on the basis of their shared "distrust in undisciplined human nature." To Burke's Shakespearian sense of "our naked shivering nature," Eliot adds an American Puritan twist: in a Calvinistic refusal of Emerson's visionary deism, he argues in effect that there is no basis for harmony between selves pursuing their own utopias. The late T. E. Hulme had maintained the metaphorical aptness of original sin for understanding the essential fallibility of human nature; Eliot, who would acknowledge his admiration for Hulme in the *Criterion*,[32] illustrated

31. I owe a debt to Charles Peake, who describes "Sweeney Erect" as "a satire of the Emersonian hero as depicted in 'Self-Reliance,' " and uncovers a number of likely echoes of Emerson in "Sweeney Erect." See Charles Peake, " 'Sweeney Erect' and the Emersonian Hero."

32. Bercovitch, *Rites of Assent*, 312. In *Literature and the American College*, Irving Babbitt distinguished between humanism and humanitarianism, which he viewed, respectively, as a "disciplined and selective sympathy" that aims at "perfecting the individual" and a sentimental program of "universal philanthropy" (8). He wrote, "Emerson's address on the American Scholar is a plea for humanism that shall rest on pure intuition; the only drawback to Emerson's programme is that he assumes genius in his scholar, and genius of a rare kind

the relevance of original sin through Sweeney, but he did so in the heat of a spiritual contest with Emerson. For Eliot, there lurked the Calvinist dogma, living still, behind the philosophical metaphor.

Having commented in several reviews of the period on "the universal sameness of men and women,"[33] Eliot wanted to convey the universal quality of Sweeney, a quality that must also have been present to Greek playwrights and Umbrian painters. In "The Development of Leibniz's Monadism," a 1916 article for the *Monist*, he discussed humankind's "universal sameness" from the standpoint of classical philosophy:

> When [Aristotle] discusses the substance of organic beings [in the *Metaphysics* and the *De anima*] we are apt to think that each individual is a substance—that the form of each body is an individual—one form for Socrates, and another for Callias. It is difficult to avoid this conclusion, but in general, for Aristotle as well as for Plato, whatever was merely individual was perishable and incapable of being a subject of knowledge. But if we say, with Burnet . . . that "Plato found reality, whether intelligible or sensible, in the combination of matter and form and not in either separately," and take the same view of Aristotle, yet we cannot say that they found it in each individual as a world apart. This is an instance of the differences between Leibniz and the Greeks. In Leibniz we find the genesis of a psychological point of view; ideas tend to become particular mental facts, attributes of particular substances. If the form or principle of Aristotle were different in each man, this form would be Leibniz' soul. For the Greek the human was the typically human, individual differences were not of scientific interest; for the modern philosopher individual differences were of absorbing importance. (*KE*, 185–86)

Eliot's focus on Sweeney's physical nature enabled him to bypass the modern concern with psychology that makes each individual a world apart and renders a theory of knowledge about the species impossible to formulate;

---

at that. On the other hand, a humanism so purely traditional as that of Oxford and the English universities has . . . certain obvious weaknesses. Perhaps the chief of these is that it seems to have forgotten real for conventional values . . ." (98). Babbitt's humanism insists on "the discipline of the central standard" (26). For H. Richard Niebuhr, see note 41. Edmund Burke, *Reflections on the Revolution in France*, 171. T. S. Eliot, "An American Critic," 284. Ezra Pound, *Polite Essays*, 14. T. S. Eliot, "A Commentary" (April 1924), 231–32.

33. T. S. Eliot, "Turgenev," 167.

equally important, it enabled him to avoid the "American introspectiveness" for which he rebuked his friend, Conrad Aiken.[34] In the Sweeney poems, Eliot's juxtaposing of historical references relies for its cogency on the classical view that the substance of *Homo sapiens* pertains, as a subject of knowledge, to the species and not the individual. If, as Eliot believed, humanity is fundamentally unchanged over the millennia, we are left to contemplate the conditions that have shaped the human substance into Sweeney: we are left with a critique of conditions.

Readers of Wyndham Lewis's *Tarr* will recognize the fierce energy of Lewis in Eliot's quatrains; Eliot had reviewed *Tarr* in 1918, and eagerly championed it. Like the Lewis of *Tarr*, the Eliot of the Sweeney poems deals roughly with unimproved human nature. The artist Frederick Tarr, reflecting on the cultural situation, tells an English acquaintance in Paris: " 'A breed of mild pervasive cabbages has set up a wide and creeping rot in the West. . . . You are systematizing and vulgarizing the individual.' " The characters in *Tarr* embody a new savagery, for which America is a prominent symbol: "money, luck, and non-personal power, were the genius of the new world. American clothes were adapted for the finer needs of the Western European; cosmopolitan Paris was what America ought to be."[35] Under American influences, the world according to *Tarr* has become an acid mixture of the mechanically and horribly comical, the appetitive, and the beastly.

Eliot's nastiness toward the Irish and the Jews is at home in this shock-aesthetic, which connects the Sweeney poems to several other works in Eliot's American volume of 1920, *Poems*. As I have suggested, Eliot intended to alarm his urbane and learned readership. He didn't set out to inflame opinion against minority groups; his art was too complex a medium for such a purpose. Christopher Ricks's take on Eliot's method, that the "crude state" of the stereotype is " 'placed' by the work of art," the stereotype thus being made available to scrutiny by the disinterested artist, seems to me utterly in keeping with Eliot's use of masks and his theory of artistic impersonality. Like other modernists, Eliot wanted to explode the mimetic and descriptive norms of authorship and subjectivity; because he insisted on critical distance from emotion, one must be especially cautious when

---

34. T. S. Eliot, "Reflections on Contemporary Poetry" (July 1919), 40.
35. T. S. Eliot, "Tarr," 105. Wyndham Lewis, *Tarr*, 25–26, 85.

reading his poetry as the witness of his personal life. Eliot at this time was insensitive to Jews—passages of Eliot's *Poems* do indeed, as Anthony Julius points out, "exploit anti-Semitism for its effects"[36]—but such insensitivity affords no greater scandal than the class prejudices of any given era.

Julius misfires in *T. S. Eliot, Anti-Semitism, and Literary Form* by ascribing a crucial place to anti-Semitism in Eliot's art and thought. Possessed of broader interests than Julius, open-minded readers may find that even Eliot's most shocking poems are much more nuanced than Julius allows. For example, while perusing James's *The American Scene* in 1918, Eliot may have come across this passage:

> I remember to have heard it remarked by a French friend, of a young woman who had returned to her native land after some years of domestic service in America, that she had acquired there, with other advantages, *le sourire Californien,* and the "Californian" smile, indeed, expressed, more or less copiously, in undissimulated cubes of the precious metal, plays between lips that render scant other tribute to civilization.[37]

Julius writes of "Sweeney Among the Nightingales": "Whatever its interpretive obscurities, we *do* know that the man with a golden grin is a Jew—one who conforms to that anti-Semitic caricature which pictures Jews' mouths as stuffed with gold fillings" (his emphasis).[38] On this point of seemingly incontrovertible anti-Semitism, the James passage undercuts Julius's assertion. He may be quite mistaken, or at least not entirely correct.

I want to suggest that a strong connection between Sweeney and Bleistein, who appears in "Burbank with a Baedeker: Bleistein with a Cigar," lies in their Americanness. Or rather, in their condition of Americanness, since Sweeney's citizenship is never stated. Bleistein is very nearly Sweeney's double:

> Apeneck Sweeney spreads his knees
> Letting his arms hang down to laugh,

36. Christopher Ricks, *T. S. Eliot and Prejudice,* 119. Anthony Julius, *T. S. Eliot, Anti-Semitism, and Literary Form,* 34. For the reception accorded *T. S. Eliot, Anti-Semitism, and Literary Form,* see my and Alec Marsh's "Pound and Eliot."

37. James, *American Scene,* 505.

38. Julius, *T. S. Eliot, Anti-Semitism,* 27.

The zebra stripes along his jaw
Swelling to maculate giraffe.
("Nightingales" 1–4)

But this or such was Bleistein's way:
A saggy bending of the knees
And elbows, with the palms turned out,
Chicago Semite Viennese.
("Burbank" 13–16)

With its Shakespearean reference to "goats and monkeys," the epigraph of "Burbank with a Baedeker" introduces the idea of humans as beasts. Eliot proceeds to invent a taxonomy for Bleistein, who, being a poor, bare, forked animal, cannot be judged according to his role in human culture. And Sweeney, we know, is virtually an ape. The *Americanum* genus of these characters, while essentially privative in its attributes, subordinates their ethnic differences under an extended metaphor or conceit of Americanness that helps drive Eliot's poetic. Both characters embody the decline of human identity in the West and, with similar force, both act as dissolvents on Europe's cultural landscape. Their names share a singsong quality, with repeating vowel sounds, signifying very little. Eliot's portraiture is appropriately cartoonlike, the poet executing in crude but ingenious strokes a rebuttal of the more optimistic Darwinians, including—in the wide cast of his intellectual net—Henri Bergson and William James.[39]

More consequential than the Sweeney poems, yet to some degree their critical counterpart, "Tradition and the Individual Talent" appeared in two installments, in September and December 1919.[40] The essay's call for an

39. For Darwin's influence on Bergson and James, see Sanford Schwartz, *The Matrix of Modernism: Pound, Eliot, and Early Twentieth-Century Thought*, 17–18, 30 n.

40. After the early successes of 1911–1912, Eliot met with a dangerous self-contradiction: "American introspectiveness" could be "fatal," as he remarked about his friend Conrad Aiken (Eliot, "Reflections" [July 1919], 40), but introspection had also been the key to much of his own work. During the mid- and late 1910s, his reaction against introspective New Englanders led to a careful and painstaking self-critique, in which he tried to distance himself from the interrelated New England traditions of idealism and skepticism—"the Boston doubt" of Emerson and Adams (T. S. Eliot, "A Sceptical Patrician," 362). In order to overcome his crippling habit of self-reflection, Eliot determined to break from his native traditions and to craft a poetry of "externals"; his admiration for the "art of caricature" in Jonson and Marlowe belongs to this anti-Boston phase. "Tradition and the Individual Talent" incorporates this phase but passes beyond it—to play on the old Hegelian dialect—into a unity of a higher kind.

"impersonal" art bespeaks Eliot's desire to escape the falsely individual and to gain the true, to distinguish between faddish novelty and genuine originality, and to strike the right balance between the present and the past. With this essay, Eliot's decade of personal cultural revolution reaches its prose denouement. The struggle with Emersonian New England culminates as insight opens into wisdom:

> To conform merely would be for the new work not really to conform at all; it would not be new, and would therefore not be a work of art. And we do not quite say that the new is more valuable because it fits in; but its fitting in is a test of its value—a test, it is true, which can only be slowly and cautiously applied, for we are none of us infallible judges of conformity. We say: it appears to conform, and is perhaps individual, or it appears individual, and may conform; but we are hardly likely to find that it is one and not the other. (*SE*, 5)

New England demanded of Eliot that literature be a force for social reform, and the literary historian must necessarily ask where Eliot's aesthetic judgments meet his arguments about society and culture. What Eliot presents here is a dialectic, and in doing so he arrives at a potent critique of Emersonian thought—namely, that it is undialectical. Eliot's view anticipates H. Richard Niebuhr's *The Kingdom of God in America*, a definitive text of the Neo-orthodox resurgence of the 1930s.[41] In his culminating chapter, Niebuhr placed Emerson and W. E. Channing in the same sociopolitical context, centered in New England, as "the great American protagonists" of "dynamic liberalism" in religion; Niebuhr maintained that Emerson and Channing had fathered an undialectical faith in redemption without law, in the coming kingdom without atonement. Eliot's interests are not specifically Christian at this juncture, but if we substitute "tradition" for "law," the comparison with Niebuhr holds up very well.

In the Emersonian camp, Kenneth Burke, writing in the 1960s, advanced a dialectical understanding of Emerson that substantially diverged from Niebuhr and the Eliot of "Tradition and the Individual Talent."[42] The differences between these points of view are fascinating. Niebuhr locates

41. H. Richard Niebuhr, *The Kingdom of God in America*, 184–98.
42. Kenneth Burke, "I, Eye, Ay—Emerson's Early Essay on 'Nature': Thoughts on the Machinery of Transcendence."

the dialectical failure of Emersonian thought in the realm of history; in this sense he is close to Eliot. Burke locates Emerson's dialectical achievement in the operations of language, and thus he helps lay the groundwork for the poststructuralist Emerson of the 1980s and 1990s. Surveying the two camps, one finds certain general tendencies confirmed: in modernism, the master trope is history; along parallel lines, the Neo-orthodox movement placed great emphasis on a radical historicizing of human knowledge and experience. For postmodernism, like poststructuralism, the master trope is the metatrope, the word that comments on other words. Hence Burke's coinage, "logology."

For Eliot writing in 1919, the self, isolated within its own circle, disappears from view. Like Sweeney, it has no social history, no history in any sense of the term, and its desires can find no justification beyond appetite. The chief social corollary of Eliot's aesthetic is that individualism had closed the door to a common culture. In theory, the way to the truly and recognizably individual, in the arts and in society, was to discover an authority outside the self. In practice, this would prove no easy matter.

4 | Forbidden Water

AT THE END OF THE LAST CHAPTER, I interpreted "Tradition and the Individual Talent" in terms of Eliot's reaction against Emerson. Here, I want to look at Eliot's seminal essay from a different perspective:

> In English writing we seldom speak of tradition, though we occasionally apply its name in deploring its absence. We cannot refer to "the tradition" or to "a tradition"; at most, we employ the adjective in saying that the poetry of So-and-so is "traditional" or even "too traditional." Seldom, perhaps, does the word appear except in a phrase of censure. If otherwise, it is vaguely approbative, with the implication, as to the work approved, of some pleasing archaeological reconstruction. You can hardly make the word agreeable to English ears without this comfortable reference to the reassuring science of archaeology. (*SE*, 3)

Sustained by his masterful prose, Eliot staked his critical fame on this opening gambit. It is worth consideration, with regard to the accuracy of Eliot's perceptions, that Arnold, in "The Study of Poetry," spoke distinctly of Chaucer and the English "tradition." Edward Thomas, a slightly older contemporary of Eliot, could typically refer to the "smooth regularity of the Tennysonian tradition," a comment on poetic style that I am sure was not intended as "archaeological." But Eliot persuaded his audience to listen to him, because neither Arnold, Thomas, nor their countrymen evinced a devotion to tradition in the sense in which he wished to foster it. As Auden would later observe, Eliot's sense of tradition must have seemed "strange" not only to the English, but to any European critic.[1]

One may compare the better Georgian poets, more generally, as adherents to a tradition in English poetry, to what Eliot proposes in his essay. To emphasize only those aspects of Georgian poetry that were self-consciously traditional, one finds a verse line that owes much to Wordsworth, and a Wordsworthian emphasis on the English landscape that is mediated, in particular, by Hardy. This tradition of Englishness is extended historically by the career of Philip Larkin, who traced the true descent of English poetry after Hardy through the Georgians and Auden.[2]

Unlike Thomas's view of England, Eliot's view of Europe is not local; in describing "the mind of Europe," he refers to a mental place more than a physical one. His idealizing perception of Europe and European culture suggests the influence of Henry James,[3] but as Eliot was quick to note, behind James, there was Hawthorne. For Eliot writing in 1918, it was Hawthorne who preceded James in "that sense of the past which is peculiarly American," and Hawthorne who thus laid the groundwork for the "historical sense" of "Tradition and the Individual Talent." By connecting James to Hawthorne, Eliot affirmed, "James is positively a continuator of the New England genius." More tellingly, Eliot explained this genius in terms of a "literary aristocracy" that was quite close to home, with a reference to "Margaret Fuller and her crew" touching on his own paternal grandfather. Eliot included Fuller, Longfellow, Emerson, Thoreau, Hawthorne, and J. R. Lowell among New England's "best people," though only Hawthorne could be singled out as "individually very important."[4]

It is not wonderful, then, that "Tradition and the Individual Talent" has an ancestor in Hawthorne's novel of cultural initiation in the temple of European art, *The Marble Faun.* One recalls, for example, Hawthorne's

1. "Chaucer is the father of our splendid English poetry; he is our 'well of English undefiled,' because by the lovely charm of his diction, the lovely charm of his movement, he makes an epoch and founds a tradition. In Spenser, Shakespeare, Milton, Keats, we follow the tradition of the liquid diction, the fluid movement, of Chaucer" (Arnold, *Prose Works,* 9:175). Edward Thomas, review of *Personae of Ezra Pound,* 627. W. H. Auden, introduction to *The Faber Book of Modern American Verse,* 18.

2. For Larkin's reaction against Eliot, see John Press, *A Map of Modern English Verse,* 251–60.

3. See Sigg, *American T. S. Eliot,* 110–53.

4. T. S. Eliot, "On Henry James," 115, 112, 113. The piece was originally published as two separate essays in 1918.

description of "Hilda the Dove," the New England maiden who tends a shrine of the Virgin in Rome and who makes her living through her spiritual powers as a copyist of European masterworks: "It strikes us that there is something far higher and nobler in all this—in her thus sacrificing herself to the devout recognition of the highest excellence in art—than there would have been in cultivating her not inconsiderable talent for the production of works from her own ideas."[5] There is a striking parallel between Hilda and the artist of "Tradition and the Individual Talent": "What happens is a continual surrender of himself as he is at the moment to something which is more valuable. The progress of an artist is a continual self-sacrifice, a continual extinction of personality" (*SE*, 6–7). Both passages convey a sense of hieratic devotion in their approach to high culture that is more austere and restrictive than Arnold's appeal to the "best self." Yet while Eliot is willing to sacrifice himself, he would also cultivate his talent within the austere framework that he devises.

When he decided to address the subject of tradition, Eliot was met with a knotty problem. One major difficulty can be stated this way: as an individual desiring to achieve artistic perfection, Eliot needed to satisfy the renunciatory demands of a civilization that gained strength by means of the high artistic ideals he would uphold. Hawthorne's Hilda meets the demands of this civilization by effacing herself, by becoming a mere copyist of the masterpieces of Europe. Having more talent to offer, Eliot must surrender more of his personality than Hawthorne's vestal heroine in order to meet his self-imposed demands.

In both Hawthorne and Eliot, the old Calvinist evil of antinomianism threatens the individual who would resist the pressures of society for the sake of his own vision. In Eliot more particularly, there is a gray area where self-sacrifice in the name of tradition becomes indistinguishable from self-asserting antinomianism. In other words, as an artist Eliot cannot be certain whether he is locating authority outside the self (i.e. in tradition), or within his individual compass. This problem of authority, which extends from the creative process to canons of taste to questions of moral and spiritual order, is central to Eliot's thinking from the late 1910s onward, and it plays a crucial role in "Gerontion" and *The Waste Land*.

A second kind of difficulty that Eliot encountered when he addressed the subject of tradition was his attempt to repair a "dissociation of sensibility," a

5. Hawthorne, *Centenary Edition*, 4:60.

degeneration in taste and feeling that allegedly had its origins in Milton and the English Civil War. I interpret this attempt as romantic and traditionalist.[6] Using materials borrowed from religion (see below), Eliot developed his own version of traditionalism, an effort to recover cultural beliefs and traditions, amounting to a lost wholeness, that were no longer socioreligious facts. The originality of "Tradition and the Individual Talent" inheres largely in its attempt to unite the effort of self-surrender, which was psychological in nature, with the sociocultural goals of traditionalism, under the heading of a single, "Impersonal theory."

"In the History of the Church no subject has been more fruitful of controversy than the Lord's Supper," wrote the young Emerson (*Works,* 11:3). A few months prior to "Tradition and the Individual Talent," in May 1919, Eliot connected Emerson's refusal of the Lord's Supper to a skeptical strain in New England thought and added that Emerson's act was "not without an austere grandeur."[7] Interestingly, during this period the controversy over the Eucharist entered into English literary criticism. Writing for the *Egoist* in 1915, two years before Eliot replaced Richard Aldington as assistant editor, May Sinclair sought to clarify the imagist poetic:

> For all poets, old and new, the poetic act is a sacramental act with its rubric and its ritual. The Victorian poets are Protestant. For them the bread and wine are symbols of Reality, the body and the blood. They are given "in remembrance." The sacrament is incomplete. The Imagists are Catholic; they believe in Trans-substantiation. For them the bread and wine are the body and the blood. They are given. The thing is done. *Ita missa est.* The formula may lead to some very ugly ritual, but that is the fault of the Imagist not of Imagism.[8]

Whether or not Eliot was reading the *Egoist* in 1915, the compelling point is that a connection between the Catholic sacrament of the Eucharist and the

6. The phrase "dissociation of sensibility" first appears in Eliot's writing in his 1921 essay, "The Metaphysical Poets" (*SE,* 247). The major critical study of the dissociation of sensibility and its relation to the movements of imagism and symbolism is Frank Kermode's *Romantic Image,* 138–61. I borrow the term "traditionalist" from Hans-Georg Gadamer's philosophy of history. Gadamer recounts four dialectical stages in the history of historical consciousness: tradition, enlightenment, traditionalism, and historicism. He defines traditionalism as a "romantic critique of the enlightenment . . . that again addresses itself to tradition and seeks to renew it" (Hans-Georg Gadamer, *Truth and Method,* 250).

7. Eliot, "Sceptical Patrician," 361.

8. May Sinclair, "Two Notes," 89.

immediacy of the imagist poetic was highly feasible. Though not an imagist himself, Eliot would have been attracted to the kind of formulation made by Sinclair, especially to her correlation of sacramentalism and poetry.

Like Arnold's "The Study of Poetry" or Mallarmé's "*Crise de vers,*" "Tradition and the Individual Talent" has a hieratic and sacramental subtext. It is through the rigor of his formulae that the American distinguishes himself. According to Eliot, "the mind which creates" will "digest and transmute the passions which are its material" (*SE,* 8). The act of transmutation occurs mysteriously and without human agency, after the mind has digested "passions" that inhere for the writer in "particular words or phrases or images" (*SE,* 8). "The poet's mind," Eliot goes on to explain, "is in fact a receptacle for seizing and storing up numberless feelings, phrases, images, which remain there until all the particles which can unite to form a new compound are present together" (*SE,* 9). These "feelings, phrases, [and] images" survive a general cultural decline, and Eliot's stress on the "material" aspect of language asserts their endurance in two related media, the letter and the body. In effect, he chooses to reverse Emerson's polemical quotation from the Gospel of John (6:63): "The flesh profiteth nothing; the words that I speak to you, they are the spirit and the life" (*Works,* 11:11). For Eliot, existent canonical language ("particular words or phrases or images") in its material aspect is transformed—inside the poet's mind, which is virtually a ciborium—into a divine flesh that profiteth all; the words of the individual, of the human agent, are likely to be antinomian babble.

Before looking at "Gerontion" and *The Waste Land,* it may be helpful to restate a few points. In "Tradition and the Individual Talent," Eliot emphasizes the material existence of tradition and hence of the cultural ideals that demand sacrifice on his part. By sanctifying poetry's physical dimension, he enables himself to demonstrate an unsurpassed reverence for high art and to play the part of the cultural priest with sacramental rigor. However, Eliot's endeavor to act selflessly is called into question by his own potentially antinomian will and by the post-enlightenment shift from tradition to traditionalism. In the pages that follow, I pay close attention to the focuses I have developed in investigating Eliot's labor to achieve a masterpiece while immolating himself upon the altar of high culture.

Written in the summer of 1919, "Gerontion" features a cast of characters who pose a problem of interpretation for the moral sensibility. The third verse paragraph contains imagery that is eucharistic: the candle-lit atmosphere reminiscent of an altar, the curious motions and devotions, the "depraved" Eastertide, suggest that Eliot is grieving for the loss of faith and meaningful ritual.[9] One is tempted to blame Mr. Silvero and the others for fostering this decadent atmosphere—the name "von Kulp" literally indicates culpability. But as Ricks notes, the people in "Gerontion" exist "in a world so wholly strange . . . as to make the distinction between strangers and others meaningless."[10] Therefore, having little basis on which to judge Eliot's characters, I will examine the moral state of the poet himself.

Over a half-century ago, Matthiessen discovered "Gerontion"'s debt to *The Education of Henry Adams*. In his magpie fashion, Eliot had culled a number of brilliant details from Adams:

> The Potomac and its tributaries squandered beauty. . . . Here and there a Negro log cabin alone disturbed the dogwood and the judas-tree. . . . The tulip and the chestnut tree gave no sense of struggle against a stingy nature. . . . The brooding heat of the profligate vegetation; the cool charm of the running water; the terrific splendor of the June thundergust in the deep solitary woods, were all sensual, animal, elemental. No European spring had shown him the same intermixture of delicate grace and passionate depravity that marked the Maryland May. He loved it too much as if it were Greek and half human.[11]

In that busy year, 1919, Eliot confided to his brother: "Henry Adams's book is more than good. It is unique" (*LTSE*, 331). One cannot doubt that he felt a shock of recognition in reading Adams, whom he could properly claim as a "cousin" (*LTSE*, 290). In the above passage, Adams brings a Paterian sensibility to his memory of an American spring, and discovers a *frisson* in his deep isolation. It is as if, before the charmed eye of the cosmopolitan spectator, Maryland's savage luxuriance were translated to a Renaissance canvas.

For Eliot, these were dazzling effects for which he felt an instinctive sympathy; but in adopting them, he accused himself of spiritual failure:

9. See Stephen Spender, *T. S. Eliot*, 59–76.

10. Ricks, *T. S. Eliot and Prejudice*, 123.

11. Henry Adams, *The Education of Henry Adams*, quoted in Matthiessen, *Achievement*, 73.

"The tiger springs in the new year. Us he devours . . ." ("Gerontion" 49). Harking back to "Christ the tiger" in line 20, the line suggests the chastisement of persons who have forsaken or provoked the Lord; similarly, the "spider" and "weevil" of the final stanza evoke the great plagues visited on Pharaoh (Exod. 7–12), as well as prophetic warnings by Jeremiah and Ezekiel. Eliot takes his scissors and paste to the Bible and Lancelot Andrewes, to morally charged texts by Chapman, Webster, Tourneur, and Middleton, in constructing an art-sermon out of his own psychomachia. Readers of "Gerontion" may well ask if the poet's form and method, his thefts and imitations arrayed in the service of an elaborate and difficult art, accord with the message he is preaching, namely, the corrosive effects of thought divorced from ultimate value. The sympathetic reader will answer yes; but even he may grant that on a basic level the poet's lucubrations disappear into Gerontion's labyrinth of reflection.

My central point is that behind the spiritual crisis of Gerontion and the characters who inhabit his brain lurks the artistic crisis of Eliot, which is surely a moral crisis as well. In weaving a cento of quotations from Andrewes and the old playwrights, the poet insinuates a comment about his general method, to the effect that his sacramental use of the letter, of the body of traditional texts, may be fraudulent—Adams, the odd carrot in this English gallimaufry, wasn't supposed to be there, and when Matthiessen pointed the echo out to him personally, the poet "expressed amazement."[12] The poem's acts of eating, dividing, and drinking suggest a parodic Eucharist that implicates Eliot in the act of composition and mimics the brokenness of the poet's form. Not being part of the sermonical and moral tradition that he reconstructs, absorbed in his own aestheticism, the poet cannot participate in the meanings sustained by that tradition. His own culpableness—I revert to the pun on the good Fräulein's name—admits of a rare definition of "culpable" meaning "artistically faulty or censurable" (OED).

Having outlined some difficulties with Eliot's method in "Gerontion," I turn now to my main concern, The Waste Land. I interpret the core of the poem as a dialectic between self-assertion and self-sacrifice, to be set forth as follows: on the one side, a style of conative metaphor developed by Emerson and Whitman, and on the other, Eliot's sacerdotal counter-romanticism, by which I refer to the hieratic view of European culture

12. B. C. Southam, A Guide to the Selected Poems of T. S. Eliot, 72.

expounded in "Tradition and the Individual Talent" and scrutinized by the self-critical poetic of "Gerontion."

One of the leading traits of Emerson's thought is his emphasis on the "fluid" quality of nature and the imagination.[13] At the conclusion of *Nature*, he cites a poet who is perhaps either Bronson Alcott or himself:

> Nature is not fixed but fluid. Spirit alters, moulds, makes it. The immobility or bruteness of nature, is the absence of spirit; to pure spirit it is fluid, it is volatile, it is obedient. . . . Build, therefore, your own world. . . . until evil is no more seen. The kingdom of man over nature, which cometh not with observation,—a dominion such as now is beyond his dream of God,—he shall enter without more wonder than the blind man feels who is gradually restored to perfect sight. (*Works*, 1:76–77)[14]

For Emerson, fluidity is a sign of the divine human will at work in nature, which regains its unfallen state by means of that will. Eliot would have objected to the wordiness and sheer cultural familiarity of the passage, which is the climax of Emerson's first book, and to Emerson's premises about individual potential and the disappearance of evil. To put the issue in stark but serviceable terms, Emerson affirms the power of the creative self to transform the world; Eliot questions not only the self's power, but whether the autonomous self ultimately exists.

Influenced by Emerson, Whitman attached a spiritual significance to metaphors of a fluid or liquid variety.[15] Such metaphors are conspicuous in "When Lilacs Last in the Dooryard Bloom'd." For example, the line "O

13. "Emerson's work is as permeated with images of flowing as you would expect from his declaration that 'the philosophy we want is one of fluxions and mobility.' In *Nature* the earth becomes 'this green ball which floats him through the heavens.' Nothing solid is left secure, since all matter has been infiltrated and dissolved by thought. He noted himself how such images were the fitting expression of a mind most of whose values were continually varying, as in his estimate of America, 'which sometimes runs very low, sometimes to ideal proportions' " (Matthiessen, *American Renaissance*, 70).

14. Other examples of this characteristic tendency in Emerson's thought occur in "Circles" ("There are no fixtures in nature. The universe is fluid and volatile" [*Works*, 2:302]); in "The Poet" ("The quality of the imagination is to flow" [*Works*, 3:34]); and in "Montaigne; or, The Skeptic," from *Representative Men* ("A man of thought must feel the thought that is parent of the universe: that the masses of nature do undulate and flow" [*Works*, 4:183]).

15. In *Democratic Vistas* Whitman calls for an American poetry that has a "freeing, fluidizing, expanding, religious character" (*CPCP*, 986). During the nineteenth century, many European poets also specialized in this kind of trope.

liquid and free and tender!" describes both the hermit thrush's song and the poet's soulful tallying of that song (*CPCP*, 463). "Floating," which occurs in three inflections, and other liquid words are similarly important. All such usages empower Whitman, the speaker of the poem, in his struggle with the "cruel hands" that signify matter and death.

Where Emerson and Whitman transform reality through the triumph of the liquid spirit over matter, *The Waste Land,* with its elaborate scholium or notes, adheres to the letter and the letter's materiality. I have discussed Eliot's sacramental interest in the physical matter of words—his quip of some years later, "And the spirit killeth, but the letter giveth life" (*FLA,* 94 n) reveals, I think, an authentic comment on his poetry. In *The Waste Land,* his primary symbols are solids, "a heap of broken images." The cultural past exists literally, in "stony rubbish" and "a handful of dust." Ezekiel, who inspires the first of Eliot's notes, is a type of *Waste Land* poet in his insistence on a collective cultural memory. Like Eliot, he emphasizes the chiastic presence of the word in the body: "Moreover he said unto me, Son of man, eat that thou findest; eat this roll [i.e. "scroll"], and go speak unto the house of Israel" (Ezek. 3:1). The prophet must ingest the word of God before he can prophesy; he must embody the sacred letter. Ezekiel's lesson is that the fate of Israel rests entirely on the Lord, not the people. Similarly, the reference to Ezekiel in *The Waste Land* evokes a moral and spiritual authority that transcends the heterogeneous desires of individuals. One infers that Eliot, as poet-prophet, seeks to be a pure vessel of tradition, a messenger of words that possess moral and spiritual authority.

Throughout the poem, there is an implicit negation of those metaphors, the poetic stock-in-trade of Emerson and Whitman, that express individual will, mastery, or power. Because Eliot resists this family of tropes, he must approach the theme of transformation in an indirect manner; he does so under the auspices of Madame Sosostris:

> Here, said she,
> Is your card, the drowned Phoenician Sailor,
> (Those are pearls that were his eyes. Look!)
> (*WL* 46–48)

In his use of the drowned Phoenician Sailor, Eliot adapts *The Tempest* for purposes of circumventing the fluid metaphors of Emerson and Whitman.

If the "fear" of "death by water" (line 55) connotes a fear of language that is self-directed in origin and effect, of language that contravenes Eliot's highly demanding versions of tradition and authority, then the "sea-change" in "Full Fathom Five" removes this impasse, because it is a transformation that follows upon a death, not upon anyone's active will. Madame Sosostris refers to the drowned Phoenician Sailor as "your card," the card shared by the poet and the reader as they set about their difficult labor of inheritance: the fate foretold of poet (and of reader, and of the poet as reader) would appear to be either a new life through a transforming death (line 48 referring us to Shakespeare's "sea-change") or antinomian self-assertion, a kind of living death. In either case, water remains—as Eliot said of Emerson's mentor, Montaigne—"a fluid, insidious element" (*SE*, 362); through Shakespeare's deeps there is at least the possibility of salvation.

In contrast to the drowned Phoenician Sailor, the Hanged Man signifies those energies in the poem that reject the liquid tropes of the antinomian will; he is a symbol of doctrine and "a member of the traditional pack" (*CP*, 70). Although the Hanged Man is elusive and doesn't appear in Madame Sosostris's tarot reading, he may be said to emerge, through the poem's subterrene network of symbols, in the "gliding" and hooded figure who resembles Jesus on the road to Emmaus (in his notes, Eliot explains, perhaps unnecessarily, that he "associated" the Hanged Man with the Hanged God of *The Golden Bough*). The Emmaus episode in Luke (Luke 24:13–48) merits close attention from readers of *The Waste Land*. Deeply literalist, it lingers over the risen body of Christ and the stigmata of that body. The pericope describes the resurrected God sharing bread with two of his followers, who naturally do not recognize him at first. Jesus eventually asks them for something more substantial to eat and, near the end of the Gospel, rises into heaven. This uncanny vision of Christ pertains strongly to the design of *The Waste Land*, where tradition—its bones, relics, and indecipherable fragments—awaits a physical resurrection.

Because Eliot resists the liquid, transformational language of Emerson and Whitman, the redemptive symbolism of water in the poem is exceptionally difficult. The poet needs to create a dialectic between past and present, the tradition and the individual. Resurrection in *The Waste Land* turns on the union of dust and water, but the self-effacing poet is reluctant in his role, with its echoes of the divine—Jehovah himself withheld his life-giving mist until he wanted to create Adam. In "What the Thunder Said," tropes of liquidity appear beside "rock," "carious teeth," and "fragments," as Eliot contemplates various types and themes of personal and cultural resurrection. The hermit thrush of Whitman's "When Lilacs Last in the Dooryard Bloom'd," particularly its liquid voice, suggests a direction, a vision *toward* a plenary world:

> If there were water
> And no rock
> If there were rock
> And also water
> And water
> A spring
> A pool among the rock
> If there were the sound of water only
> Not the cicada
> And dry grass singing
> But sound of water over a rock
> Where the hermit-thrush sings in the pine trees
> Drip drop drip drop drop drop drop
> But there is no water
>
> (*WL* 346–59)

The literal, onomatopoeic treatment of water allows Eliot to wield the liquid power of figuration, which he needs as a poet, in the name of tradition, the ideal order that demands surrender to its models of representation. In the musicality of the passage, which is intensified by the onomatopoeia, one may see Mallarmé's ideal realized: a seamless correspondence between language and reality, "a total word" in poetry that gives unmediated expression to the senses and the referential world. But then, the redemptive water doesn't quite materialize. True to his "Calvinistic heritage" and "Puritanical temperament" (*OPP*, 209), the poet resists assent to a vision that may not transcend the self. In fact, he has it both ways, for despite his assertion that "there is no water," there surely is: an intense subjectivism unsettles the chronological sequence. As the poet yields to the reader, and hence to fate, which will decide whether he has succeeded in his task, an important question surfaces about these ambiguous acts of writing: do Eliot's subjectivist procedures offer an adequate mimesis—do they renew or destroy the inherited modes of perception? Sphinx-like, the poet brings one's readerly destiny to the riddle.[16]

Continuing with Eliot's dialectic of self-assertion and self-sacrifice, I want to examine the numerous figures of drowning in the poem, which include the drowned Phoenician Sailor and Phlebas the Phoenician. The specific quality of language that connects these figures receives some important attention from Eliot in *The Use of Poetry and the Use of Criticism*: "The imagery of ['Kubla Khan'], certainly, whatever its origins in Coleridge's reading, sank to the depths of Coleridge's feeling, was saturated, transformed there—'those are pearls that were his eyes'—and brought up into daylight again" (*UPUC*, 139). Here Eliot is responding to Coleridge by way of J. L. Lowes's *The Road to Xanadu: A Study in the Ways of the Imagination*. Lowes undertook to solve the mystery of "Kubla Khan"'s many sources. He did not, however, cite "Full Fathom Five" as an emblem of the creative process, and it is revealing that Eliot should make this identification after using Ariel's song in *The Waste Land* to develop the symbolic resonance of the drowned Phoenician Sailor. Following this clue, I am led to consider the drowned Phoenician Sailor and the figures that radiate from him, such as Phlebas, as symbolic actors in Eliot's creative process.[17] The kind of writing I see Eliot engaged in is related to the *art poétique* of Valéry, described by Eliot in later years as "the penetration of the poetic by the introspective critical activity" (*TCTC*, 41); but a moral spur, leading to the symbolic action of psychomachia, precludes the metalinguistic narcissism that Eliot disliked in Valéry.

Phlebas—who embodies Eliot's own transformative, creative energies—converges in the poem's discarded drafts with the doomed New England fisherman, a quester who evokes Dante's Ulysses and Coleridge's Mariner. The dilemma facing Eliot in his representation of these figures, a representation that is severely, almost despairingly truncated in the final version of the poem, is the impossibility of effecting a saving transformation without

16. For the crisis in mimetic values brought about by subjectivism in modernist literature, see Erich Auerbach, *Mimesis*, 525–57. For the interplay of objectivism and subjectivism in Eliot's critical writings, see Richard Shusterman, *T. S. Eliot and the Philosophy of Criticism*, 42–46.

17. In *Harmony of Dissonances: T. S. Eliot, Romanticism, and Imagination*, John Paul Riquelme also observes Eliot's use of Ariel's song in connection with the writing process; Riquelme views Eliot's work as primarily metalinguistic and reads Eliot as a precursor to Paul de Man.

committing an act of will by which the poet locates authority (the power of creating and judging) in himself. Put another way, a compositional crisis occurs because, while the poet needs his assorted questers to generate his poem, they are symbols of individual agency in a work that forbids such agency. Though tradition cannot be allowed to calcify, and though the past must be transformed through the new social and cultural arrangements of the present, the individual has no authority to effect this transformation.

Let us consider two of the rejected drafts. First, a fragment:

> Those are pearls that were his eyes. See!
> And the crab clambers through his stomach, the eel grows big
> And the torn algae drift above him,
> And the sea colander.
> Still and quiet brother are you still and quiet.
>
> (*WLF*, 123)

I interpret the quotation from Shakespeare as an emblem of unconscious creative forces in Eliot, who is baring his own psychic depths. With the image of digestion in the second line, recalling "Us he devours" from "Gerontion," we are reminded of the vengeful power of Eliot's tradition, of the *lex talionis* that pursues transgressors. The next two lines belong to a familiar type of Eliotic lyric, and anticipate "the more delicate algae and the sea anemone" of "The Dry Salvages." Most important, the final line recalls Baudelaire, as quoted in "The Burial of the Dead." Eliot, hypocrite writer and reader of the traditions he transmits, cannot exorcise the ghost of his own will, who, as the inverted syntax would suggest ("are you still and quiet [?]"), may yet be eerily unstill and unquiet.

In "Dirge" (*WLF*, 121), "your Bleistein" replaces the anonymous corpse. Bleistein's "sea-change" has no saving effect on his eyes or face—he is in a sense a bad poet (accompanied by Prufrockian lobsters and a bathetic "stare of dull surprise") who mocks Eliot's willful, antinomian desire to transform tradition; it is a small step to see him as a figure of authorial anxieties.[18] The guilt that Eliot incurred in arrogating the mantle of tradition to himself is transferred in "Dirge" to a scapegoat figure who, as a Jew, defines (from

18. Finding a sustained comparison in Eliot's poetry between Judaism and Unitarianism, William Empson interprets the Bleistein of "Dirge" as a symbol of Eliot's father. See William Empson, *Using Biography*, 189–200.

the outside) the tradition that Eliot would represent. A tasteless if cleverly juvenile parody of Shakespeare, "Dirge" issues from self-directed pity and anguish. As a comment by Eliot on his own authorial problems, it answers to a notion of civilization that is to the utmost degree renunciatory.

Returning for a moment to "Gerontion," I want to suggest that had Pound agreed to that poem's being prelusive to *The Waste Land,* it would have served to introduce the idea of Eliot's assimilation of Europe. By "assimilation," I refer in general to the assimilative powers of a Henry James, to the ability of a sophisticated expatriate to study the cultural landscape of Europe and, with the acute self-consciousness of a foreigner, to record European life more keenly than those who were born to it.[19] More specifically, though, I refer to Eliot's assimilation of European history within the framework of the self; it is in this regard that his work evinces suggestive parallels with Emerson and Whitman.

In his essay "History," Emerson develops a model of the self that has humanistic origins in his reading of Montaigne, who had defended his own self-explorations with the credo that every man carries within himself the complete pattern of human nature. Drawing on this humanistic aspect of Montaigne as well as on Hegelian notions of *"Geist"* or universal mind, Emerson crafts an argument for the radical autonomy of the individual:

> There is one mind common to all individual men. . . .
> This human mind wrote history, and this must read it. The Sphinx must solve her own riddle. If the whole of history is in one man, it is all to be explained from individual experience. . . . Of the universal mind each individual man is one more incarnation. All its properties consist in him. Each new fact in his private experience flashes a light on what great bodies of men have done, and the crises of his life refer to national crises. (*Works,* 2:3–4)

To the extent that *The Waste Land* is about "the whole of history," this whole exists in the figure of Tiresias, a universal subject for whom all history is the predicate. It is true that, unlike Emerson's "individual man," Tiresias is not an active figure. Emerson champions "the advancing man" who realizes a personal significance in the annals of history; by contrast,

19. "It is the final perfection, the consummation of an American to become, not an Englishman, but a European—something which no born European, no person of any European nationality, can become" (Eliot, "On Henry James," 109).

Tiresias neither advances nor looks for significance—he is therefore the vehicle of irony, the classical irony of fate. But behind *The Waste Land*—"behind" in a self-critical fashion that challenges the abiding readerly norms of romanticism—is Eliot. And, like Emerson, Eliot turns autobiography into history: he interprets personal crises in terms of national crises, and finds a personal significance in history and myth.

In the figure of Tiresias, Eliot construes a model of the self that contains not only a multitude of characters, but age upon historical age. Whitman had achieved a similar effect in "Passage to India," in recording an optative mood that was—like Eliot's melancholy—at once personal and public. In both "Passage to India" and *The Waste Land,* history is shown to exist stratum by stratum in the multifold present of the self; in both poems a quotation from (or reference to) the ancient Indo-European language of Sanskrit affirms the universality of the poet's perspective; both meditate, with Emersonian precedent, on Indic religion. The chief difference between Whitman's and Eliot's constructions of the self can be measured in Whitman's active response to history. For Whitman, the transforming self is the literary and cultural agent of the progressive history set down, albeit with reservations, in *Democratic Vistas.* Grounded on visible experience, Whitman's poetic catalogs represent the spiritual promise of an idealized American democracy.[20] Spurning the idea of historical progress, Eliot adopts Whitman's imaging consciousness but disperses the Whitmanian agent among its collective perceptions: through the passive medium of Tiresias, he converts *Song of Myself* into *Song of My Selves.*

Like Emerson and Whitman in their writings, Eliot erects a universal subject; unlike them, he wants to characterize the self as passive before the power of fate. Yet he is writing a masterpiece. This is precisely "The Problem," as Emerson presents it in his poem of that name:

> The hand that rounded Peter's dome
> And groined the aisles of Christian Rome
> Wrought in a sad sincerity;
> Himself from God he could not free; . . .
>
> (*Works,* 9:7)

---

20. Kenneth Burke observed of Whitman, "In his 'oceanic' accumulation of details, the catalogues that characterize most of his longer poems . . . , there is obviously the 'spiritualization' of matter" (Kenneth Burke, "Policy Made Personal," 82–83).

When we place these lines in their context, we see Emerson's meaning: Michelangelo cannot escape the un-Christian truth of his own divinity. No Prufrock now, but a Michelangelo at work, Eliot meets with a cognate problem: does the ultimate meaning of culture inhere in a spiritual authority outside the circle of the self, or is there no such authority beyond the self? This line of inquiry, or inquisition, can be extended: is Eliot satisfied with intensely fine poetry that mourns the loss of authority, or is he in deadly earnest, trying to escape the divine self of Emerson and come unto that which is greater than the self?

The Waste Land's final section, "What the Thunder Said," looks for a signal from the cosmos, from a God of thunder, that will affirm the poet's subordinate place in the divine order. It is Eliot's task to interpret the thunder, and thus to mediate between the human and the divine.[21] He succeeds insofar as he translates the thunder's primal word into three Sanskrit words, *datta, dayadhvam, damyata,* meaning "give, sympathize, control." But he has not really escaped Emerson's problem, because he is still both thunderer and scribe:

> DA
> *Datta:* what have we given?
> My friend, blood shaking my heart
> The awful daring of a moment's surrender
> Which an age of prudence can never retract
> By this, and this only, we have existed
> Which is not to be found in our obituaries
> Or in memories draped by the beneficent spider
> Or under seals broken by the lean solicitor
> In our empty rooms
>
> (*WL* 401–10)

A primal force disturbs the self complacent in its "prudence" and tears the drapery of convention. The speaker recognizes the need to give himself (or herself) up—perhaps to God, though the passage is closer (as the notes suggest) to Webster than religious drama. In any case, the speaker's "memories" lie in physical ruin, so that Eliot's hypostatizing of the past,

21. See Marc Manganaro, *Myth, Rhetoric, and the Voice of Authority: A Critique of Frazer, Eliot, Frye, and Campbell,* 83–90.

a process that has informed his dialectical configurations throughout the poem, gains a new twist. No longer a temple of literalist devotion, the past appears as something uncongenial and even macabre, a dead hand. The Emersonianism of this is clear: divinity and meaning reside in the present.

When it works—as it does here—the modernist technique of abrupt transition heightens intensity. Eliot's ambiguous syntax creates a rapid shift of perspective, as "In our empty rooms" yields unexpectedly to "I have heard the key":

> DA
> *Dayadhvam:* I have heard the key
> Turn in the door once and turn once only
> We think of the key, each in his prison
> Thinking of the key, each confirms a prison
> Only at nightfall, aethereal rumours
> Revive for a moment a broken Coriolanus
> (*WL* 411–17)

The notes provide two glosses for the above passage: one from the *Inferno* and one from *Appearance and Reality,* by F. H. Bradley.[22] The allusion to Dante is to the story of Count Ugolino (*Inferno* 33), who tells of being locked in the "horrible tower" where he and his children gradually starved. As one of the damned, Ugolino is cut off from the God of Dante's faith. The

---

22. As Louis Menand and others have noticed, the quotation is not fully representative of Bradley: when Eliot cited the same passage (in its entirety) in a philosophy article of 1916, he remarked that it was an "extreme" statement of one point of view, and noted that, from another point of view in Bradley, "experience is in principle essentially public" (*KE*, 203–4). Hence, I agree with Menand that Eliot's allusion to Bradley signifies a solipsistic mood or perspective within the poem that is not its sole mood or perspective (Louis Menand, *Discovering Modernism: T. S. Eliot and His Context,* 29–53). Nonetheless, Eliot's description of the self as a "prison" and the quotation from Bradley's *Appearance and Reality* comment on a culture of solipsism that was the dark side of Unitarian reverence for the sanctity of individual worship. Nathaniel Alden, the Boston landlord and High Church Unitarian of Santayana's *The Last Puritan,* provides a good example: "He had certain secret convictions, one of which was this: that human beings could be united only in the common sphere of their actions; they remained for ever separate and solitary in their thoughts—when, indeed, they had any" (George Santayana, *The Last Puritan,* 38). Eliot's graduate work on Bradley didn't change the nature of his own self-immurement, which we recognize in the worlds of "Prufrock" and "Portrait of a Lady." As an older poet, he used philosophy as a means of ordering and objectifying feelings that were basic to his poetic endeavor.

reprobated Count would thus provide a symbol of the individual locked within himself.

Though Bradley's world is distant from the world of Dante, Eliot's quotation from Bradley consorts with this reading of Ugolino: "My external sensations are no less private to myself than are my thoughts or my feelings. In either case my experience falls within my own circle, a circle closed on the outside; and, with all its elements alike, every sphere is opaque to the others which surround it. . . . In brief, regarded as an existence which appears in a soul, the whole world for each is peculiar and private to that soul" (*CP*, 75). Academic, comparative, the note suggests that the poem is explicating Dante for the modern era, positing his universality with the one hand, but with the other undermining his religious authority. In citing Bradley alongside Dante, Eliot declines to clarify the link between his cultural and religious aspirations; likewise, his dialogue between Christianity, Hinduism, and Buddhism is experientially compelling but intellectually incomplete.[23] As readers, we long for "the key" to the poem's elliptical narrative and its encounter with tradition; the divine thunder promises such a key, a revelation telling where ultimate value resides, but the scholium imprisons us in books.

We come to the mellifluous lines: "Only at nightfall, aethereal rumours / Revive for a moment a broken Coriolanus." Eliot's Coriolanus is a personalized version of Shakespeare's sublime egotist, and here he bears romantic markings that recall the demonism of a romantic Cain. The expansive movement, the movement of spiritual release or sympathy with creation that Coriolanus feels, is decidedly self-oriented: revival occurs during the romantic interlude of "nightfall" or dusk in the field of personal consciousness.[24]

With the thunder's final word, the poet seeks to transcend psychic prisons. The polysemous "sea" conveys the anagogical meaning of a triumphant passage toward one's ultimate destiny:

23. A. D. Moody credits Eliot with a more precise intention. He writes: "The extended allusion to the Upanishads doesn't so much supply the major structure as subserve the quest to recover a Christian form of life" (A. David Moody, *Tracing T. S. Eliot's Spirit*, 24). Not finding a decisively Christian quest in *The Waste Land*, I am more sympathetic to John Mayer's view of the poem's spiritual ambiguity and its openness to "each individual's vision"; see Mayer, *T. S. Eliot's Silent Voices*, 290–91. For Eliot and Indic religion, see Cleo McNelly Kearns, *T. S. Eliot and Indic Traditions: A Study in Poetry and Belief.*

24. For the romantic and modernist topos of twilight, see Hugo Friedrich, *The Structure of Modern Poetry*, 10–11.

DA
Damyata: The boat responded
Gaily, to the hand expert with sail and oar
The sea was calm, your heart would have responded
Gaily, when invited, beating obedient
To controlling hands

(*WL* 418–23)

It is hard to say whether these are images of self-discipline or images of the self yielding to an authority from without: distinctions between inner and outer authority cannot be discerned. The poet both creates the figure of a sailboat and sails the boat he has created. In addition, he compares "your heart" to the boat: if "your heart" denotes the poet's own heart, then the movement of energy and concentration is decidedly inward, not outward; if "your heart" addresses the reader, then the poet is affirming his own power and authority. We cannot say whether God or the sea or the poet is doing the inviting. Whose hands are in control?

The final third of the triptych is more religious in feeling than "the awful daring of a moment's surrender," the allusions to Ugolino and Bradley, or the lines about Coriolanus, but the idiom may strike us as similarly psychological or egocentric. Although this loosely punctuated, highly enjambed passage suggests a more spiritual surrender and revelation, Eliot doesn't succeed, as Dante succeeded, in imaging a spiritual communion with an external God. Doubt exists as to whether he has even tried. The use of the conditional mood ("your heart would have responded / Gaily") implies an elegiac sense of loss, as if the invitation never came, as if a spiritual consummation were beyond the poet's reach. Eliot's intentions remain elusive, hidden behind a screen of dazzling effects. He pursues—structurally, through his triptych—a tortuous quest for God. The resulting poetry is of a very high order. But is the pursuit of God, of a spiritual authority behind the poem's incarnation of high culture, merely a vehicle for that poetry? If the poet, the tradition, and the divine are one, hasn't Eliot in fact illustrated the force of Emerson's "problem"?

In 1923, the year after *The Waste Land* was published, Eliot wrote "The Function of Criticism." At the core of the essay is his debate with John Middleton Murry:

"Catholicism," [Murry] says, "stands for the principle of unquestioned spiritual authority outside the individual; that is also the principle of

Classicism in literature." Within the orbit within which Mr. Murry's discussion moves, this seems to me an unimpeachable definition, though it is of course not all that there is to be said about either Catholicism or Classicism. Those of us who find ourselves supporting what Mr. Murry calls Classicism believe that men cannot get on without giving allegiance to something outside themselves. I am aware that "outside" and "inside" are terms which provide unlimited opportunity for quibbling, and that no psychologist would tolerate a discussion which shuffled such base coinage; but I will presume that Mr. Murry and myself can agree that for our purpose these counters are adequate, and concur in disregarding the admonitions of our psychological friends. If you find that you have to imagine it [i.e "spiritual authority"] as outside, then it is outside. (*SE*, 15)

The passage addresses the interpretation of Eliot that I have put forward in this chapter. As a critic, Eliot describes a need to locate spiritual authority outside the self. He acknowledges the validity of psychological analysis, which has the power to undercut the distinctions that he wants to make, between the Catholic-classicist position and the Protestant-romanticist position. Then, by an imaginative and personal gesture, he rebuilds the boundaries in question, between inner and outer, between the individual and a transcendent spiritual order. Readers of *The Waste Land* must choose whether or not to sympathize with him on this score; in either case, the poem retains its enigmatic beauty.

5 | Lost Kingdoms

FRANK KERMODE HAS WRITTEN insightfully on the theme of exile in Eliot, which he finds "most obvious in *Ash-Wednesday,* where exile has to be accepted with patience as the human condition. . . ."[1] Kermode suggests that exile was a "dominant trait" of Eliot's personality. Both in his personal relations and in his art, Eliot kept aloof, his true attachments being to ideals that were more absent than present: ideals of European order, of an empire laid up in heaven, of a meaning or pattern in history that completes individual destinies. It was faithfulness to these ideals that enabled Eliot to develop his conception of the classic, a conception to which neither American nor English national literature has warmed very much, for the reason that it locates authority in the symbol of the *urbs aeterna* and hence consigns modern nations and their vernacular languages to a provincial status. As a self-declared *"metoikos"* or stranger, Eliot remained perpetually in-between: at once exiled from the ideal, because it was by definition otherworldly, and not at home in the real and present, because it evoked in his haunted mind the absent ideal.

In this chapter, I explore how Eliot's Americanness informs the related themes of exile and disinheritance in "The Hollow Men" (1925) and *Ash-Wednesday* (1930). More precisely, I chart a course from the symbolist idiom of "The Hollow Men" to the Anglo-Catholic ethos of *Ash-Wednesday,* using

1. Frank Kermode, *An Appetite for Poetry,* 109.

Eliot's continuing engagement with America as my polestar. Edgar Poe, Henry Adams, and other American writers will assist in this cartography. First, though, it will be helpful to look at how exile and disinheritance enter into two of Eliot's earlier poems, "The Love Song of J. Alfred Prufrock" and *The Waste Land.*

Ronald Schuchard and others have suggested that the ending of "Prufrock" echoes *"J'ai rêvé dans la grotte où nage la syrène,"* a line from Nerval's sonnet *"El Desdichado"* ("The Disinherited One"), which Eliot had seen quoted in Arthur Symons's *The Symbolist Movement in Literature* (*VMP*, 154 n).[2] If this echo holds true, one may infer that Eliot had "Prufrock" in mind when he spoke of Nerval's alexandrine as poetry of "the daydream type" (*VMP*, 153–54), for both poets employ the daydream as an expression of disinheritance. By virtue of being a daydream, an egocentric fantasy of sexual and aesthetic pleasure, Prufrock's vision of "sea-girls" registers Eliot's resistance to the social and psychological demands of his family; it is "the chambers of the sea" that mark his ultimate retreat from the "human voices" of familial duty (see Chapter 2). "Prufrock" is not a poem of exile, for the protagonist does not seek after his native land and traditions, but it is a poem of disinheritance, and it reveals a division between the identities of a dutiful son and a maturing poet.

With regard to motifs of exile in *The Waste Land,* Kermode names three personages: Tristan, the Psalmist, and Coriolanus.[3] Of these, Coriolanus bears most centrally on Eliot's oeuvre. Coriolanus's memorable remarks, "There is a world elsewhere" and "I banish you," do not suggest an Ovidian *tristitia,* a forlorn banishment from the cosmopolitan center; rather, they signify a willful and angry rejection of Rome. But where Shakespeare's tragic hero is obdurate in his aristocratic disdain for Roman politics, *The Waste Land*'s Coriolanus admits to being "broken": he combines a demonic self that rejects history with an elegiac self that suffers a traumatic loss; in this elegiac aspect, he differs from Shakespeare's character. As in "Prufrock," Eliot symbolically severs his heredity, but in *The Waste Land* this heredity survives in the mournful music of exile.

2. *"J'ai rêvé dans la grotte où nage la syrène"* is quoted by Arthur Symons, *The Symbolist Movement in Literature,* 20. Symons's book, the modernist Rheingold discovered by Eliot in December 1908 in the library of the Harvard Union, introduced him to Laforgue, Rimbaud, and presumably Nerval.

3. Kermode, *Appetite,* 110.

Now, in adapting the figure of Coriolanus to *The Waste Land*, was Eliot describing himself as an exile from America, in the sense that Coriolanus was an exile from Rome, an aristocrat at odds with his native polity? Or was it as a more general symbol of the human condition that Shakespeare's character drew Eliot's attention? A reader of the unfinished *Coriolan* sequence, which was conceived in the early 1930s, might well defend the latter choice—exile as an emblem of the human condition. But there is an interesting piece of evidence connecting Eliot's figurations of Coriolanus to his private quarrel with American history. I refer to a draft of the suppressed "Ode," entitled "Ode on Independence Day, July 4th 1918."[4] In the draft, as well as in the rare Ovid Press edition, *Ara Vus Prec* (1920), the "Ode" bears an epigraph from *Coriolanus*. Eliot both (very slightly) misquotes his text and omits the opening line from the speech in which Coriolanus reveals himself to his former enemies, the Volsces—the English, I think, in Eliot's equation. With the first line restored in brackets, the original runs:

> [My name is Caius Marcius, who hath done]
> To thee particularly and to all the Volsces
> Great hurt and mischief . . .
> (Coriolanus 4.5.70–72)

Having dropped the speech's opening line, Eliot uncorks an ambiguity: is he wishing harm upon the "Volsces," or admitting that he has done them "hurt and mischief"? Where, precisely, are his allegiances? There is no answer, nor does the "Ode" provide one, but in the epigraph, a tie between Coriolanus, in exile from Rome, addressing his recent enemies, and Eliot, the American in England on Independence Day, reflecting on the twists of his personal history and allegiances, is apparent. And if Shakespeare's Coriolanus enabled Eliot to comment on his increasing distance from his native country, then there is good reason to approach the leitmotif of exile in Eliot's work as in other respects rooted in his Americanness.

The figures of exile in *The Waste Land*, to which I would add Ezekiel, who prophesied during the Babylonian captivity, are accompanied by two figures that convey the theme of a lost or imperiled inheritance: Nerval's *"Le Prince d'Aquitaine à la tour abolie"* and the Fisher King. In the notes to *The*

4. TS, Berg Collection; *IMH,* 383.

Waste Land, Eliot alludes to the Fisher King in his introductory statement: "Not only the title, but the plan and a good deal of the incidental symbolism of the poem were suggested by Miss Jessie L. Weston's book on the Grail legend: *From Ritual to Romance.*" There has been a long controversy about the notes and the large place in the poem they claim for Weston, as well as for the anthropologist James Frazer. My view, in brief, is that Eliot digested his Frazer readily (having first read him at Harvard), that Frazer more than Weston influenced the thinking behind the poem, and that Eliot's use of the Grail legend (by way of Weston) is less significant than the understanding of myth, magic, scientific method, and primitive religious consciousness that enters the poem through *The Golden Bough.*[5]

If Weston does not adequately elucidate the Fisher King in Eliot, then Eliot's use of the figure becomes more subjective. The act of fishing and the word "vegetation" (as in "vegetation deity") make for a curious connection between Weston's Fisher King and *The Tempest,* but the most worthwhile result is an original *persona,* direct in utterance and forceful of vision:

> A rat crept softly through the vegetation
> Dragging its slimy belly on the bank
> While I was fishing in the dull canal
> On a winter evening round behind the gashouse
> Musing upon the king my brother's wreck
> And on the king my father's death before him.
> (*WL* 187–92)

Behind the kaleidoscope of source materials (including Joyce's *Ulysses*), autobiography lends an ulterior coherence. While Shakespeare's Ferdinand has a sister but no brother, the speaker's reference to his father and older brother accords with the patriarchal order of succession in Eliot's own family. Untitled aristocrats, the Eliots, like the family of Brooks and Henry Adams, belonged to a displaced species of New Englander, a ruling class supplanted by a new breed of industrialists during the economic revolution known as the Gilded Age.[6] When viewed through the lens of Adams's *Education,* Eliot's myriad figures of exile and disinheritance become expressions

5. For Eliot's debts to Frazer, see Jewel Spears Brooker, *Mastery and Escape: T. S. Eliot and the Dialectic of Modernism,* 110–22.

6. While the Eliots don't have quite the same status, sociologically, as the monumentally displaced Adams clan, I would propose that Eliot himself saw suggestive parallels.

of late-Puritan anomie. In some sense, *The Waste Land*—which all but begins with the voice of a displaced aristocrat, Countess Marie Larisch[7]—is a threnody of dominion lost; the modern wasteland was for Eliot, at least originally and in memory, a post–Civil War America in which the Eliot family had relinquished its position of moral and spiritual leadership.[8] Eliot as Fisher King is Eliot stripped of his antebellum pride of place, at best an inheritor of property that has no historical consequence:

> I sat upon the shore
> Fishing, with the arid plain behind me
> Shall I at least set my lands in order?
> (*WL* 424–26)

Eliot's words about Henry Adams were not without personal relevance: "The American was born to the governing-class tradition without the inherited power, and he was born to exercise governance, not to acquire it."[9] As the Adams-like poet, Eliot found other imagoes in Prince Ferdinand and *le Prince d'Aquitaine,* as well as in the Hamlet (or "not Prince Hamlet") of "Prufrock." All are princes without kingdoms—"kingdom" preceding "my lands" in a surviving draft of *The Waste Land* (*WLF,* 78).

The word "kingdom" links the aforementioned draft to "The Hollow Men," where it occurs a talismanic seven times. One finds "death's other Kingdom" (line 14), a place of self-abnegation and innocence; "death's dream kingdom" (lines 20 and 30), a realm "between life and death" (I quote "The wind sprang up at four o'clock"), where the poet's muse, more properly his Beatrice, is sought, and where the landscape intimates her remote presence until the poet stumbles on his own lack of affirming will; "the twilight kingdom" (line 38), where spiritual reality is immanent and judgment presumably at hand; "death's other kingdom" (line 46) or mortal life itself (also known as "the dead land"), which for Eliot and his "hollow men" resembles a Coleridgean Life-in-Death, again marked by the absence of an affirming will; "This broken jaw of our lost kingdoms" (line 56),

---

7. See *WLF,* 125–26, and Empson, *Using Biography,* 189–90.

8. "The real revolution in [the United States] was not what is called the Revolution in the history books, but is a consequence of the Civil War; after which rose a plutocratic élite . . ." (*NDC,* 118).

9. Eliot, "Sceptical Patrician," 361.

which evokes, through the allusion to Samson's heroic feat with the jaw bone of an ass (Judges 15:15–19), the redemptive history of God's chosen people; "death's twilight kingdom" (line 65), much the same as "the twilight kingdom"; and "For Thine is the Kingdom" (lines 77 and 91), which is taken from the Lord's Prayer.[10]

I am especially interested in "This broken jaw of our lost kingdoms" because it recalls the desolation of Nerval's "*El Desdichado*" and the Fisher King. Moreover, I see a trace of Eliot's lost American patrimony in the phrase—in its implication of a broken covenant. The state of the hollow men, "In this hollow valley / This broken jaw of our lost kingdoms" (lines 55–56), mirrors the spiritual paralysis described by Henry Adams: "The American people . . . were wandering in a wilderness much more sandy than the Hebrews had ever trodden about Sinai; they had neither serpents nor golden calves to worship. They had lost the sense of worship. . . ."[11] Adams's passage foretells the mood of "The Hollow Men" very accurately, and both authors draw a certain pathos from the memory of their American ancestors, who envisioned themselves as prophets. Like *The Education of Henry Adams,* "The Hollow Men" describes an agony of skepticism that leads to a worldview divorced from ultimate value and a concomitant loss of faith in life. The works are further alike in transforming a particular historical and cultural episode into a universal statement of cosmic collapse. If elegiac poetry, such as Donne's Anniversary poems, had a long tradition of monumental gloominess, Adams and Eliot succeeded in applying the elegiac strain to their tragic sense of history.[12]

A palimpsest of autobiographical and American materials underlies "The Hollow Men," providing a basis for the poet's more impersonal meditations on existence and history. In his "Ode," Eliot had connected descriptions of self-doubt and sexual anticlimax to the Fourth of July. Against the background of Guy Fawkes's Gunpowder Plot, "The Hollow Men" builds to the anticlimax of a world ending "Not with a bang but a whimper." In both

10. Northrop Frye observes, "The worlds of experience and innocence, the subway and the rose garden, may be called respectively, using terms from 'The Hollow Men,' 'death's dream kingdom' and 'death's other kingdom'" (Northrop Frye, *T. S. Eliot: An Introduction,* 56).

11. Adams, *Education of Henry Adams,* 328.

12. Bercovitch remarks: "Adams is not a Victorian sage calling halt to a rampant industrial capitalism. He is a prophet reading the fate of humanity, and the universe at large, in the tragic course of American history" (*American Jeremiad,* 195).

poems, there is the tendency to interpret the private self through the history of nations. It can be argued that both poems rely, antithetically, on the optimism of conventional July Fourth rhetoric—I would agree with Hugh Kenner that the comparison between Guy Fawkes Day and Independence Day is virtually inevitable for an American.[13] But an equally significant point may follow. One may look on Guy Fawkes Day as a demonic inversion of the Fourth, a mocking of America as an idea that could not translate into reality. From this angle, the English fireworks become the vehicle of what was, for the poet, an absurdly bitter expression of cultural loss.

Like the Adams of *The Education,* the Eliot of "The Hollow Men" cannot profess faith in the kingdom of God. And yet his ancestral vocation, to advance the kingdom, is not wholly absent from the poem. This calling, figured as a distant bourne or spiritual goal, emerges faintly in section 4, where the covenantal theology of Eliot's American Puritan ancestors is accommodated and transformed by a symbolist concern with musicality and *le rêve.* While "The Hollow Men" is in a theological sense dualistic, differentiating the realms of God and humankind with Calvinistic rigor, the poet's incantatory and visionary idiom makes counterclaims for a transcendent and healing symbolism. As commentators have noted, much of the symbolism is Dantean: the "perpetual star" and "multifoliate rose" direct us to the *Paradiso.* The issue I am considering is this, however: how does the emotional and intellectual burden of "our lost kingdoms" inspire the poet's visionary longing?

Extending a pattern that goes back to "Preludes," Eliot arouses feelings of spiritual renewal only to quell them; for the last section of "The Hollow Men" denies all possibility of spiritual progress on earth. One will recall that Eliot had addressed the hiatus between existence and essence in "Mr. Eliot's Sunday Morning Service," where his American contexts were never far from view. In "The Hollow Men," a "Shadow"—the shadow of original sin or Hulmean discontinuity—falls between the conception and the creation of a millennial kingdom: a dark *coup de grâce* and a final blow against ancestral Pelagianism. The imagery and tone of the previous section harbor the exile's dream of return to a lost covenant and dispensation, but the poem ends with a "whimper" that bespeaks both personal breakdown and the defeat of theocratic history. It is this ruined hope that informs Eliot's echoing of

13. Kenner, *Invisible Poet,* 187.

Poe's "Eldorado" ("And o'er his heart a shadow / Fell . . ." [*PT,* 101]), verses that share a strong verbal and cultural resonance with the climactic, or anticlimactic, refrain of "The Hollow Men": "Falls the Shadow."

In discussing "The Hollow Men," I have highlighted a theme that is familiar to readers of English romantic poetry, for the anticipation of a heavenly kingdom on earth plays a large role in the literary history both of Britain and the United States. After the brutal end of the revolutionary project in France, two generations of British poets invented what M. H. Abrams called "alternative ways to the millennium": if the kingdom of God were not to be realized through political revolution, it could be pursued through the redemptive powers of the imagination.[14] Even in "The Hollow Men," the powers of human consciousness hold out the possibility of salvation, despite a strongly articulated dualism and the crippling burden of sin. As in *The Waste Land* and *Four Quartets* (though not in *Ash-Wednesday*), Eliot shelters a millennial "hope," and his poetry has a revolutionary element in its drive to transcend history's monotony of chaos.

In his 1926 Clark Lectures, Eliot digresses during a talk on Donne to expound a theory of poetic "doubleness"; the theory indicates how the redemptive possibilities of his symbolism and the often inverted (but not entirely abandoned) hope of a millennial kingdom interact. Eliot finds the properties of doubleness (also called the "otherworld type" of writing) in Chapman, Dostoyevsky, and "in a more obvious form," in Browning's "Childe Roland to the Dark Tower Came" (*VMP,* 151–53). A writer's doubleness or "double world" can only be sensed; it is essentially an indirect expression, a correlative, of a personal quest for God. It is mystical. What I wish to stress is that an author's doubleness is as personal as his signature; on this subject Eliot is concerned with personality as the basis for an expression "from which we [as readers] are shut out."[15]

In his digression, Eliot distinguishes between the daydream and the "double-world type" of poem, a distinction that implies he is observing his own progress, from the daydream of "Prufrock," which yielded abstraction without spiritual manna, to the double world of "The Hollow Men," where,

---

14. M. H. Abrams, *Natural Supernaturalism,* 56–65.

15. Eliot returned to the theme of doubleness in his 1934 essay on John Marston, which I have quoted (T. S. Eliot, *Elizabethan Essays,* 190).

by exploring his psyche through an idiosyncratic arrangement of prayer, nursery rhyme, choric utterance, and Dante, as well as through a peculiar suggestiveness of syntax and poetic language, he paved a mystical way to, or towards, God.[16] My argument gathers support from the fact that Symons's quotations of Nerval, in *The Symbolist Movement in Literature*, provided the groundwork for Eliot's taxonomy of poetic types. Among Eliot's examples of the daydream type is the line from "*El Desdichado*," which he first encountered in Symons, and which, as I have proposed, directs us to "Prufrock": "*J'ai rêvé dans la grotte où nage la syrène.*" Doubleness is exemplified by another of Symons's touchstones: "*Crains, dans le mur aveugle, un regard qui t'épie!*" taken from Nerval's "*Vers dorés.*" I think it likely that this last line of verse, received explicitly in the context of Symons's discussion (*VMP*, 154), inspired the images of disembodied and judgmental eyes that people "The Hollow Men" and earlier stages of the work such as "Doris's Dream Songs." Other sources for the eyes are relevant (in Crashaw, Shelley, Baudelaire, and Poe, for example), but Symons in particular would have enabled Eliot to organize his development of such imagery. For Symons, the line from "*Vers dorés*" betokened "the mystery lurking behind the world,"[17] a broad but invaluable symbolism in light of the material Eliot was working with. Eliot would have found support in Symons's reading of Nerval for an analysis by which he could both coordinate different moments in his career, and bring order to his mystical preoccupations.

Eliot wanted "the mystery lurking behind the world" to have a moral dimension. In his final Clark Lecture, he discussed a tradition of "Satanism," a path that leads from Byron—in whom "the cultivation of Evil" was basically "a pose," but nonetheless a "revival of morality"—to Poe, Baudelaire, and Wilde (*VMP*, 209–10). With its dark radiance, "The Hollow Men" owes a debt to this particular strain of symbolism. Eliot's repetition of "kingdom" points to Poe's mesmerizing use of the same word in "Annabel Lee," where Poe's Byronic ancestry is quite conspicuous; the Satanic strain of symbolism, the falling shadow, the lost kingdom, and the inverted Fourth of July all bear the stamp of Poe.

16. Denis Donoghue aptly refers to "a strange quality of Eliot's poetic language, its observance of other duties than denotation" (Denis Donoghue, "Eliot's 'Marina' and Closure," 377).

17. Symons, *Symbolist Movement,* 11; cited by Schuchard (*VMP,* 154 n).

Of the two modes of poetry, Satanism and mystical doubleness, the former is open, the latter opaque to the reader. It is a problem for Eliot that these modes do not necessarily work to parallel ends. Doubleness is mystical and psychological, and it flirts with psychosis: it pertains to the self's isolated pursuit of the divine, but at least the divine is, in some sense, accessible. By contrast, the nineteenth-century strain of Satanism meets Eliot's definition of metaphysical poetry by providing an emotional equivalent for thought, and an intellectual counterpart for feeling, through an obsession with sin that refers, by way of Byron, to Calvinism. And sin is a very workable, very solid foundation for giving a definite shape to the emotions. But Satanism, the aesthetic of hell, is in another sense an admission of despair and an abandonment of duty.

In considering the interaction, in both his poetry and critical writings, of Eliot's symbolism and the idea of a millennial kingdom, I have arrived at an Eliotic crux—it is a version of a question that pursued him through all his major poems, the question of the use of poetry, and of the moral defensibility of his work. During the period of "The Hollow Men" and the Clark Lectures, it arose with the recognition that the double world failed to share its harvest of moral and spiritual truth. This is not quite the dilemma of *The Waste Land,* for in the present case the poet may embark on a journey to God, may even achieve a knowledge of God's presence radiating from outside the self, and yet needn't communicate that presence to the reader. If the kingdom of God were to be a realizable telos for society, Eliot could not rest with the personal satisfaction of doubleness: he needed to bring private mystical insight, which remained important in his later poetry, into harmony with moral and religious tradition. In order to redeem the time of his exile, he needed to redeem the time of his people.

But who were his people? In the first two Ariel poems, "Journey of the Magi" (1927) and "A Song for Simeon" (1928), Eliot sought to integrate private and public religious experience by assuming the identity of biblical figures. It has never been remarked that he was preceded in this tradition by his grandfather. William Eliot wrote "Nunc Dimittis" in 1886, on the eve of his death and his grandson's birth. Charlotte Eliot printed it in her biography, *William Greenleaf Eliot:*

> Fain would I breathe out that gracious word,
> Now lettest thou thy servant, Lord,

> Depart in peace.
> When may I humbly claim that kind award,
>   And cares and labors cease?
>
> With anxious heart I watch at heaven's gate—
>   Answer to hear;
> With failing strength I feel the increasing weight
>   Of every passing year.
> Hath not the time yet fully come, dear Lord,
>   Thy servant to release?[18]

This short poem, inspired perhaps by Browning's religious monologues, is based on the Gospel of Luke. By virtue of his pious old age, the biblical Simeon is an appealing figure. Of particular interest here is that, as a witness to his people's redemption, he speaks for the nation of Israel.[19]

In adopting the role of Simeon, Eliot would have remembered his grandfather's poem and his grandfather's life. And it happens, for Eliot's was a very literary family, that we have a good idea of what such a memory meant to the poet. In *William Greenleaf Eliot,* Charlotte Eliot follows her quotation of "Nunc Dimittis" with some eulogistic remarks:

> What was the secret of Dr. Eliot's power? Above all else, his absolute self-consecration to the service of God and man, which was to him not only a duty but a divine instinct inspired by love. This it was that impelled him to leave home and friends and the attractions of the older communities to work in the then "far West," and later to resist the temptation to return eastward under favorable auspices. He went to St. Louis not only as an evangelist, a missionary of a liberal faith to spiritualize Unitarianism in the West, but as an educator, a philanthropist, a patriotic citizen of the Republic, to assist in founding institutions of learning, in advancing all humane objects, and in making Missouri a free State.[20]

Eliot inherited from his mother and grandfather a missionary idealism, which they had expressed through the typological use of biblical figures and topoi. Within this typological framework, Missouri was William Eliot's

---

18. Quoted in Charlotte Eliot, *William Greenleaf Eliot,* 351–52.
19. See John Timmerman, *T. S. Eliot's Ariel Poems: The Poetics of Recovery,* 119.
20. Charlotte Eliot, *William Greenleaf Eliot,* 352–53.

Israel; as a type of Simeon, he had dedicated his life to fulfilling the Christian promise of the American West.

"A Song for Simeon" addresses this powerful inheritance. Eliot's poem of "dust in sunlight and memory in corners" is, I want to suggest, a form of conversation between the living and the dead, a conversation about family responsibilities:

> I have walked many years in this city,
> Kept faith and fast, provided for the poor,
> Have given and taken honour and ease.
> There went never any rejected from my door.
> Who shall remember my house, where shall live my children's children
> When the time of sorrow is come?
> They will take to the goat's path, and the fox's home,
> Fleeing from the foreign faces and the foreign swords.
>
> ("Simeon" 9–16)

One can imagine—the thought has a Jamesian piquancy—that it is the ghost of the grandfather, William Eliot, who speaks of his life of ministry, of walking "many years" in the city of St. Louis, and who ponders the fate of his "children's children" and his "house"; I note the echo in Simeon's "kept faith and fast" of Prufrock's "I have wept and fasted," the earlier poem reacting, in my view, against the grandfather's legacy (see Chapter 2), while the later poem returns to it as a paradoxical source of identity. The living poet, for whom "the time of sorrow is come," has fled from America, fled its "foreign faces" and "foreign swords," and consequently no longer has an Israel to serve. His experience, like his description of spiritual birth, is self-directed:

> Now at this birth season of decease,
> Let the Infant, the still unspeaking and unspoken Word,
> Grant Israel's consolation
> To one who has eighty years and no to-morrow.
>
> ("Simeon" 21–24)

The poem's many antitheses cover, one feels, an eerie stillness. Where in *The Waste Land* and "The Hollow Men" the idea of Israel lived in the poetry's exilic pathos, the exhausted speaker of "A Song for Simeon" verges on abandoning "Israel" emotionally, on reducing it to a gesture. Worn out with his ancestral calling, the poet is summoned by his grandfather's ghost, and communicates his sense of futility and lassitude: "Grant me thy peace," he intones, "I am tired with my own life and the lives of those after me."

In "Animula" (1929), Eliot resumed the difficult task of integrating personal feeling with Judeo-Christian traditions. The verses about child-hood epitomize what we know of Eliot's youth: the servants, the moral expectations, the sea's presence, the love of books. In this autobiographical (and rather Wordsworthian) context, the scene of reading the encyclopedia opens a metanarrative, as the author's life begins to appear as a book among a constellation of other, related books. One thinks of the young Jane Eyre tucked away in her window seat ("amazingly good stuff," Eliot told his mother [*LTSE*, 219]). But only in a nominal sense is the *Encyclopaedia Britannica* a book; more accurately, it is a patchwork in which no single vision prevails, and thus an emblem of the young soul's confusion.

Connected to the scene of the child's reading the encyclopedia is an-other, equally troubling one: Eliot's reading of Dante. The two moments of reading create a circuit. In refiguring the division between the soul and God that Eliot's opening quotation articulates (by way of the theological passage on which "Animula" is based, in *Purgatorio* 16), the reading of the *Encyclopaedia Britannica* foreshadows the adult poet's spiritual crisis. Rhetoricians would call this interplay of texts a "metalepsis," an elliptical form of attributing a consequence (Eliot's recognition of himself in Dante's explanation of human errancy) to an antecedent (the child's reading the patchwork encyclopedia), with an accompanying transformation of fact (the encyclopedia and its version of reality) into value (the Dantean un-derstanding of alienation from God). Through both moments of reading, the poet marks his distance from an ideal Christian order; only through the reading of Dante, however, is this distance made self-conscious, and finally expressed in an autobiographical portrait of the poet as a young and isolated reader.

Eliot underscores the metaleptic relation between the scenes of reading by placing line 23, "Behind the *Encyclopaedia Britannica*," alongside a restatement of the opening line—with the word "God" changed to "time." This restatement ushers in a passage about adult life, where the distance between self and God has widened disastrously. It becomes apparent that the cost of healing this break is the poet's identity, his craft and imagination:

> Issues from the hand of time the simple soul
> Irresolute and selfish, misshapen, lame,
> Unable to fare forward or retreat,
> Fearing the warm reality, the offered good,
> Denying the importunity of the blood,
> Shadow of its own shadows, spectre in its own gloom,
> Leaving disordered papers in a dusty room;
> Living first in the silence after the viaticum.
>
> ("Animula" 24–31)

As a "shadow of its own shadows, spectre in its own gloom," the soul ironically recapitulates a process of interiorization, a turning inward for spiritual strength, that began in English poetry with Spenser and Milton and found renewed expression in Wordsworth and Coleridge, as in Whitman and Poe. Here the process constitutes a flight from God, and the poet claims not to draw strength from it; only after receiving the viaticum, the final communion given to the dying, does the soul live for the first time. Indeed, the mood is rather grim. Rejecting his more immediate poetic forebears, perhaps overwhelmed by Dante's moral and artistic superiority, the poet would renounce his poetic vocation (symbolically foregrounded by a closing triplet), which has brought him to "disordered papers in a dusty room."[21]

"Animula" ends with a coda, an attempt to reconcile personal mysticism with formal Christian prayer. Seeking to escape his spiritual isolation, the poet grafts the mysterious, Adonis-like image of Floret onto the structure of a Roman Catholic prayer, the "Hail Mary." But the result has the opposite effect: a confirmation of the young boy's loneliness and the soul as a "spectre in its own gloom." The fragmentary and allusive cast of the reference to Floret, with its cryptic symbolism of "boarhound" and "yew trees," makes the ritual seem intensely private.

Published by Eliot in 1930, *Ash-Wednesday* is contemporaneous in some of its sections with several of the Ariel poems and reflects their preoccupations on a larger scale and through a more varied verse-medium. It returns to the problem of integrating private experience with public forms of worship and confession, but, as a major work, fully engages the emotional

---

21. I am borrowing from Vinnie-Marie D'Ambrosio, who treats the link between "the drug of dreams" and Eliot's adolescent development in her rewarding study of Eliot and FitzGerald's *Rubáiyát;* see Vinnie-Marie D'Ambrosio, *Eliot Possessed: T. S. Eliot and FitzGerald's "Rubáiyát,"* 17–28.

and intellectual sources of Eliot's poetry, including the stimulus of Poe. In *"Note sur Mallarmé et Poe,"* which appeared in Paris in November 1926, Eliot formulated a defense of Poe that presaged the method he would employ for *Ash-Wednesday.* I translate the closing paragraph:

> It is arguable that "metaphysical poetry" precedes or follows philo-sophical poetry, and that it appears in the absence of an established philosophy. In Poe and Mallarmé, philosophy is to some degree re-placed by an element of *incantation.* In "Ulalume," for example, and in *Un Coup de Dés,* this incantation, which insists on the primitive power of the Word *(Fatum),* is obvious. In this regard, Mallarmé's phrase, which applies so well to himself, constitutes a brilliant analysis of Poe: *donner un sens plus pur aux mots de la tribu.* The effort to restore the power of the Word, which inspires the syntax of both writers and leads them away from pure sound or pure melody (which both men, had they desired, could have exploited to no end), this effort, which prevents the reader from swallowing whole their phrasing or verse-line, is one of the qualities that the poets most have in common. There is also the sureness of their steps as they pass from the tangible world to the world of phantoms.[22]

Eliot compares his subjects on the basis of Mallarmé's words in *"Le Tombeau d'Edgar Poe":* their uncommon labor was, as Eliot would later write, "to purify the dialect of the tribe" (LG 127). They share an incantatory style in which the gravity of syntax mediates the ether of pure sound. In conse-quence, they "restore" to the tribe a mystical potency of language. Here, and in their ability "to pass from the tangible world to the world of phantoms," they connect the common walks of society to the double-world.

In equating the "primitive power of the Word" to Fate, Eliot hints at the equivalence of this "primitive power" with the Word of God, and ponders the capacity of the poet, as seer, to become a channel for Fate. It was in the opening passage of *Ash-Wednesday* 5, which dates from 1928, that he found a chance to test the religious implications of his poetic:

> If the lost word is lost, if the spent word is spent
> If the unheard, unspoken

22. T. S. Eliot, *"Note sur Mallarmé et Poe,"* 526. The translation into French is by Ramon Fernandez; to my knowledge, the original English text is lost. I am grateful to my colleague Margaret Spires for her assistance with my translation.

> Word is unspoken, unheard;
> Still is the unspoken word, the Word unheard,
> The Word without a word, the Word within
> The world and for the world;
> And the light shone in darkness and
> Against the Word the unstilled world still whirled
> About the centre of the silent Word.
>
> (*AW* 149–57)

This is where Bishop Andrewes meets the author of "The Bells." The technique of Andrewes, as Eliot understood it in 1928, had been summarized by Andrewes's recent editor: "Andrewes develops an idea he has in mind: every line tells and adds something. He does not expatiate, but moves forward: if he repeats, it is because the repetition has a real force of expression; if he accumulates, each new word or phrase represents a new development, a substantive addition to what he is saying. He assimilates his material and advances by means of it."[23] By combining a similarly repeating, accumulative style with a poetry of incantation, Eliot created the opening passage of *Ash-Wednesday* 5. Shunning the Byronic Poe, the Poe of sin and revolt, he attempts to bring the poet's word, the "lost" or unredeemed word of his poetic calling, into harmony with the divine Logos. Throughout *Ash-Wednesday,* the poet seeks to relinquish the Satanic strain of "The Hollow Men" by enacting, through the mutual operations of language and belief, a trancelike state of heightened receptivity to God. Eliot shares Poe's obsession with intense rhyming and incantatory repetition. His unique success is to fuse Poe's aesthetic to poetry that has a redemptive element.

The fifth section features an antiphon: "O my people, what have I done to thee" (lines 158 and 176) and "O my people" (line 184). These choric reproaches are from the liturgy for Good Friday; the "people" are the people of Israel, reproached by Christ as he takes the cross. The effect marks another poetic success for Eliot: where "Animula" had ended on a note of isolation, here the devotional lyric and liturgical structure suggest a correspondence between the mystical quest for personal salvation and public forms of worship. Though his theme is one of human deafness to God, the poet's mystical pursuit of the Word is fittingly answered and strangely affirmed by the voice of Christ.

---

23. F. E. Brightman, quoted in Eliot (*FLA*, 11–12).

One difficulty remains. In looking at "A Song for Simeon," I argued that Eliot's naming of "Israel" was rhetorically hollow—perhaps deliberately so. Because Eliot doesn't resolve the meaning or identity of Israel in *Ash-Wednesday,* he risks the same effect. As a self-conscious poet, he wavers between two traditions, that associating Israel with America in American Puritan culture, and the corresponding tradition of English poets in the Miltonic line. He draws on Ezekiel's account of the valley of dry bones (Ezek. 37) for section 2, but where Blake, in *The Marriage of Heaven and Hell,* had discovered a nexus between the resurrected bones of "the whole house of Israel" and the redemption of humankind through the French Revolution, Eliot turns his back on history:

> Under a juniper-tree the bones sang, scattered and shining
> We are glad to be scattered, we did little good to each other,
> Under a tree in the cool of the day, with the blessing of sand,
> Forgetting themselves and each other, united
> In the quiet of the desert. This is the land which ye
> Shall divide by lot. And neither division nor unity
> Matters. This is the land. We have our inheritance.
>
> (*AW* 89–95)

The bones do not unite, the desert replaces the promised land, and the inheritance is otherworldly. In his shifting and circular use of personal pronouns ("we," "each other," "themselves," "each other," "ye," "we"), the poet weaves a net of collective address around himself and his readers. His aim is not only quietism: it is to make the allure of ascetic withdrawal palpable. The poem's recurring Marian figure, whom Eliot describes in the fourth section as "Talking of trivial things / In ignorance and in knowledge of eternal dolour," represents a cathexis of devotional quietism.

It would thus appear that Eliot has abandoned the millennial vocation of his ancestors. For Allen Tate, discussing the poem in the early 1930s, such a passage communicated the poet's "humility," "a self-respect proceeding from a sense of the folly of men in their desire to dominate a natural force or situation." Eliot had cited Tate approvingly in "American Critics,"[24] a

---

24. Allen Tate, *On the Limits of Poetry: Selected Essays, 1928–1948,* 346. Eliot, "American Critics," 24. In this essay, Eliot connects Tate, as a member of "the third generation of modern American criticism," to Irving Babbitt and P. E. More, representatives of the first generation,

1929 review, and one finds evidence, both in *Ash-Wednesday* and in Tate's interpretation of it, of a reaction against the political and social legacy of the North after the American Civil War.

In the notorious Page-Barbour Lectures of 1933, Eliot expressed his sympathy with the Southern Agrarian movement, of which Tate was a prominent member. Ruminating over the ills of the "industrial expansion of the latter part of the nineteenth and the first part of the twentieth century," Eliot pronounced the Civil War to be "certainly the greatest disaster in the whole of American history," adding, "it is just as certainly a disaster from which the country has never recovered, and perhaps never will . . ." (*ASG*, 16). This opinion severely questions his family's heroic military and personal sacrifice for the Union cause. It also suggests why Eliot would be willing to renounce history, to forego questions of "division" and "unity," and to seek the peace of the desert. In eschewing all causes, the Eliot of *Ash-Wednesday* lent support to Tate's growing New Critical consensus (discussed in Chapter 7). But Eliot's rejection of his family's old commitment to the historical millennium would not extend to *Four Quartets*.

In the sixth and final section of *Ash-Wednesday*, the poet turns unexpectedly to America, a place that does not promise redemption, but that nonetheless inspires his poetry. The section's opening lines reprise those of the first section, and thus restate the theme of exile, for as Kermode observes, "The poem of Cavalcanti [that Eliot] echoes here, '*Perch'io non spero di tornare mai*,' is a poem of exile, and *tornare* really means not 'turn' but 'return.' "[25] It appears rather suddenly that Eliot is in some sense writing about his exile from America—from the New England of youth and memory. The poet confesses, "I do not wish to wish these things," and conscience balks, for the "lost heart" that rejoices in the pleasures of earth rebels from its God. Images of New England and America, the "granite shore," "lilac," and "golden-rod," bring concreteness to a poem that is generally very abstract,

---

who were balanced in their reaction against "the influence of President Eliot, of Harvard. . . ." The second generation, represented by H. L. Mencken and Van Wyck Brooks, stands outside the main current—Mencken is cranky and Brooks "merely querulous." (Mencken, when he met Eliot a few years later, was politely bored.) Eliot goes on to suggest that Babbitt, More, and T. E. Hulme were kindred minds (T. S. Eliot, "Mr. P. E. More's Essays," 136); he thus campaigned for an American criticism originating in a judicious reaction against the progressivist ethos of Harvard (and his own family) after the Civil War.

25. Kermode, *Appetite*, 110.

but they may be delusions, since it is traditionally false dreams that issue from the "ivory gates." The parenthetic and somewhat confessional "(Bless me father)" ambiguously raises the matter of fathers and patrimonies, worldly and spiritual: the phrase, as if it were nearly repressed and had crossed the threshold into being only through a parenthetical change of tone and voice, belongs to a mysterious index of hidden vistas in Eliot's poetry—the strain of doubleness that materializes from time to time.

As a denouement to the larger poem, the final section is fraught with ironies. Having forsaken history for the desert, the poet elected an otherworldly inheritance in section 2; he abandoned hope of the millennium and accepted exile as the human condition. In section 6, exile becomes more particular, an expression of the poet's desire to "recover" what he had earlier forsaken as "lost" and the root of "loss." What Eliot moves to "recover" (a nicely ambiguous word) is the fertile memory of America, which is precisely what he had renounced in November 1927, when he became a British citizen by naturalization and, during the same fall months, turned his back on history by declaring (under the title, "Salutation," later section 2), "We have our inheritance." Two years later, the lost heart, exiled from its homeland, rejoices in that homeland, which is itself "lost," like the "word" of the poet's calling in section 5.

Ash-Wednesday proved to be the beginning of Eliot's poetic *nostos*. In "Marina," written in 1930 and closely connected to the final section of *Ash-Wednesday,* he resumed his journey to the New England coast, but with the redemptive promise of his native shore mysteriously restored.[26] From the standpoint of Eliot's oeuvre, *Ash-Wednesday*'s closing prayer for reconciliation and return would be granted.

26. A. D. Moody finds that " 'Marina' originated in the drafting of *Ash-Wednesday*" (A. David Moody, "The American Strain," 86). Moody's essay is a first-rate introduction to the American Eliot, and I am indebted to it.

6 | The Soul's Mysterious Errand

Life only avails, not the having lived. Power ceases in the instant of repose; it resides in the moment of transition from a past to a new state, in the shooting of the gulf, in the darting to an aim. This one fact the world hates, that the soul *becomes;* for that for ever degrades the past, turns all riches to poverty, all reputation to a shame, confounds the saint with the rogue, shoves Jesus and Judas equally aside. Why, then, do we prate of self-reliance? Inasmuch as the soul is present, there will be power not confident but agent. To talk of reliance is a poor external way of speaking. Speak rather of that which relies, because it works and is.   (*Works,* 2:69–70)

ELIOT WOULD PROBABLY HAVE responded to this celebrated passage from "Self-Reliance" by contending that if you "shove Jesus and Judas equally aside," you will have small matter left for moral argument and the feelings that morality inspires. Such a response would not be unusual: Emerson's inconsistencies in the field of ethics are widely noted. As Stephen Whicher observed, Emerson's "faith in the Soul" could not resolve the conflict between his ideals of power and law, of "life and moral perfection."[1]

Yet even in 1919, a week after telling the readers of the *Athenaeum,* "the essays of Emerson are already an encumbrance," Eliot could write in the

---

1. Stephen Whicher, *Freedom and Fate,* 49. Committed to the social foundation of morals, Eliot arrived at a diametrical remove from what Whicher called Emerson's "radical egoistic anarchism."

same pages: "The Arts insist that a man shall dispose of all that he has, even of his family tree, and follow art alone. For they require that a man be not a member of a family or of a caste or of a party or of a coterie, but simply and solely himself." This is very close to Emerson, and the general sentiment informs not only the Divinity School Address,[2] but the Emersonian culture of New England, including the writings of Charlotte Eliot. In her *Savonarola*, Charlotte dramatizes the moment when the hero finds his calling and his mother realizes that she must lose him:

> Savonarola:
> > Go mother, go. I hear the sweet bells chime.
> > And now my father calls thee. It is time
> > That thou depart. So, let me kiss thy hands.
> > Through many years fulfilling love's commands,
> > How beautiful they are! Lay them on me
> > And consecrate my destiny.
> Elena (anxiously):
> > Thy destiny? My son, with heavy heart
> > I leave thee if I must. I know we part
> > But for a little while, yet fears oppress
> > Vague, undefined. Give me a last caress
> > And then, farewell.[3]

Eliot's high regard for Machiavelli marks yet another point of controversy between him and his mother, whose heritage had made Savonarola—onetime head of the Florentine Republic, victim of Pope Alexander VI, and idealist foil to Machiavelli's political realism—a kind of Puritan saint. But the continuities between mother and son are ultimately more important than their differences. In keeping with his Unitarian and Emersonian parentage, T. S. Eliot in 1919 recasts Christ's injunctions concerning the costs of discipleship (Luke 14:25–35); upholding a family tradition of personal calling, he transfers his activities to the sphere of art.

By 1935, the year of "Burnt Norton," Eliot had fully reclaimed his broader social and religious interests: "To be free we must be stripped,

2. T. S. Eliot, "A Romantic Patrician," 266–67. In the Divinity School Address, Emerson asks: "Where now sounds the persuasion, that by its very melody imparadises the heart, and so affirms its own origin in heaven? Where shall I hear words such as in elder ages drew men to leave all and follow—father and mother, house and land, wife and child?" (*Works,* 1:136).

3. Charlotte Eliot, *Savonarola,* 5–6.

like the sea-god Glaucus, of any number of incrustations of education and frequentation; we must divest ourselves even of our ancestors. But to undertake this stripping of acquired ideas, we must make one assumption: that of the individuality of each human being; we must, in fact, believe in the soul." One should approach these remarks through the context of Eliot's Christian response to the political turmoil of the 1930s.[4] It was in "the needs of the individual soul" that he found a defense against the "regimentation and conformity" that threatened all Western culture (*ICS*, 18). Whereas "a society with a religious basis" would foster individuality, the modern secular nation, whether democratic or fascist or communist ("If you will not have God . . . you should pay your respects to Hitler or Stalin" [*ICS*, 50]), inclined toward "the subduing of free intellectual speculation, and the debauching of the arts by political criteria" (*ICS*, 34); the real issue was not, as was commonly assumed, democracy versus totalitarianism, but paganism versus Christianity. As if to underscore his contention that only a religious culture can tolerate a gadfly, Eliot writes as a Christian apologist in 1935, but he challenges the more traditional Christian public: instead of hymning High-Church conservatism, he alludes ambiguously to a sea god—to a world that is too much with us—and thus conveys the impression that his view of the soul is not predictably orthodox.

But can his view be called Emersonian? The meaning of the word "soul" in "Self-Reliance" poses a crucial problem for students of American literary and intellectual history. Critic Richard Poirier discusses Emerson from a standpoint that is at once pragmatist, mediated by a rather despiritualized version of William James, and theoretical, by way of poststructuralism and Jacques Derrida.[5] For Poirier's Emerson, the soul

> is not to be imagined as an entity; it is more nearly a function, and
> yet no determination is made as to when the function occurs or from

4. T. S. Eliot, "Notes on the Way," 89. On the subject of Eliot's cultural politics in the 1930s, see Jeffrey Perl's *Skepticism and Modern Enmity: Before and After Eliot*, 86–112. From an adversarial position, the best analysis of Eliot's cultural writings is Raymond Williams's *Culture and Society, 1780–1950*, 227–43.

5. Poirier's definition of the soul as function echoes a well-known passage from Derrida: "It was necessary to begin thinking that there was no center, that the center could not be thought in the form of present-being, that the center had no natural site, that it was not a fixed locus but a function . . . in which an infinite number of sign-substitutions came into play" (Jacques Derrida, *Writing and Difference*, 280).

where it emanates. The soul has no determinable there or then, no here or now; rather, as [Emerson's] italics insist, it only *"becomes,"* only promises to make its presence known. That is, the soul appears or occurs only as something we feel compelled to live into or to move toward *as if* it were there. . . .

The creative impulse which is the soul discovers in the very first stages of composition that it wants to reach out beyond any legible form, that it wants to seek the margins, to move beyond limits or fate.[6]

As a reading of Emerson, the passage reflects indirectly on many American writers, not least the Eliot of *Four Quartets.* In his poem's succession of houses—the estate at Burnt Norton, the ephemeral houses of East Coker, the St. Louis home of "The Dry Salvages," and the Anglican church at Little Gidding—Eliot constructs dwellings for what he calls the "soul" and "spirit," then time and again abandons these stopping places in favor of "a moving toward" more adequate moments of insight. But if Poirier is very good at observing the improvisatory brilliance of Emerson's writing, he is willfully blind to the Transcendental and religious dimension of the historical Emerson—I take issue with that *"as if."* While following Poirier's insights into the soul's "becoming" as in some respect a compositional process, I want to keep hold of the austere spirituality that connects Emerson to Eliot.[7]

In this chapter, I approach Eliot's Emersonianism through what may seem an eccentric hypothesis: that beginning with the final section of *Ash-Wednesday* (discussed in Chapter 5), the expatriate poet and High-Churchman returned to his native traditions in order to set down the spiritual experience that culminated in *Four Quartets.* I explore this ambivalent and difficult return through Eliot's relation to several authors, but chiefly through his likeness to Emerson in their respective discourses on the soul. Matthiessen's much repeated statement, "[Eliot] once remarked to me . . . of his sustained distaste for Emerson," seems to have cut off investigation

6. Richard Poirier, *Poetry and Pragmatism,* 23–25.

7. I am seeking some middle ground in the debate over the poststructuralist Emerson. Michael Lopez advances the cause of poststructuralism during a helpful discussion of Emerson's ties to nineteenth-century romantic thought more generally; see Michael Lopez, "De-transcendentalizing Emerson." Offering a more traditional perspective, Alan Hodder surveys the contentious field of Emerson studies in his fine historicist essay, " 'After a High Negative Way': Emerson's 'Self-Reliance' and the Rhetoric of Conversion."

into the Emersonian aspects of *Four Quartets*. Indeed, one measure of Eliot's success in legislating his academic reception is the absence of Emerson's name from the subject index of Mildred Martin's weighty *A Half-Century of Eliot Criticism*.[8] Here I want to build on my argument of previous chapters, that Emerson was a vital part of Eliot's cultural inheritance. I will develop two focal points: one, where Eliot adapts Emersonianism to his own purposes, and two, where he successfully departs from it, thus challenging American readers, past and present, about what constitutes American poetry.

In "the still point of the turning world" (line 62), the poet of "Burnt Norton" resurrected a concept that had seen earlier use in *Coriolan* 1, "Triumphal March" (1931). Eliot never finished the *Coriolan* sequence, and one may wonder if the plan of that sequence, to describe a spiritual progress in the modern world, failed because his symbolism was inadequate to the task. The still point of *Coriolan* inheres in a supreme and abstract reality, which resembles the Hindus' *Nirguna Brahman*:

> O hidden under the dove's wing, hidden in the turtle's breast,
> Under the palmtree at noon, under the running water
> At the still point of the turning world. O hidden.
> ("Triumphal March" 32–34)[9]

When Emerson wrote his famous poem "Brahma," he imagined a similarly impersonal version of the divine: it was perhaps the utter remove of such high-order abstractions that drove Eliot to change his poetic tack. In *Four Quartets,* the still point continues to be the "hidden" core of reality, knowable only through grace and spiritual discipline; however, as the theme is echoed and elaborated, stillness itself takes on new significance in the poem as the goal of an emergent quest—a quest with visible and personal

8. Ronald Bush anticipates my line of thought: "No matter how hard the later Eliot tried to accept received dogma and received ritual, his striving betrayed an Emersonian quest to renew and purify the spirit" (Ronald Bush, " 'Turned toward Creation': T. S. Eliot, 1988," 1:42). The references are to Matthiessen, *Achievement*, 8, and Mildred Martin, *A Half-Century of Eliot Criticism: An Annotated Bibliography of Books and Articles in English, 1916–1965*. John Clendenning's lonely article of 1967, "Time, Doubt and Vision," is brief but insightful in comparing Eliot and Emerson, with emphasis on "the Boston doubt."

9. Eliot was recalling a poem from his pre–*Waste Land* days, "Hidden under the heron's wing" (*IMH*, 82), which, with its singing "lotos-birds," suggests the influence of Indic religion.

contours. As a goal, the still point develops affinities with Eliot's symbolism of the New World, a class of symbolism that he was also extending during the 1930s.

In lines 70–78 of the first *Quartet* ("The inner freedom from the practical desire . . ."), the still point retains much of its abstractness. Eliot carves out a mode of contemplation, which he approaches first in contrast to the "practical," then through a hint of feeling, a "grace of sense / a white light still and moving," then through an abstract series of near paradoxes. Like the "still point" that it explicitly resembles, the "new world" is at this juncture largely conceptual. Only at the end of "Burnt Norton" does it begin to take shape in three dimensions:

> Sudden in a shaft of sunlight
> Even while the dust moves
> There rises the hidden laughter
> Of children in the foliage
> Quick now, here, now, always—
> (BN 169–73)

In his short lyric "New Hampshire" (1934), Eliot had described "Children's voices in the orchard / Between the blossom- and the fruit-time" (*CP*, 138). In "Burnt Norton" 1, he deliberately resumes this line of imagery: a 1941 letter to John Hayward refers to "the children in the appletree meaning to tie up New Hampshire and Burnt Norton."[10] At the poem's conclusion, he builds on the images of "New Hampshire" and "Burnt Norton" 1 until they begin to form a theme or pattern, a recurring symbolism of a longed-for paradise that is always "a new world."

I will cast one more backward glance in observing Eliot's symbolism of the New World, as that symbolism developed in the years leading up to *Four Quartets*. Written in 1930, "Marina" dramatizes an anagnorisis that occurs on the New England coast.[11] As in *Four Quartets*, the beauty of a landscape conduces to a moment of spiritual reflection, though here Eliot uses the

10. Quoted in Helen Gardner, *The Composition of "Four Quartets*," 29.
11. In 1930, Eliot told a friend that his New England was more closely tied in memory to Maine than to Massachusetts (letter to William Force Stead, June 20, 1930). In another letter of 1930, he said that England couldn't inspire his natural imagery, and that, to write about nature, he had to imagine Missouri and New England (letter to William Force Stead, August 9, 1930).

high romantic trope of the divine wind or afflatus to express a visionary state. The poet leaves behind a world of "Death," identified by preparations for war, by vanity, stasis, and animal pleasure, which

> Are become unsubstantial, reduced by a wind,
> A breath of pine, and the woodsong fog
> By this grace dissolved in place
>
> ("Marina" 14–16)

It would be facile to say that the poet has abandoned Europe for America; rather, he has assimilated America and its redemptive mythology to his own journey. Thus, in writing "Marina," Eliot discovered a more adequate symbol for the movement toward spiritual fulfillment than the still point of *Coriolan*. As *Four Quartets* unfolded, he drew on "Marina" to bring a concrete and affecting reality to the intangible paradox of stillness (the "still and moving"), which consequently became associated with "the frontiers of the spirit."[12] "Marina" was a breakthrough because it portrayed America, the New World, as a spiritual frontier.

One way, rarely if ever explored, of interpreting the *Quartets* is through their relation to Hart Crane's *The Bridge* (1930), where the crossing from an old to a new world is a central theme. Much of Crane's work enters into dialogue with Eliot, and it is virtually certain that Eliot noticed his influence on a younger contemporary whose work he admired. Having published "The Tunnel," the penultimate section of *The Bridge*, in a 1927 issue of the *Criterion*,[13] Eliot may have had his eye on it while composing the tube scene in "Burnt Norton" 3; I will quote Crane, and then Eliot:

> In the car
> the overtone of motion
> underground, the monotone
> of motion is the sound
> of other faces, also underground—
>
> . . . .

12. T. S. Eliot, "A Commentary: That Poetry Is Made with Words," 27. One may compare Eliot's remark of 1942: "If, as we are aware, only a part of the meaning can be conveyed by paraphrase, that is because the poet is occupied with frontiers of consciousness beyond which words fail, though meanings still exist" (*OPP*, 30).

13. In the *Monthly Criterion* 6 (November 1927), 398–402.

> Toward corners of the floor
> Newspapers wing, revolve and wing.
> Blank windows gargle signals through the roar.[14]

> Only a flicker
> Over the strained time-ridden faces
> Distracted from distraction by distraction
> Filled with fancies and empty of meaning
> Tumid apathy with no concentration
> Men and bits of paper, whirled by the cold wind
> (BN 99–104)

Like Dante before the city of Hell (possibly evoked by the iteration, "Dis . . . dis . . . dis"), Eliot remains spiritually aloof. The train is his symbol of how "the world moves / In appetency, on its metalled ways" (BN 124–25), but his is not among the faces beleaguered and run over by time. By comparison, Crane achieves the eerie effect of mechanizing language and his own voice through the repetition of "motion," "tone," and "ground," by personifying (or demonizing) the "blank windows" that "gargle" (the word derives from the Old French *gargouille,* "throat," and is cognate to "gargoyle"), and through the synaesthetic convergence of the "sound" of these words with the entire field of figuration and imagery. Though Crane as narrator merges with his environment and Eliot does not, each writer faces an existential blankness, and each depicts a journey through a dark night of the soul. Through parallels of setting, mood, and theme, Eliot and Crane pursue a conversation about ends that are desired but in doubt, about their respective quests as poets, and about the destination or *telos* towards which their societies should be directed.

In "The Tunnel" Crane asks: "did you deny the ticket, Poe?";[15] that is, did you, Poe, disavow the physical and spiritual transit, the millennial promise of self and nation? The question is not merely rhetorical and awaits an answer for the reason that "Poe" comprises many figures. He is the historical Edgar Poe, author of "To Helen," "The Raven," and "The City in the Sea," poems that Crane weaves into his own writing. He is also Crane's antiself, a doubter and an agent of irony, "The Tunnel" being the womblike/tomblike

---

14. Crane, "The Tunnel," 98, 100, in *Poems.*
15. Ibid., 99.

space of struggle between the two poets. But Crane has more in mind than competition—he wants to transform his adversary. Rewriting Poe's "Nevermore" as "O evermore," he seeks to change the meaning of Poe's work, to absorb him within the utopian trajectory of *The Bridge*. Granted christological qualities, Poe becomes a kind of martyr who hovers on the brink of resurrection. And it is likely that this new status for Poe takes its epistemological sanction from Eliot's perspective toward literary tradition: "the past should be altered by the present as much as the present is directed by the past."

I want to suggest that Eliot detected a challenge in Crane's question to Poe. During his career Eliot had often championed Poe, and he sympathized with Poe's aversion to the myth of America, the very inspiration of *The Bridge*. On his part, Crane, to judge both from his letters and from his use of *Waste Land* imagery, had grouped Eliot with Poe among the dystopians.[16] Now what was Eliot's answer to Crane? Although the poet of *Four Quartets* refuses to vouchsafe the kind of vision that concludes *The Bridge*, that is, a dream of self, nation, and history redeemed through the mystical power of language, he does not entirely "deny the ticket"—indeed, Eliot shared with both Crane and Poe a belief in that mystical power. Eliot's response to Crane, or to the dialogue that Crane enacts in *The Bridge*, is to correlate the fate of the self neither to America nor to England exclusively, but to a community of the living and the dead in which conventional ideas of nationhood are modified and personalized. Crane, I would argue, had fired Eliot's imagination by replacing the stale rhetoric of nationalism with an America of the spirit. But where Crane had used mythopoesis to connect the past to the present, Eliot turned to his own ancestors: the key to Eliot's community of the living and the dead, and to its central role in the later *Quartets*, is the history of the Eliot family.[17] Implicit in this Eliotic response,

16. For Crane's uses of *Waste Land* imagery in *The Bridge*, see Harvey Gross, *Sound and Form in Modern Poetry*, 217–21.

17. Eliot was intensely conscious of family ancestry. At his Crawford Street flat in the late 1910s he kept a kind of shrine in a corner adorned with family photographs and silhouettes. His letters to his mother give further evidence of his deep concern with ancestry. He wore the family ring, and his nickname, "the elephant," derives in part from an elephant on the family crest. See Ackroyd, *T. S. Eliot*, 91; *LTSE*, 268, 274; and Lyndall Gordon, *Eliot's New Life*, 253. Eliot wrote Herbert Read in 1928 that as a "small boy" he "felt that the U.S.A. up to a hundred years ago was a family extension" (Sir Herbert Read, "T. S. E.—A Memoir," 15). My concern here is to show that Eliot's strong sense both of family and of the United States—as intimately

finally, is a criticism of Crane's position, insofar as Crane upholds a secular myth of America, while Eliot, in keeping with his cultural writings and theocratic ancestry, rejects a secular basis for even the idea of America, let alone its national reality.

In "East Coker" 1, the poet commences with a theme of houses and beginnings. East Coker is the village in Somerset, England, from which Eliot's forefather, Andrew Eliot, set out for Massachusetts in the years following the Restoration. When he published "East Coker" in the *New English Weekly* in 1940, Eliot wrote *aresse* for *arras* (EC 13) in order to follow Sir Thomas Elyot's *The Boke of the Governour* (1531). The poet's namesake and distant ancestor, Sir Thomas was both an East Coker native and a vanguard figure in the English Renaissance. His presence in "East Coker" suggests that the poet is fusing self-inscription with historiography; by alluding to Sir Thomas Elyot, Thomas Stearns Eliot asserts a personal tie to English history and the history of the English language, which developed a perhaps unparalleled range and subtlety in the sixteenth century.

This personalizing of the past differs in spirit from the lesson of Emerson's "History": "The student is to read history actively and not passively" (*Works*, 2:8)—Eliot is devoutly literal in his reading, Emerson more figurative. But the wartime *Quartets* are Eliot's most Emersonian work, for in them he reads public events through the prism of personal experience, without recourse to a poetic mask or persona. "In my beginning is my end" (EC 1)—not "In the beginning God created the heaven and the earth," but the cosmological transformed into autobiography. Avoiding self-reliant egotism, the speaker achieves what is more truly Emersonian: a prophetic self-consciousness, extending from the profound to the seemingly trivial. Behind the high and biblical style of "East Coker"'s opening, a private world revolves, replete with personal and familial associations, some of which are quite ordinary. The description of the "rise and fall" of houses evokes a memory of the old Eliot home at 2635 Locust Street, St. Louis, which the family surrendered to a burgeoning warehouse district during T. S. Eliot's Harvard days.[18] The

---

connected to his family's history and identity—emerged as a major force in the symbolism of *Four Quartets*: "When I speak of the family, I have in mind a bond which embraces a longer period of time than this [i.e., longer than two or three generations]: a piety towards the dead, however obscure, and a solicitude for the unborn, however remote" (*NDC*, 116).

18. In a letter reminiscent of Henry James's *The American Scene*, Eliot told Stead that the Missouri of his youth had been swept aside by progress (letter to William Force Stead, June

humble "field-mouse" apparently comes from the Eliots' "country house" on Cape Ann.[19]

For the poet of "East Coker," the relation of beginnings to ends inspires a meditation on the act of writing, on literary tradition, and on public and private history. The arras, shaking in the wind like the "bits of paper" in "Burnt Norton" 3, a page from an unbound book, furnishes a locus for this meditation. As commentators have noted, the silent motto on the arras is in one respect that of the Eliot family, which is indeed a motto of silence: *"tacuit et fecit,"* "he was silent and acted." Yet, by characterizing the motto as "silent," the poet implies that it too is "removed" from the thoughts, words, and deeds of a living generation. Perhaps we should infer that the motto is superannuated or even simply illegible. More in keeping with the poem's trial of knowing and unknowing, however, is for the motto's silence to recall the silence of all texts until the capable eye confers meaning on them. The motto is silent until illuminated by a pattern of readings, corresponding to a pattern of generational risings and fallings, of beginnings and ends, that directs the progress of the poem's ideal reader, who is the poet in the act of writing and meditating on his writing.

Complicating this larger gestalt, a principle of hermeneutic uncertainty operates in the *Quartets.* By virtue of this uncertainty, the future does not merely repeat the past; the poet can both belong to a family or house, and be freed from the identity that is imposed by houses. He is both part of an established pattern, and freed from that pattern because the pattern is, from his point of view, still forming, not yet fully formed. Thus, after his description of the rural dance at East Coker, Eliot concludes the first section of the poem with lines that liberate him from his ancestral community:

> Dawn points, and another day
> Prepares for heat and silence. Out at sea the dawn wind
> Wrinkles and slides. I am here
> Or there, or elsewhere. In my beginning.
>
> (EC 47–50)

20, 1930). When this author visited the site of the old Eliot home in 1992, he encountered a parking lot—very nearly vacant.

19. Responding to John Hayward's inquiry about the "field-mouse," Eliot wrote: "*Field-mice. They did* get into our country house in New England, and very pretty little creatures too: we always restored them to the Land, and only slew the housemice. But the particular point here is that the house is supposed to have been deserted or empty" (his emphasis; quoted in Gardner, *Composition,* 97).

Though in one sense the village of East Coker marks his beginning, the poet indicates other beginnings in other places. The gate of his choosing, of being "here / Or there, or elsewhere," remains open. One recalls Poirier's observation: "The soul has no determinable there or then, no here or now. . . ." Determination lingers, however, in the dawn's "point[ing]"— a gesture of fate that singles out the poet, that chooses him, limning his identity so that, coincident with the suggestion of a mysterious destiny, a recognition of otherness literally dawns. This otherness is transcendent, withheld in the antelucan hour, but enduring behind and beyond the play of signification that animates a series of near personifications: "dawn," "day," "heat," "silence," and "wind."

The freedom to unhouse the self has rich American precedents, not least famously in Whitman, who exhorted his readers: "Unscrew the locks from the doors! / Unscrew the doors themselves from the jambs!" (*CPCP*, 50). In the essay "Fate," Emerson observed, "Every spirit makes its house; but afterwards the house confines the spirit" (*Works*, 6:9). The "soul" that waits patiently for "the darkness of God" in "East Coker" 3 enters into a visionary mode rather foreign to our own fin de siècle; but Emerson's "way of life" that "is by abandonment" (*Works*, 2:321–22) constitutes an American negative way with strong parallels in Jonathan Edwards's "rhetoric of negation or apophasis." In the manner of Edwards and Emerson, Eliot explores his *via negativa* with a repetitious tenacity that says he is not wholly satisfied with it; it too will be abandoned:[20]

> You say I am repeating
> Something I have said before. I shall say it again.
> Shall I say it again? In order to arrive there,
> To arrive where you are, to get from where you are not,
>   You must go by a way wherein there is no ecstacy.
> In order to arrive at what you do not know
>   You must go by a way which is the way of ignorance.

20. Hodder, " 'After a High Negative Way,' " 438; Hodder compares Edwards's apophasis to "the *via negativa* of the medieval mystics." I have found Paul Fry's odic genealogy for *Four Quartets* to be very instructive. One of Fry's more general reflections on the nature of odes throws considerable light on the passage at hand: "The quest for voice is by no means confined to the ode; it is possibly the theme of all writing, and it is certainly the theme of the quieter lyrics to which the ode is related in its sphere of concern, the Meditative Lyric and the Conversation Poem. But whereas the lyric that is not an ode seeks voice without fanfare, as if by a spontaneous course of thought, the ode denies itself the illusionism of full-throated ease and writes itself hoarse" (Paul H. Fry, *The Poet's Calling in the English Ode*, 9).

> In order to possess what you do not possess
>   You must go by the way of dispossession.
> In order to arrive at what you are not
>   You must go through the way in which you are not.
> And what you do not know is the only thing you know
> And what you own is what you do not own
> And where you are is where you are not.
>
> (EC 133–46)

Eliot derived this passage from *The Ascent of Mount Carmel* by St. John of the Cross, the sixteenth-century Spanish mystic. The allusive technique recalls *The Waste Land,* but a notable difference emerges. The Old World of Europe tends in *The Waste Land* to be melancholy—beautiful, but moribund; "staring forms" lean out, "hushing" a room that is "enclosed" in sepulchral air (lines 104–5); such forms conjure a world that, like the House of Usher, might be better lost. It is not to detract from Eliot's historical reach to say that in *Four Quartets* the past lends a momentary framework to experience that is present and unfolding: age-old wisdom is rediscovered and renewed. The mystic's paradoxes do not appear as a set piece or brilliantly preserved relic; they constitute a sympathetic effort of articulative skill within a larger meditation.

Like Emerson in his essays and journals, Eliot in the *Quartets* repeats himself, doubles back on his thoughts, appears in two places at once. For both writers, the innermost self, the soul, goes about its mysterious errand. Repetition is not simply repetition, and arrival not exactly arrival, because they are dual aspects of a journey that cannot be fully comprehended. Throughout the *Quartets,* poetic style is possessed and dispossessed by the poet in what he calls "the intolerable wrestle / With words and meanings" (EC 70–71).[21] One might interpret the metaphysical stanzas of "East Coker" 4 (or any of the fourth sections) as one stylistic experiment among many and not the dogmatic heart of the poem. As "rooms," the *stanze* provide a

---

21. Finding that the Eliot of *Four Quartets* accepted "a set poetic structure of the kind he had always struggled to avoid," Ronald Bush avers: "The formal lyrics of . . . 'East Coker' and 'The Dry Salvages' were written to 'fit.' Exchanging the authority of his own voice for the impersonality of an orchestra, Eliot frequently lost his touch. Sometimes, his simulated voices fail to convince" (Ronald Bush, *T. S. Eliot: A Study in Character and Style,* 222). By contrast, I would say that the formal lyrics of "East Coker" and "The Dry Salvages" are spiritual exercises for the personal voice, not impersonal structures.

habitation for the soul and an experiment in Christian identity. Here I am certainly not questioning Eliot's religious conviction, I am suggesting that his religious sincerity was closely tied to artistic sincerity, and that as an artist Eliot felt impelled to reinvent himself constantly. Eliot's insistence on stylistic innovation bespeaks his spiritual questing. Emerson asked, "Is not prayer also a study of truth—a sally of the soul into the unfound infinite?" (*Works,* 1:74). In their protean and dynamic aspect, Eliot's stanzas represent a relentless sallying forth of the soul; in their repetition and structure, they mark the basic, material conditions of time and mortality to which the soul must return.[22]

"The Dry Salvages" (1941), the third *Quartet,* dramatizes the metaphor of crossing from an old world to a new. In autobiographical terms, the poet retraces the Atlantic voyages of his English ancestors, Andrew Eliot and Isaac Stearns, who sailed to America in the seventeenth century. Their crossings, and their shared Puritan mission to build a New Israel, acquire fresh significance in light of the poet's journey.

"The Dry Salvages" begins, as do the previous *Quartets,* at the scene of a house, here the Eliot home in St. Louis, near the Mississippi River. In Whitmanian tones of almost painful simplicity, Eliot characterizes the Mississippi as "a strong brown god," a pagan conception that is soon amplified in a description that echoes Tennyson's "Ulysses": "The sea has many voices, / Many gods and many voices" (DS 24–25). Paganism is important in this poem; the first hint of pagan themes occurs almost immediately, in the note subjoined to the title: "The Dry Salvages—presumably *les trois sauvages*—is a small group of rocks, with a beacon, off the N.E. coast of Cape Ann, Massachusetts." In lines 26–48 ("The sea howl . . ."), Eliot explores the savage world of river and sea through a synthesis of romantic sublimity and imagist particularity, Pound having applied the latter to the pagan seas of the early *Cantos.* Eliot thus creates his own version of the Homeric voyager sailing by *periploi,* rounding the coast "homewards." Recording the questions—of cosmology, beginnings, ends, and the riddle of time—that the natural world compels the conscious mind to frame, Eliot, following Dante, conceives nature in itself as removed from grace; the "granite teeth"

22. Cf. Elisa New: "The Emersonian afflatus gives the American poet reach. . . . And yet the poet stretched beyond his limits or past her reach must, in the end, come back to his powerlessness, back to her purblindness" (Elisa New, *The Regenerate Lyric: Theology and Innovation in American Poetry,* 25).

are teeth of primary rock—no subtle change has acted on them. Terror and beauty, the "menace and caress of wave that breaks on water," captivate the imagination, but convey a "distant" cosmos, a "time not our time," while the powers that "howl" and "yelp" are alien to human ears.

Emerson had considered a similar kind of beauty:

> In history, the great moment is, when the savage is just ceasing to be a savage, with all his hairy Pelasgic strength directed on his opening sense of beauty:—and you have Pericles and Phidias,—not yet passed over into Corinthian civility. Everything good in nature and the world is in that moment of transition, when the swarthy juices still flow plentifully from nature, but the astringency or acridity is got out by ethics and humanity. (*Works*, 6:70–71)[23]

At the end of "The Dry Salvages" 1, Eliot approaches what Emerson calls "the great moment," a sublime interlude that challenges Eliot's own religious and social convictions. Emerson selects as his example the golden age of Athens, in the fifth century B.C. Eliot's Ulyssean sailor inhabits a roughly analogous setting, where Pelasgic strength is also directed on an opening sense of beauty—though beauty of a less anthropocentric kind. Unlike Emerson, Eliot does not attach "ethics and humanity" to the moment and place of crossing. To speak of America in its spiritual sense, Emerson's America is the very nexus of transition—one may compare "the imagined land" of Wallace Stevens's "Mrs. Alfred Uruguay." For Emerson's self-reliant individual, America as nature is a source of strength, a birthright. For Eliot, America as nature is a place not fully humanized, where the sunlight of Ithaka yields to a Cimmerian dark, where past and present do not meet, and where ends are very much in doubt. America stands outside the Christian dispensation at this stage in the *Quartets,* Eliot's perspective thus coinciding with that of his seventeenth-century ancestors, who came to build Christ's kingdom among the so-called savages.

In the sestina that begins the next section, the poet owns a profound doubt. His question is age-old: for what purpose do generation after generation undergo the trials of beauty, terror, and death? He loads the question with harrowing and relentless force. As he does so, an intricate

---

23. Quoted in Bloom, *Poetics*, 312. I am indebted to Bloom's pithy essay "Emerson: Power at the Crossing" to the extent that this chapter originated as a response to it.

pattern of feminine (or double) and triple rhymes establishes itself and unfolds, like a numerical series, with the effect that the lyric's surface makes great demands on the eye, which finds "no end" or resting place, only "addition." Eliot exploits this effect to describe "a future that is . . . liable / Like the past, to have no destination" (DS 71–72). The "autumn flowers," the "drifting boat with a slow leakage," the fishermen "forever bailing / Setting and hauling," signify cosmic and personal exhaustion. By juxtaposing his sublime sea lyric with the sestina, the poet suggests that the Emersonian "moment" cannot be sustained as a way of life, that eventually nature and time will crush a man. The sestina's catalog of objects and images fails to cohere spiritually, fails to grant the promise that Whitman, in his poetic catalogs, could triumphantly locate. On the abyss's edge, Eliot can only imagine an "end" to history in "the hardly, barely prayable / Prayer of the one Annunciation" (DS 83–84). Thus, in *Four Quartets,* the saving move by consciousness is faith: William James would call this expression of belief a "live hypothesis." From a Christian standpoint, Eliot's challenge was to make the ancient message of the Incarnation new, to dramatize the vitality of a dogmatic truth. The doctrinal theme of course distances him from Emerson. But the severity of his spiritual quest connects Eliot to Emerson's poetic heirs, such as Frost, for whom "the height of poetic thinking" was the "attempt to say matter in terms of spirit and spirit in terms of matter."[24] Eliot takes this attempt to an extreme, before turning to Christian prayer.

"Little Gidding," the final *Quartet,* integrates the many crossings of the larger poem with the theme of Christian pilgrimage. Approaching the church at Little Gidding on a "rough road" in the Huntingdonshire countryside, the poet orders the scene with details conjoining the pedestrian and the numinous:

> When the short day is brightest, with frost and fire,
> The brief sun flames the ice, on pond and ditches,
> In windless cold that is the heart's heat,　　`
> Reflecting in a watery mirror
> A glare that is blindness in the early afternoon.
> And glow more intense than blaze of branch, or brazier,
> Stirs the dumb spirit: no wind, but pentecostal fire
> In the dark time of the year. Between melting and freezing

24. Robert Frost, *Selected Prose of Robert Frost,* 41.

> The soul's sap quivers. There is no earth smell
> Or smell of living thing. This is the spring time
> But not in time's covenant. Now the hedgerow
> Is blanched for an hour with transitory blossom
> Of snow. . . .
>
> (LG 4–16)

It appears that Eliot is echoing his own echo-laden writing, the Belladonna scene from *The Waste Land* (lines 77–89, "The Chair she sat in . . ."). For it is not likely that "branch," "flames," "reflecting," "stirs," and "glow" would have recurred in "Little Gidding," in a passage of nearly identical length to the *Waste Land* passage, purely by chance. Looking at the manuscript record in Helen Gardner's *The Composition of* Four Quartets, one finds that "is blanched" had earlier been "glitters," so that the drafts yield yet another echo of *The Waste Land*.

In his 1941 essay "Rudyard Kipling," Eliot referred to Enobarbus's speech (the point of departure for the Belladonna passage) as "highly decorated," but noted that "the decoration has a purpose beyond its own beauty." This usage of "beyond" is clarified in the essay by Eliot's adoption of Henry James's phrase "the figure in the carpet" to describe the master form suffusing all details, the latent unity emerging out of the variety of a great poet's work, that he saw in Shakespeare (*OPP,* 235–36).[25] Eliot himself pursued such a "figure," and in *Four Quartets* undertook a creative reevaluation of his earlier writing, with the intended result that, in our example, the passages from "Little Gidding" and "A Game of Chess" should modify each other. In a sense, we are met again with Eliot's maxim: "the past should be altered by the present as much as the present is directed by the past."

To what end, precisely, are "Little Gidding" and "A Game of Chess" brought into conjunction? What is the figure in Eliot's carpet? For an answer, I turn once more to Poe, for as Grover Smith has convincingly shown, the language and imagery of the Belladonna scene have a major

---

25. Eliot also used James's phrase with reference to Shakespeare in his introduction to *The Wheel of Fire.* It has a close analogue in Eliot's perspective on rhythm: "Rhythm, of course, is a highly personal matter; it is not a verse form. It is always the real pattern in the carpet, the scheme of organization of thought, feeling, and vocabulary, the way in which everything comes together" (T. S. Eliot, "Marianne Moore," 595).

source in two of Poe's tales, "The Assignation" and "Shadow—a Parable," mentioned by Eliot in a 1921 *Chapbook* article.[26] "Little Gidding" doesn't repeat the same extensive borrowing from Poe that Smith uncovers in *The Waste Land* (though the later Eliot does in fact reecho the "flames," "mirror," "glare" sequence that Smith observes in a short passage from "Shadow—a Parable"), but verbatim repetition isn't central to my point. I am suggesting that if the Belladonna scene displays Poe's specular opulence, the scene from "Little Gidding" directs Eliot's earlier, Poe-like writing to a more spiritual desideratum. This would accord with the mystical reading of Poe's poetry that Eliot developed in the later 1920s.

Looting Poe's tales for "A Game of Chess," the younger Eliot created a brilliant pastiche, a baroque pleasure-dome for the literary connoisseur. Two decades later, Eliot stresses that such aesthetic experience is not an end in itself, but a means to an end that, however elusive and problematic, remains desirable and mysteriously intact. His impulse is therefore to regard *The Waste Land*'s aestheticism as a prelude to, and hence a part of, the *Quartets*' spiritual autobiography. This autobiography is the true pattern underfoot, the basis for a self-criticism centered upon questions of personal, artistic, and spiritual authority.

Eliot would write soon after the war: "Esthetic sensibility must be extended into spiritual perception, and spiritual perception must be extended into esthetic sensibility and disciplined taste before we are qualified to pass judgment upon decadence or diabolism or nihilism in art" (*NDC*, 103). One might say that the two elements of Eliot's chiasmus, "esthetic sensibility" and "spiritual perception," amount roughly to the two halves of Eliot's career, pre- and postconversion. But that is not quite right, because Eliot's aesthetic sensibility was always haunted by his spiritual restlessness. It would therefore be more accurate to say that the two halves of Eliot's career are, to use terms he applied to other poets, immaturity and maturity, for only the mature poet is in a position to judge the relative merits of the different types of art, including types that he had formerly practiced. As his most mature work, *Four Quartets* would express Eliot's aspirations to realize an integrated sensibility, to instantiate the highest principles of taste and judgment through a continuing critique of his past and present writing. An Olympian gambit of this kind must rely upon a comprehensive

26. Grover Smith, *"The Waste Land,"* 123–25.

and highly confident knowledge of one's culture, a knowledge that Eliot cultivated through his views on religion.

In "Little Gidding" 1, thoughts of a "broken king" again recall *The Waste Land* (especially its more Shakespearian moments), as Eliot makes his pilgrimage to the stone church with its memorable history:

> If you came at night like a broken king,
> If you came by day not knowing what you came for,
> It would be the same, when you leave the rough road
> And turn behind the pig-sty to the dull façade
> And the tombstone. And what you thought you came for
> Is only a shell, a husk of meaning
> From which the purpose breaks only when it is fulfilled
> If at all.
>
> (LG 26–33)

In a stripped-down, Puritan plain style that is logical and sequential, yet shades toward the use of typology, the poet reflects on the life of Nicholas Ferrar and on Charles I's flight from the Roundheads. As a last bastion of Anglican community before the regicide, Little Gidding embodied English tradition for Eliot.[27] And yet, with that severity of thought that characterizes him, he discovers: "what you thought you came for / Is only a shell, a husk of meaning." Tradition thus has an Emersonian edge. Shunning mere nostalgia, the poet must build his house anew, must construe identity, knowledge, and consciousness as unfolding rather than fixed. It is not that human history, in its institutions and channels of authority, is corrupting and should be discarded. Rather, it is that what one may choose to keep—a place of prayer, a memorial—reminds one of failure more than triumph. Having failed in the past to live up to our ideals, we must try again; we must purify our motives, and continue the soul's errand in order to fulfill our purposes and recover meaning. Emerson, though a man of many moods, says this over and over again, from "Experience" to "Days."

For the Eliot of *Four Quartets,* poetic language must burn with a purgatorial (and at times pentecostal) "fire" that unites aesthetic sensibility with spiritual perception. In the Dantean passage from "Little Gidding"

---

27. See Ronald Schuchard, " 'If I think, again, of this place': Eliot, Herbert, and the Way to 'Little Gidding.' "

2, the place "between three districts where the smoke arose" is a version of purgatory, though the ghost's "brown baked features" add an infernal touch. Evidently, Eliot wanted a purgatorial meeting, but couldn't wholly escape the demonic.[28] With World War II in the very near background, he observes himself in the act of composition; I am reminded of the encounter with Stetson in *The Waste Land:*

> So I assumed a double part, and cried
> And heard another's voice cry: "What! are *you* here?"
> Although we were not. I was still the same,
>   Knowing myself yet being someone other—
>   And he a face still forming; yet the words sufficed
> To compel the recognition they preceded.
>
> (LG 97–102)

Though the words only "suffice," they reveal a prophetic power in "pre-ced[ing]" the thoughts of the poet who writes them, in making him their conduit. The scene is, on the one hand, improvisatory, its pragmatic authority based on "a sense of power and accomplishment in language";[29] on the other hand, it is sustained by a numinous language that embraces the living and the dead. Whether or not we want to ascribe, as Eliot did in some phases, a metaphysical force of fate or destiny to such writing, the use of a scene of instruction, with cultural roots in Dantean and ultimately Virgilian allusiveness, marks one of Eliot's great contributions to American literature. The Emersonian legacy does not entail meetings of this kind.

The ghost's speech is a rather bitter if stately comment on the life of poets, characterized as a hellish purgatory for speech-driven prophets, a slow and painful crossing towards an unseen paradise. The line adapted from Mallarmé, "To purify the dialect of the tribe" (LG 127), which Eliot connected in 1928 to "the primitive power of the Word," bespeaks the poet's capacity as a vehicle of fate, while it conveys an ideal of social responsibility that is foreign to Mallarmé's *art poétique*. On a related plane, the ghost's revisiting London streets parallels Eliot's own revisiting England and New England in *Four Quartets,* and points (along with the general delineation of

---

28. Eliot wrote Hayward: " . . . I wished the effect of the whole [encounter with the ghost] to be Purgatorial which is much more appropriate" (quoted in Gardner, *Composition,* 64–65).
29. Eliot, introduction to *The Wheel of Fire,* xvi.

the poet's life, i.e., the life of all poets) to an underlying design of repetition and analogy in Eliot's cosmos. Yet the purport or end of this design, like the truth in poetry itself, cannot be firmly grasped; for this reason the poet's spirit, like the ghost, is "unappeased and peregrine" in a ceaseless pilgrimage.

Despite the "partial horror" of slow decrepitude, the loss of "promise" and the "bitter tastelessness of shadow fruit," the paradise that Eliot seeks throughout the poem, through the purgatory of words and history, is earthly. The union of "the fire and the rose" that ends the *Quartets* suggests a union of spirit and matter, not a reign of paradisal spirit. The Incarnation is the governing idea behind this and similar passages in the poem where the timeless intersects with time, whereas in Emerson, Whitman, and Crane, the Incarnation is assimilated, alongside other biblical and sacramental themes, into syncretic modes of thought. By restoring a formal religiosity that rejects emotional nostalgia, that insists on intellectual substance, Eliot presents a worthy alternative to Emersonian canons. Yet in his concern with the old Puritan ideal of a common errand, Eliot does not follow Dante in imagining heaven, but, like Emerson at the conclusion of *Nature,* devotes himself to a vision of the redeemed earth.

In the final lines of "Little Gidding" ("We shall not cease from ex-ploration . . ."), an American sense of vastness, expressed by imagery of the New World, the longest river and the apple tree, animates a call for exploration that is private and public, voiced in the third-person plural. This new world is no particular place, but an idealized frontier: it is "here, now, always," a perpetual spur to thought, labor, and poetry. Eliot had a similar notion in mind when he wrote in 1939, "we have to remember that the Kingdom of Christ on earth will never be realised, and also that it is always being realised . . ." (*ICS,* 47). The "children in the apple-tree" (LG 248) are the children of Adam, renewed to the innocence that was lost through original sin (Eliot strengthens this suggestion by placing "-fall" at the end of line 247). Poetically, their import has changed, grown more polysemous, since "New Hampshire" and "Burnt Norton," for they hint at the fulfillment of the Eliot family's quest in America, and evoke Christ's equation of "little children" with the kingdom of God (Matt. 19:14). In the final union of "the fire and the rose," the poet enacts a communal prayer for a closure that he cannot achieve by himself: "the fire and the rose are one"—they must be "won" by the collective "we," as well as given from above. As I have suggested, Eliot advances his Christian belief polemically, through dialogue with, among others, Emerson, the non-Christian inheritor of American Puritan culture. Finally, Eliot's vast and vastly refined sensibility is itself the means by which he would persuade us that Christianity is necessity and truth, that history, the history of America, of any and all new worlds, of individuals and their societies, can only cohere, from origin to end, through a Christian grace that leads to a meaning beyond the reach of words. *Four Quartets* is its own best argument for the culture of Western Christendom that it represents.

The "condition of complete simplicity / (Costing not less than every-thing)" (LG 253–54) recalls the imperative of self-surrender that Eliot had put forward in "Tradition and the Individual Talent." But in his refinement of the will to a purgatorial intensity, the poet relies not on tradition so much as on the mysterious destiny of the soul. *Four Quartets* is a record of the soul, and the world of the poem is, in large measure, an image of the soul's becoming. The end of this becoming, the bourne of the soul's transitions, is glimpsed in a vision of an earthly paradise attained through purgatorial fire. The site of this paradise is not determined, but Eliot's final rose harks back with poignancy to the landscape of "The Dry Salvages":

> The salt is on the briar rose,
> The fog is in the fir trees.
>
> (DS 25–26)

Here the setting is undoubtedly, as in "Marina," New England. Briar roses are humble flowers, and the salt from the sea air adds to the feeling of commonness. But there is also a touch of surprise in the image, an unexpected combination of textures, while the fog in the fir trees blurs the distant outlines and wakes us to the unfolding possibilities of the concrete and immediate present. In this discovery of the uncommon promise of common things, the poet, like Emerson's blind man "gradually restored to perfect sight," enters the New England of his literal and spiritual ancestors.

7 | Prophecy and Postmodernism

WHEN HELEN VENDLER OPENED *The Harvard Book of Contemporary American Poetry* with twenty-two pages of Wallace Stevens and included none by Eliot, no one was very surprised. After all, she had long ranked Stevens as the most influential and important of American modernists. With no malice toward that very fine poet, I think that Vendler's appraisal, representative of her generation of critics, will fail—is failing—to convince younger readers, for whom Eliot's preeminence among twentieth-century American poets appears as a given, an obvious and neutral fact supported by every form of media. Still, my real quarrel with Vendler concerns the significance, not the extent, of Eliot's impact. In her view, "experiments in perception, in memory, [and] in language" supply the vital link between modernism and its heirs, while the social bearing of Eliot's work lacks consequence.[1] I believe that criticism needs to look at how aesthetic, moral, and cultural issues interact; if American poets have encountered Eliot on grounds other than formal innovation and experiments in consciousness, let us explore those grounds in detail.

In assessing Eliot's long-term significance, I will focus on his role as a poet who contemplated the nature and meaning of history. I will look at how he shapes and informs the historical thinking of three poets: John Ashbery, Elizabeth Bishop, and Robert Lowell. And I will question prevailing critical narratives about recent American poetry. First, however, I would linger

1. Vendler, "Contemporary American Poetry," 3.

over my principal terms: *modernism* and *postmodernism*. For the historian of literature in English, the postmodern dates from the 1940s. Laboring to distinguish Lowell from the modernists, Randall Jarrell, for example, saw fit to use the adjective "post-modernist" in his 1947 review of Lowell's *Lord Weary's Castle*. Having noted the book's biblical trajectory, Jarrell construed Lowell's postmodernism as "a unique fusion of modernist and traditional poetry." This definition strikes me as rather halting: modernism was itself steeped in traditional forms, and Jarrell, though a superior critic, wobbles a bit by offering "anti-modernist" as an alternative—the one thing needful was not to introduce Lowell as an epigone. Though Jarrell hesitated to say so, *Lord Weary's Castle* pays tribute to the epic heroism of Eliotic modernism, to the hope of redeeming, and not merely repeating, the time. Surveying Western culture in "The Drunken Fisherman," Lowell had given voice to an apostolic anguish when he asked, "Is there no way to cast my hook / Out of this dynamited brook?" Such poetry may be postmodern in Jarrell's limited and local sense, which rightly stresses Lowell's "dramatic, dialectical internal organization," but by current standards it is not. Because Lowell, both early and late, refused to sever the tie between what he called "a murky metaphysical historic significance" and the self, he emerges as an heir to Eliot.[2]

As opposed to Eliotic modernism, which addresses the past in order to renew a covenant of works, postmodernism shows a tendency to domesticate history, and thus to abandon its public aspect. A textbook example of this would be James Merrill's "Days of 1964," where the poet hires a Greek cleaning-woman named Kleo. Kleo does her work around the house, while an off-hours glimpse of her sexual escapades moves Merrill and his lover to breathless laughter: Merrill's tableau—Ovidian, Spenserian—is distinctively rich and allusive. In "English: An Ode," Robert Hass wants to "imagine . . . a language . . . purged of history" because English is a vehicle for imperialism; he longs for a linguistic wholeness that is "Adamic / electrified by a clear tension / like the distance between a sparrow and

2. For other approaches to Eliot's influence on recent American poetry, see Charles Altieri, "Eliot's Impact"; James E. B. Breslin, *From Modern to Contemporary: American Poetry, 1945–1965;* and Daniel Hoffman, ed., *The Harvard Guide to Contemporary American Writing*. For his dating of the postmodern and his citation of Jarrell, I am indebted to James Longenbach, *Modern Poetry after Modernism*, 177. Randall Jarrell, *Poetry and the Age*, 195. Robert Lowell, *Lord Weary's Castle*, 38. Lowell, *Collected Prose*, 213.

a cat."[3] This imagery conflates Eden and suburbia. Poems by Sylvia Plath also exhibit the postmodern tendency to domesticate history, to transform, for example, the worlds of classical epic ("The Colossus") and Auschwitz ("Daddy") into a grammar of family and self. When the postmodernist extends the Emersonian call to understand private experience in terms of "what great bodies of men have done," he avoids heroic narratives that are, to quote Whitman, "common to all, typical of all."[4] Contemporary literature features a host of bourgeois writers who, seeking the moral authority of victims, appropriate the darker passages of history, the Holocaust in particular, through personalizing and familiarizing metaphors. The question becomes whether such writers abandon Clio, Auden's "Muse of the unique / Historical fact," or diminish her.

For John Ashbery, like Merrill in this regard, history is largely a private affair. Ashbery equates history with personal experience: he treats it as a romance between one or possibly two people, while a realm of otherness, a community of friends, associates, and readers, oscillates nearby. Sometimes there is a fine line between domesticating history and making public use of it, and in this and other respects the difference between Eliotic modernism and postmodernism can be difficult to judge. Other critics, moreover, formulate postmodernisms quite different from my own: Michael Beehler, in comparing Eliot's moral critique of symbolism in "From Poe to Valéry" to the ethics of Emmanuel Levinas, places Eliot under the rubric of a postmodernism sympathetically characterized by its chastened humanism.[5] And to offer yet a further qualification, I am not at all sure that the problem of postmodernism furnishes the best interpretive framework for recent poetry. But if my basic distinction leads to meaningful criticism, it will serve its purpose.

Were Ashbery scorned by the cultural establishment, I would be tempted to defend him. His astringent aestheticism, its seriousness and wit, brings High Modernism to an accomplished, mannerist close. Like many self-consciously late artists, he achieves a sophisticated elegance, a self-referential style that complements his obsessive reading. And like all important poetry,

3. Robert Hass, *Sun under Wood,* 68.

4. For a related discussion, see Christopher Lasch, *The Revolt of the Elites: And the Betrayal of Democracy,* 86–91.

5. Michael Beehler, " 'Riddle the Inevitable': Levinas, Eliot, and the Critical Moment of Ethics."

his writing conveys a valuable critique of the language. What concerns me here is Ashbery's position as a cultural authority; I refer especially to certain pseudomoral occasions in his writing that critics have amplified in their response to him. As an example, in his justly praised "Self-Portrait in a Convex Mirror," Ashbery defends the serious "play" of his own art, and does so compellingly; but then, irritated by someone, he lashes out:

> "Play" is something else;
> It exists, in a society specifically
> Organized as a demonstration of itself.
> There is no other way, and those assholes
> Who would confuse everything with their mirror games
> Which seem to multiply stakes and possibilities, or
> At least confuse issues by means of an investing
> Aura that would corrode the architecture
> Of the whole in a haze of suppressed mockery,
> Are beside the point. They are out of the game,
> Which doesn't exist until they are out of it.[6]

Ashbery wants the existentially authentic: I hope we all do. But when he slams others for "mirror games," he is attacking, one suspects, anyone who adheres to a metaphysics of history or a Western religion. And there is a cost to Ashbery's jealous atheism: nowhere does he show the power to measure what Lowell so profoundly calls "man's lovely / peculiar power to choose life and die." Unable to dramatize moral choices because he lacks a workable structure for doing so,[7] refusing the limitations that such choices impose— in myriad ways—on the self and the other, Ashbery asserts his idea of the good with a wordy and unreal freedom.

Though Ashbery's best work is probably his "Self-Portrait," it will be helpful to study one of his prose poems in order to consider more closely his

6. John Ashbery, *Self-Portrait in a Convex Mirror*, 79–80.

7. The sentence beginning "They are out of the game" recalls a highly nuanced passage from *Song of Myself*: "Looking with side-curved head curious what will come next, / Both in and out of the game and watching and wondering at it" (*CPCP,* 191). The quotation is from "For the Union Dead," in Robert Lowell, *For the Union Dead,* 71. Ashbery refers to this structure as "the problem of pathos vs. experience" (*Self-Portrait,* 70): for Ashbery, these poles have lost their dialectical capacity, and hence they cannot sustain a moral denouement or scene of anagnorisis; Ashbery's poetic domain is thus the reflective space of his purely lyrical "vs." (or *verses*).

postmodern response to Eliot and Eliotic versions of history. "The System" was first published in 1972 as the centerpiece of Ashbery's *Three Poems,* and then reprinted by the poet in his 1985 *Selected Poems.* It comprises some twenty-five sections of various length, in which Ashbery describes an episodic journey of the mind through winter and spring. Along the way, he borrows continually from *Four Quartets.* The key to Ashbery's encounter with Eliot is a passage from "Little Gidding":

> And the end of our exploring
> Will be to arrive where we started
> And know the place for the first time.
> (LG 240–42)

Ashbery echoes and alludes to these lines repeatedly, and takes the odic and variegated rhythm of Eliot's more discursive passages to an extreme of prosiness. Often there is a process of dilution at work, as if Ashbery were exploring Eliot's ideas in a draft for a poem: " . . . This place of joining was indeed the end, and . . . it was the very place you set out from, whose intolerable mixture of reality and fantasy had started you on the road which has now come full circle." The theme lends itself to numerous variations: " . . . And this whole surface of daylight has become one with that other remembered picture of light, when you were setting out. . . ." And interspersed throughout "The System" are catch phrases from Eliot: " . . . just, I say, as we begin each day in this state of threatened blankness which is wiped away so soon, but which leaves certain illegible traces, like chalk dust on a blackboard after it has been erased, so we must learn to recognize it as the form—the only one—in which such fragments of the true learning as we are destined to receive will be vouchsafed to us, if at all."[8] That "if at all" is a mannerism—it recalls Eliot's "husk of meaning / From which the purpose breaks only when it is fulfilled / If at all" (LG 31–33). Wearing certain obvious poststructuralist influences, Ashbery converts Eliot's rhetoric of negation into a purely compositional experience, with "blankness," the white of the page, supplanting all other origins, historical and religious. The result, I find, is a mishmash of feeling. Are we meant to laugh ("chalk dust on a blackboard after it has been erased" seems pure bathos), to meditate, to sympathize, to feel sad? If my puzzlement is not unusual, can such tonal confusion bode well for poetry?

8. John Ashbery, *Three Poems,* 90, 80, 79.

In the following passage, one may see a connection between teleology and an aspect of *Four Quartets* that Ashbery disapproves of:

> . . . What was wanted and was precisely lacking in this gay and salubrious desert was an end to the "end" theory whereby each man was both an idol and the humblest of idolaters, in other words the antipodes of the antipodes of his own universe, his own redemption or his own damnation, with the rest of the world as a painted backdrop to his own monodrama of becoming of which he was the lone impassioned spectator.[9]

Lowell once remarked, "Eliot's real all through the *Quartets*. He can be very intelligent or very simple there, and *he's* there, but there are no other people in the *Quartets*." Less sympathetic, Ashbery finds in Eliot's poem a mode of spiritual autobiography that isolates the individual soul. Ashbery implies that, by ending "the 'end' theory," the self will become more genuinely social. The problem is that Ashbery never substantiates this implication, nor does he say why teleological beliefs should be intrinsically isolating. A moral balloonist at home among the cloud tops, he one day proposes that he can walk on them—one looks in vain for the saving irony of Shelley or Baudelaire. And yet, admirers of Ashbery would raise their poet's stock by interpreting stylistic maneuvers as moral choices, by discovering a deep sagacity in the endlessly permutating minutiae of Ashbery's eternal now.[10]

Three Poems enters into crisis whenever Ashbery would distinguish his thought from Eliot's. Ashbery likes the more purely poetic qualities of the *Quartets*, but one may ask how far these qualities exist apart from the hints of salvation, the subtly assumed narrative of ends that Eliot unfolds. This is a question that Ashbery doesn't entertain as he labors to pare Eliot's text away from Eliot the poet:

> These people [Ashbery is speaking of "spiritual bigots"] are awaiting the sign of their felicity without hope. . . . So great is their eagerness that they believe they have already absorbed it, that they have attained that plane of final realization which we are all striving for, that they have

9. Ibid., 64.

10. Lowell, *Collected Prose*, 265. It is unsurprising to read, in a review of one of Ashbery's recent volumes: "Yet ['Tuesday Evening'] . . . articulates an almost moral imperative to explore the positive aspects of the new [postmetaphysical] dispensation, to experience its freedoms as fully as we can" (Mark Ford, "Nothing and a Lot").

achieved a state of permanent grace. Hence the air of joyful resignation, the beatific upturned eyelids, the paralyzed stance of these castaways of the eternal voyage, who imagine they have reached the promised land when in reality the ship is sinking under them. The great fright has turned their gaze upward, to the stars, to the heavens; they see nothing of the disarray around them, their ears are closed to the cries of their fellow passengers; they can think only of themselves when all the time they believe that they are thinking of nothing but God. Yet in their innermost minds they know too that all is not well; that if it were there would not be this rigidity, with the eye and the mind focused on a nonexistent center, a fixed point, when the common sense of even an idiot would be enough to make him realize that nothing has stopped, that we and everything around us are moving forward continually, and that we are being modified constantly by the speed at which we travel and the regions through which we pass, so that merely to think of ourselves as having arrived at some final resting place is a contradiction of fundamental logic. . . . Yet this is not so bad; we have at any rate kept our open-mindedness. . . . [11]

Words and images borrowed from the third section of "The Dry Salvages" serve several purposes for Ashbery. They supply him with raw material; they enable him to adopt Eliot's skeptical intelligence; and they become arrows aimed at Eliot in a rebuke of theism. Both poets explore the Buddhist—or by parallel Humean—insight that space and time disrupt self-knowledge. But where Eliot envisions the possibility of an unmoved center, of which the still point is a type, Ashbery parodies the still point, calling it a "fixed point" ("do not call it fixity," wrote Eliot) and heaping abuse on "idiot[s]" who don't agree with him.

As Vendler would say, Ashbery's apperceptive journey is "a form of repetition . . . the returning upon an orbit already traced."[12] Introducing her anthology, Vendler argues in effect that lyric poetry (and she includes the prose poem) should have no teleological perspective. And this is an odd thing for an American critic to do, because American poets have traditionally made a great deal of the belief that America would redeem the time—that America embodied the teleological principle in history. What

11. Ashbery, *Three Poems*, 73–74.
12. Vendler, "Contemporary," 2. She is echoing Keats on the "simple imaginative mind," valued by Keats for "the repetition of its own silent working coming continually on the spirit with a fine suddenness."

Vendler actually characterizes is postmodernism, in which the repetitive element of American lyric poetry undergoes hypertrophy, and does so at the expense of the teleological element that is its counterpart; in this respect she is completely undialectical. I must be very careful here, for lyric poetry in general does not require a teleological framework, nor need the idea of a telos be more than hinted at to be effective. My point is that because the pursuit of ends has played an exceptionally strong role in American lyric poetry, and a defining role in American society, nonteleological poets rarely if ever achieve major status in the national culture: they are simply not representative enough. Hence the fate of John Crowe Ransom, born the same year as Eliot. Complex and various, Eliot's American sense of providential history links him to Poe, Whitman, Pound, Crane, and Lowell. Bishop, who wrote her undergraduate thesis on Cotton Mather, is canny in her use of this legacy.

In referring to "ends," Ashbery alludes to American redemptive history, to the New Jerusalem and the kingdom of God, but these allusions fail to cohere for the poet or the reader, and sound like the murmurings of a solipsist. Recognizing the dialectical character of Eliot's poetic, Ashbery refuses it, thus divorcing Eliot from his social concerns and re-creating him in Ashbery's own image, as a writer of pure poetry. Unlike Ashbery, Eliot coordinates repetition, the formal and thematic repetition of the *Quartets*, with *telos*. Eliot's ability to see experience in the light of historical patterns serves to connect his present to his past, and lends a contractual force to his teleology. He persuades us to consider his collective vision, to agree to his terms of reference in the linguistic sense, and to regard ourselves, though our self-knowledge is imperfect, as agents in a world where our beginnings and ends are meaningful, because meaningfully related. The moral of the *Quartets*, for later poets at least, may be that a narrative of history, applying in some degree to a common culture, is an indispensable resource.

I turn now to one of the very good poems in Vendler's anthology: Bishop's "At the Fishhouses," which appeared in 1947, not many years after *Four Quartets*. It is based on a visit Bishop made to Nova Scotia, where she had lived for a time with her maternal grandparents. Bonnie Costello and other critics cite Wordsworth's "Resolution and Independence" as an ancestor of the poem, and this background is important in what I have to say.[13] To readers of "The Dry Salvages," Bishop's landscape will appear

---

13. Bonnie Costello, *Elizabeth Bishop: Questions of Mastery*, 111–12.

familiar, in part because Nova Scotia and the Dry Salvages inhabit the same northeastern seaboard. With its nets, jagged rocks, and local fishing industry, Bishop's shoreline looks like Eliot's New England. I know of only two poems where "lobster pots" crop up: "The Dry Salvages" and "At the Fishhouses." And there are other echoes and likenesses. Bishop's "element bearable to no mortal" is suggestively close to Eliot's "human kind / Cannot bear very much reality" (BN 42–43), while the sea's burning "as if the water were a transmutation of fire" has an analogue in the fires of "Little Gidding."

Beyond these details, Bishop's engagement with Eliot provides what is arguably the dramatic basis for her poem:

> Although it is a cold evening,
> down by one of the fishhouses
> an old man sits netting,
> his net, in the gloaming almost invisible,
> a dark purple-brown,
> and his shuttle worn and polished.
> The air smells so strong of codfish
> it makes one's nose run and one's eyes water.
> The five fishhouses have steeply peaked roofs
> and narrow, cleated gangplanks slant up
> to storerooms in the gables
> for the wheelbarrows to be pushed up and down on.[14]

Though no one has said so, Bishop's "old man" among his "fishhouses" recalls Gerontion, an "old man" in whose house shuttles weave not fishing nets, but the wind. In other respects, he recalls the "familiar compound ghost" of "Little Gidding." Bishop meets him in the twilight and, in the routines of his trade, sees him as an ancient craftsman:

> He has scraped the scales, the principal beauty,
> from unnumbered fish with that black old knife,
> the blade of which is almost worn away.

The poet refers to the "old man" as "a friend of my grandfather"—a clue that encourages us to think in genealogical terms. Now, if the Wordsworthian

---

14. "At the Fishhouses," in Elizabeth Bishop, *The Complete Poems, 1927–1979*, 64–66.

framework alerts us to approach the poem as a text about poetic vocation, then genealogy becomes literary genealogy and, given the conjunction of Eliotic motifs with Wordsworth's narrative, Bishop's fisherman may be interpreted as a compound father figure—a ghostly compound. Marked by his "invisible" net in the gloaming, the fisherman's ghostliness is all along part of his appearance. Thus, "At the Fishhouses" would represent a second meeting in Bishop's writings between the Wordsworthian and the Eliotic, the first being her short story of 1937, "The Sea and Its Shore."[15]

But I would go a little further. A corollary instance of Bishop's penchant for genealogies occurs in "In the Waiting Room"; for when Bishop's narrator hears the "family voice" in her throat, the sound is "not very loud or long," a phrase that echoes the Spenserian Eliot of "The Fire Sermon." That Bishop's sense of literary tradition owes a great deal to Eliot seems to me beyond cavil; her poetic sensibility is in profound ways Eliotic. "At the Fishhouses" partakes in a Virgilian allusiveness, a particular method of cultural instruction (piquantly individualized by Bishop), that distinguishes Eliot and his American legacy from that of Emerson. (Interestingly, this allusiveness has proved serviceable to poets writing in a colonial context— one thinks of Seamus Heaney, E. K. Brathwaite, and Derek Walcott.) "At the Fishhouses" alludes not only to "Gerontion" and *Four Quartets*, but, in the long view, to such Virgilian encounters as the uncanny scene in the *Aeneid* (3.588 ff.) on the island of Sicily, where Aeneas and his men discover a lone survivor of Odysseus's meeting with the Cyclops. The surviving Greek, Achaemenides, appears near the shore in the morning twilight, much as Bishop and Eliot develop liminal moments in which to encounter the past.[16]

Like the house of "Gerontion," Bishop's fishhouses reverberate with history sacred and secular. With their "steeply peaked roofs," the fishhouses are churchlike structures; fish is an apostolic symbol; the "ancient wooden capstan" on the slope behind the houses is a kind of cross with "melancholy stains, like dried blood, / where the ironwork has rusted." This Christian symbolism revolves around the apostolic figure of the old fisherman (one thinks of fishing motifs throughout Eliot and in Lowell's first two volumes), who is a vestige of the Christian mission in America, a seemingly lost mission

15. For an interpretation of this allegorical tale, see Costello, *Elizabeth Bishop*, 186–87.
16. Bishop, *Complete Poems*, 160–61. Cf. Virgil: "*Hic me, dum trepidi crudelia limina linquunt / immemores. . . .*"

to which the Bishops, like the Eliots, had strong ties. What I am chiefly suggesting is that Bishop, in the first half of her poem, gives us a complex of details that assimilates Eliot's tradition to a quasi-allegorical landscape.[17]

By way of a short middle section that describes a "long ramp / descending into the water" and alludes to the underworld, Bishop turns from the land to the sea. Her language heightens as she waxes prophetic, but suddenly slips back into a conversational or epistolary register. A seal catches her eye: he is a counterpoint to the fisherman, and signifies an aspect of Bishop that cannot be known through poetry. He is a seal who belies his name, for he cannot be tied to "seals," linguistic contracts of any variety, including the hymns she sings to him. Behind this oddly communicating couple, "a million Christmas trees stand / waiting for Christmas." The image recalls the symbolism of the first section, but works to place Christian eschatology in doubt.

Turning from the sea to the earth to the heavens, the poet, throughout her final stanza, alternates between modes of poetic speech, from apparent small talk to vatic utterance. Her surprising shifts of tone enable Bishop to parry the master's echo, to provide a critical distance for herself from the spiritual and moral prejudices of tradition, and to realize her full range by getting a word in edgewise. With characteristic self-restraint, and after weaving together numerous rhetorical styles, she describes a momentary transcendence:

> The water seems suspended
> above the rounded gray and blue-gray stones.
> I have seen it over and over, the same sea, the same,
> slightly, indifferently swinging above the stones,
> icily free above the stones,
> above the stones and then the world.

17. Recent commentary on Bishop's debt to Eliot is pertinent here. James Longenbach reads Bishop's 1933 undergraduate discussion of "Tradition and the Individual Talent" as a "theory of hermeneutic indeterminacy." Longenbach finds that Bishop seized on a legitimate but daring interpretation of Eliot—an interpretation that establishment critics of the day overlooked. By way of Bishop's unusual emphasis, "Tradition and the Individual Talent" became her manifesto of liberation from the "monuments" and "order" of a restrictive and moribund tradition (James Longenbach, "Elizabeth Bishop and the Story of Postmodernism"). In her *Elizabeth Bishop,* Costello maintains that "Tradition and the Individual Talent" provided a major point of departure for Bishop; Costello generally reads Bishop as reversing Eliot's emphases and gives perhaps too little attention to continuities between the two authors.

The visionary observer ascends among waters, like those described in the opening chapter of Genesis, which are above the earth. Following Emerson, she has become "a transparent eyeball"; following Eliot, she grounds her mimetic subjectivism on a kind of absolute technical rigor.

As a developing poet, Bishop shared in the revival of Donne that Eliot helped precipitate, and her letters show that she received her Donne through Eliot's criticism.[18] Eliot was both an influence and an atmosphere, and Bishop thrived in the heady air. In "At the Fishhouses," her final, oracular description of the sea appeals, as Eliot said of Donne, to the "cerebral cortex, the nervous system, and the digestive tracts" (*SE*, 250):

> If you tasted it, it would first taste bitter,
> then briny, then surely burn your tongue.
> It is like what we imagine knowledge to be:
> dark, salt, clear, moving, utterly free,
> drawn from the cold hard mouth
> of the world, derived from the rocky breasts
> forever, flowing and drawn, and since
> our knowledge is historical, flowing, and flown.

It may seem odd at this point to advert once more to "Gerontion," but Bishop is writing in the vein of that poem, though not in the monologue form; in any event, the modernist impulse is to interweave forms and genres within lyric poetry. "Gerontion" helps claim history for the modernist poet,[19] and one may see a parallel between the end of "At the Fishhouses" and the end of Eliot's poem, where history has broken down, and Fresca and the others are "whirled / Beyond the circuit of the shuddering Bear / In fractured atoms." In both poems, knowledge of this world proves to be poisonous, and absolute freedom to be icily dark. Shunning the imaginative compensations of Wordsworth, Bishop, like Eliot's Gerontion, ends on a note of resignation.

According to my working definition, Bishop is very nearly a postmodernist. By the end of "At the Fishhouses," she has abandoned history as a narrative with a beginning, a middle, and an end. On the other hand,

18. Bishop, *One Art*, 10, 13.
19. For "Gerontion" and Eliot's modernist turn toward history, see Gregory S. Jay, *T. S. Eliot and the Poetics of Literary History*, 22–30; for a wide-ranging discussion of history in modernist contexts, see James Longenbach, *Modernist Poetics of History: Pound, Eliot, and the Sense of the Past.*

though, she does not cashier her inherited traditions or distance herself entirely from her past. There is no epochal break from history, just an expression of its, and our, contingency in a godless world—the poem's statement of this contingency has a Protestant resonance, except for the stark fact that God is entirely absent. Bishop thus discovers the ultima Thule of modernism. Like Lowell, she pursues, or at least entertains, the modernist question of how autobiography connects to tradition and an idealized sense of history. Eliot had developed this question in "Tradition and the Individual Talent," an essay on which Bishop based a theory of the novel while still an undergraduate. But if she inherits Eliot's dialectic, Bishop resists any metaphysical sanction for its authority, or for the authority of her poems. She pragmatically accepts what fate has given her, not with an eye towards an epic binding of past, present, and future, but because to renounce history would be to renounce poetry and one's identity as a poet.

Robert Lowell's debt to Eliot underlies an important debate about the legacy of American modernism. In *Hart Crane and Allen Tate,* a fine study that promises to be influential, Langdon Hammer offers an interpretation of American modernism that concludes with a chapter on Lowell. According to Hammer, Crane and Tate became allies through their "mutual dedication to the formal, self-reflexive properties of art."[20] As Tate's disciple, the young Lowell inherited Tate's approach to Eliot, which served to bolster Tate's formalist poetic and Southern Agrarian cultural values; so strong was Tate's influence on Lowell that, for Hammer, *Life Studies* becomes a perverse riff on the mentor, Tate.

In conceiving Lowell's relation to Eliot through the intermediary of Tate, Hammer perpetuates a misreading of American modernism that I want to question. At stake in this misreading, I would argue, are the related questions of whether we choose to see Eliot's legacy as principally formalist, a view countenanced by Hammer and Vendler, and whether we grant an authentic moral vision to Eliot and Lowell. Lowell's writings and interviews show that Eliot exerted a direct and personal influence on Lowell, and our idea of American modernism needs to address this poetic commerce, which was regulated neither by Tate nor the professorial circles that Lowell frequented. As Lowell himself commented in the 1960s, Southern Agrarianism "was partly a continuation of Pound and Eliot and partly an attempt to make

20. Langdon Hammer, *Hart Crane and Allen Tate: Janus-Faced Modernism,* x.

poetry much more formal than Eliot and Pound did." Under the pressure of academic canons, the clear difference that Lowell recognized between Eliot and the formalists has all but vanished.[21]

Among the many expressions of Lowell's filial piety toward Eliot, who was in fact a distant relation, "My Last Afternoon with Uncle Devereux Winslow," from part 4 of *Life Studies,* strikes me as the most interesting.[22] Beneath his title, Lowell sets the scene for his reader in italics, *"1922: the stone porch of my grandfather's summer house."* He then begins:

> "I won't go with you. I want to stay with grandpa!"
> That's how I threw cold water
> on my Mother and Father's
> watery martini pipe dreams at Sunday dinner.
> . . . Fontainebleau, Mattapoisett, Puget Sound. . . .
> Nowhere was anywhere after a summer
> at my Grandfather's farm.
> Diamond-pointed, athirst and Norman,
> its alley of poplars
> paraded from Grandmother's rose garden
> to a scary stand of virgin pine,
> scrub, and paths forever pioneering.

21. Lowell quoted in Breslin, *From Modern to Contemporary,* 13; though they vary crucially on other matters, Breslin and Hammer uphold much the same view of Eliot's formalist legacy for Lowell. Hammer adopts David Bromwich's classification of Lowell: "Tate may almost be said to have created Lowell. He gave him not only advice, friendship, and idea of modernity, but a complete set of mannerisms to study, down to the very inflections of the Eliotic-Agrarian accent which Lowell picked up early and never wore out" (Bromwich, *Choice of Inheritance,* 240; quoted in Hammer, *Hart Crane and Allen Tate,* 217). With Tate as his book's central subject, Hammer observes a distinction between "Eliotic modernism and its New Critical permutations," but presents Eliot as a "tastemaker," a writer of aesthetic treatises, and the father of an "aesthetic ideology" (Hammer, *Hart Crane and Allen Tate,* 7)—there is certainly truth to this version of Eliot. In his recent biography of Lowell, Paul Mariani continues the decades-old neglect of Eliot's larger influence on Lowell: "By 1955 Lowell had paid his debt to Tate and Ransom and Eliot and had become uncomfortably 'conscious of the burden and the hardening of the old New Formalism' " (Paul Mariani, *Lost Puritan: A Life of Robert Lowell,* 243). As Lowell knew intimately well and as Jeffrey Perl has demonstrated (*Skepticism,* 30–31, etc.), Eliot never was a "New Formalist." An exception to the prevailing view of Lowell's formalist inheritance is the fine section on Lowell in Stephen Stepanchev's *American Poetry since 1945: A Critical Survey,* 17–36.

22. I am also partial to Lowell's mischievous parody of the Wagnerian Eliot of *The Waste Land:* " 'Weelawaugh, we-ee-eeelawaugh, weelawaugh,' shrilled Mother's high voice" (Robert Lowell, *Life Studies,* 19).

One afternoon in 1922,
I sat on the stone porch, looking through
screens as black-grained as drifting coal.[23]

Like "At the Fishhouses," this is a very brilliant instance of a poet establishing a genealogy. Lowell is intent on his grandfather: the father has gotten in the way—a familiar scenario for writers. Beyond the literal memories of Arthur Winslow, Lowell's maternal grandfather, Eliot's presence haunts the entire passage. The lines "its alley of poplars / paraded from Grandmother's rose garden" recall "Burnt Norton"—the "rose-garden" and "empty alley" of section 1, Lowell's rose garden being similarly placed in his poem's opening stanza. By beginning "One afternoon in 1922," the next stanza iterates, and thus draws attention to, the date. It is perhaps no accident that 1922, the year of *The Waste Land,* is so prominent: Lowell readily admitted to introducing fictional elements into *Life Studies.* Moreover, one may hear an echo of *The Waste Land,* close on the heels of "1922": "I sat on the stone porch, looking through . . . ," which compares rather closely with "I sat upon the shore / Fishing . . ." (*WL* 423–24). The effect is cumulative: the echoes of *Four Quartets,* the date of *The Waste Land* (twice), the mimicry of the latter poem. Then there is the matter of inheritance. "Shall I at least set my lands in order?" asked Eliot in *The Waste Land* (*WL* 425). Here those lands find their claimant, through whom they are rendered new and expansive, "virgin" and (with a fine tinge of irony) "forever pioneering."

Using the family-romance model, which is implicit in Hammer, one may conclude that Lowell came to select Eliot, no less than Tate, as his poetic father. Lowell began pursuing a friendship with the older poet after the war, and Eliot publicly endorsed him in the early 1950s. Citing a "New England connection" between Eliot and himself,[24] Lowell revered no one else so intensely and consistently. With the aim of further recovering this Eliotic inheritance, I turn to an autobiographical talk by Lowell dating from just after *Life Studies:*

When I was growing up in the twenties, moving into the thirties, it was a very peculiar period, it seems to me, particularly in America. It was a time of enormous optimism. The kind of argument that the world

23. Ibid., 59.
24. Lowell, *Collected Prose,* 263.

was getting better and better, and there would be no more wars, and so forth, that seemed very much in the air. . . . Yet there was the huge jar of the first world war behind us . . . and soon you had a feeling that the violence was arising. . . . [At that period] someone writing poetry perhaps had three choices. One, which was hardly a choice, was the kind of poetry the public wanted, which was a rather watered-down imitation of 19th century poetry, that really had gone completely dead. The other was an *engagé* poetry, and the only kind that really seemed to inspire that kind of conviction was the Marxist, usually pro-Russian. And the third group, which I more or less belonged to, I think it derives somewhat from Yeats and from Eliot, and in this country friends of mine, Allen Tate and John Crowe Ransom. . . . And we believed in form, that that was very important, and for some reason we were very much against the Romantics.

Lowell names Eliot as a source for his group, and I infer that the example of *The Waste Land,* as a brooding reaction against the culture of progress, is somewhere in the background of Lowell's account. To anyone exploring the nexus of Lowell's poetics and his beliefs about culture, it is instructive that he would respond to William Carlos Williams's denunciation of Eliot, to the effect that "*The Waste Land* was an act of treachery," by remarking, "I don't think *The Waste Land* would have been more authentic if Eliot had never left Boston." Like many of his generation, Lowell read *The Waste Land* as a poem about the decline of the West,[25] but Lowell in particular saw the poem as issuing from the "authentic" viewpoint of old New England, where writers had a tradition of speaking as the guardians and privileged inheritors of Western culture. Lowell's reminiscence evokes an atmosphere of crisis in which both he and Eliot, as the heirs of American Puritanism, would have felt at home. In terms of the "New England connection" adduced by Lowell, their kindred instinct would have been to frame and uphold a moral idea of society.

To make a point, I have, I hope not unfairly, adopted italics for a clause elided in Hammer's citation of the following passage, which continues Lowell's autobiographical musing:

25. Ibid., 274. I agree with Mark Rudman that Lowell, like most intellectuals of his day, read *The Waste Land* "as a tract on the decline and fall of Western civilization. . . ." But Rudman finds that *Lord Weary's Castle* "marks the end of [*The Waste Land*] tradition in American poetry" (Mark Rudman, *Robert Lowell: An Introduction to the Poetry,* 18), while I see Lowell developing that tradition in *Life Studies* and beyond.

We would say that the ideal poet is Shakespeare, who is not a poet of ideology but a poet of experience, and tragedy, and the sort of villains to us were people like Shelley—that he used too much ideology— and Whitman, the prophet, who also seemed formless. And one felt that what poetry could do was have nothing to do with causes, *that if you—that might get into what you wrote but you couldn't do it at all directly;* and something like Aristotle's purging by pity and terror, that of going through a catharsis, that that is what was suitable, rather than to persuade people to do anything better or to make the world better. And I think that is the position that is perhaps only intelligible in the thirties, when the danger of being swept into a cause was so great.[26]

"Causes" is the crucial term here, a suggestive word that extends from political to final causes and that carries an Aristotelian resonance. Lowell's comment about "indirectly" expressing causes points to a latent social critique, and the references to Shelley and Whitman make it clear that a subtext of debate about the culture was present to Lowell's imagination during the days of his apprenticeship; I will shortly attempt to ground this subtext on some particulars. Fighting in the 1930s against the politicizing of art, Lowell had to insist on the integrity of his craft. But an aesthetic ideology never appealed to him as it did to Ransom and Tate.

Though it does not speak directly to Eliot's influence, "Words for Hart Crane" merits discussion here because it highlights Lowell's ideas about the uses of form, while it engages the larger aesthetic and cultural issues that surround Lowell's response to Eliot. The poem, which is a sonnet, bears dramatic weight as the climax of part 3 of *Life Studies,* where Lowell, in examining his personal and literary relations to Ford Madox Ford, Santayana, Delmore Schwartz, and finally Crane, stakes an impressive claim to being the heir apparent of modernism in America. I quote both the poem and an earlier, typescript version, with the earlier version first:

"(An) Enlishman [*sic*] Abroad (1950)"
"When England gives the laurel to some dope
Or screw, who scrubs Catullus' tongue with soap,
I hope she will consider why I took

26. Lowell quoted in Ian Hamilton, *Robert Lowell: A Biography,* 85; the original transcript is at the Houghton Library, Harvard University. It is quoted in part by Hammer, *Hart Crane and Allen Tate,* 227.

This crooked turn, instead of Uncle Sam's
Good offices that only health can buy.
Because I knew my classics like a book,
Stranger from England, tell the Brittish [sic], I,
Catullus Redivivus, once the rage
Of Rome and Paris used to play your role
Of homosexual wolfing the stray lambs
Who hunger by the Place de la Concorde.
My profit was a pocket with a hole.
Who asks for *X,* the Shelley of the age,
Must pay pound sterling for his bed and board."[27]

"Words for Hart Crane"
"When the Pulitzers showered on some dope
or screw who flushed our dry mouths out with soap
few people would consider why I took
to stalking sailors, and scattered Uncle Sam's
phoney gold-plated laurels to the birds.
Because I knew my Whitman like a book,
stranger in America, tell my country: I,
Catullus redivivus, once the rage
of the Village and Paris, used to play my role
of homosexual, wolfing the stray lambs
who hungered by the Place de la Concorde.
My profit was a pocket with a hole.
Who asks for me, the Shelley of my age,
must lay his heart out for my bed and board."[28]

Lowell included "(An) Enlishman Abroad (1950)" in a 1954 letter to Pound at St. Elizabeth's Hospital. Whoever "*X*" may be, I would suggest that Lowell follows *Hugh Selwyn Mauberley* in rebuking literary and national establishments. I would also note that Lowell, in the same batch of letters, addresses the matter of his and Pound's masterful Latin at some length, and writes about "tumbling" through prodigious quantities of Virgil in a single sleepless night. Like Pound, Lowell knew his "classics like a book"—it is the autobiographical ingredient within his earlier monologue, combined

27. Robert Lowell to Ezra Pound (March 26, 1954). Hammer's reading of this sonnet is very different from my own; see Hammer, *Hart Crane and Allen Tate,* 230.
28. Lowell, *Life Studies,* 55.

with the base provided by the Poundian model, that enabled Lowell to rewrite "(An) Enlishman Abroad (1950)" successfully. Moreover, a quality of feeling joins Lowell's two versions: this feeling does not stem from what is often too vaguely called "social consciousness"; it arises from Lowell's self-consciously masculine desire to be a national prophet. Uniting the primitive instinct for power with a highly refined sense of law, morality, and duty, the prophetic impulse confirms the poet's role as a true and virile son of his culture, at the same time that it distances him, in a triumphant manner, from uncles and sheep. It was really Whitman's alleged formlessness, not his prophesying, that Lowell distrusted. He told Pound: "a man must sweat for his meters, if he is ever going to be a fabbro, and not just a prophet."[29] The speaker of "(An) Enlishman Abroad (1950)" sweats for his iambics in vain: as Lowell may well be suggesting, modernist writers must inevitably give up the prophetic for the sake of "profit."

My central point is that "Words for Hart Crane," with its references to "Uncle Sam's phoney gold-plated laurels," "Whitman," and "America," resonates within an epic tradition, dating back to Barlow and earlier, which was developed by Whitman, Eliot, Pound, Crane, Langston Hughes, and others. The sympathetic anger of Lowell's poem arises from the poet's fraternal regard for Crane, who, apart from being a superb elegist, uttered prophecy to a nation incapable of moral and spiritual action; in the early version of the poem, this fraternal spirit may explain Lowell's signing his letter to Pound, "*Vale,* Cal"—a possible reference to the great elegy that concludes "*ave atque vale,*" written by Catullus (cf. line 2 of the early version) for his lost brother. In terms of the dramatic structure of *Life Studies,* the terror and pity of the occasion emerge in a catharsis experienced by Lowell and communicated by him to that (rather too) rarefied audience of poets and critics who may share in it: "Crane," in calling himself "the Shelley of my age," evokes the "beautiful and ineffectual angel" memorialized by Arnold. I use Arnold as a compass point; what counts is the potential identification with the fey Shelley. Alive, both intellectually and emotionally, to the subtext of cultural debate enacted by *The Waste Land, The Bridge,* and numerous other important works, Lowell must align Crane with Shelley (and Whitman) on the side of a valiant but failed idealism, with the lost prophets. It is precisely like Lowell that he employs a sonnet, well wrought,

29. Lowell, letter to Ezra Pound (March 30, 1954).

metrically resourceful, formally impressive, to present a trenchant and complex argument about American literary culture.

By "Skunk Hour" and the end of *Life Studies,* Lowell had placed himself with Eliot in pursuing a course of moral realism. Informed by the dialectic between individuality and conformity in "Tradition and the Individual Talent" (see Chapter 3), the realist position does not relinquish the duty to have ideas and grapple with the world. Rather, it begins in reaction against a failed idealism (an impractical dream of social change based on false notions about the self's prerogatives) by seeking to define the field of action within which ideas can live: for Eliot, that field was religious community; for Lowell, it was often a matter of remembering "our tougher roots."[30] Above all, realism prefers a dialectical to an absolutist moral stance: one's heart is just too high a price to pay for another's—even Hart Crane's—"bread and board." The poet cannot cling singularly to his own vision, but must negotiate with community, tradition, law—that which is greater and more permanent than himself—in order to gain sustenance, support, and social authority. It was one of *Life Studies'* little ironies that a poet could aspire to moral realism, only to find himself, like Pound, in the madhouse.

Life Studies extends Eliot's tradition along several lines: it echoes Eliot; it combines traditional and experimental forms in ways that are intensely refined and richly coded; it advances the side of moral realism in a debate with the moral idealist, Crane; and, in connecting the self's history to the history of nations, it relies on teleology as an ulterior frame of reference. What Lowell found in Eliot, "a continuation and a criticism of the [New England] tradition,"[31] applies of course to Lowell himself. Both poets' ancestors came to America to build Christ's kingdom, and neither Lowell nor Eliot lost track of their failure. One can trace this pyrrhic continuity through much of *Life Studies,* which, in surveying the infertility, dead religion, and capitalist mania of New England and the United States, effectively interprets *The Waste Land* as a New England poem. Like *The Waste Land,* "Skunk Hour" reflects on a final cause that no longer, apparently, obtains, but that, in its demonic inversion or its absence, informs every level of human experience—the skunks themselves are robustly exempt from the burdens of history. From the opening poem of *Land of Unlikeness* (1944), the very

30. Quoted from "Sheep" in Robert Lowell, *History,* 37.
31. Lowell, *Collected Prose,* 263.

title of which carries an Eliotic echo, Lowell dwells on the fate of "New World eschatologies," and one cannot really understand his career without bearing in mind his deep familial and imaginative ties to what he called "the Promised Land foreseen in Plymouth."[32] Thus, while the later Lowell renounces formal belief, he is a late modernist according to the distinctions I have set up: however bittersweet, American providential history retains its hold on him.

In the past, critics have understood Eliot's poetics of history along the lines of what Northrop Frye called a "mythology of decline."[33] Populating this mythology were, more or less, the dissociation of sensibility, the English Civil War, Donne rising, Milton sinking, and the fact that in some moods Dante was about the only author that Eliot would prescribe for his public. Throughout his oeuvre, though, and with culminating clarity in *Four Quartets*, an American sense of providential history impels Eliot's writing. For Lowell, Eliot's most revealing reader, the mythology of decline is more conspicuous than, but secondary to, the impetus to lead a people out of history's cunning passages and toward the promised land. It is, I want to suggest, Eliot's commitment to a future good, his belief in a future good, and not his nostalgia for lost origins or a golden age, that will imbue any future American poetry that takes on an Eliotic cast. Such poetry will be late modernist rather than postmodernist, and it will present a salutary challenge to contemporary wisdom about the future of our culture.

32. Quoted from "The Park Street Cemetery," in Robert Lowell, *Land of Unlikeness*, no page number.
33. Frye, *T. S. Eliot*, 24.

Appendix | The "Patient Etherised"

THE OPENING LINES OF "THE LOVE Song of J. Alfred Prufrock" are a touchstone for twentieth-century poetry in English.[1] Here, I would briefly consider the origins of the lines and their bearing on literary history:

> Let us go then, you and I,
> When the evening is spread out against the sky
> Like a patient etherised upon a table; . . .
>   ("Prufrock" 1–3)

The source for the image of the "patient etherised" may well be William James, who retired from Harvard University in 1907 when Eliot was a freshman. Eliot's student notes on James's *The Varieties of Religious Experience* fill the ruled sides of four index cards in the Eliot Collection at Harvard, and belong to a batch of about fifty four-by-six-inch note cards that record Eliot's reading on mysticism and religion. Lyndall Gordon places the entire group of cards from 1908 to 1914.[2] Her dates strike me as reasonable because,

1. For the rival schools of interpretation, see Leonard Unger, "Actual Times and Actual Places," 99.
2. For James in the context of modernism, see Schwartz, *Matrix of Modernism,* 34–49. Gordon, *Eliot's Early Years,* 141–42. Elsewhere reliable, Gordon misdates some of the books, and cites the wrong study by Henri Delacroix. The six cards on Delacroix pertain to the *Etudes d'histoire et de psychologie du mysticisme* (Paris: F. Alcan, 1908) and not to the *Essai sur le mysticisme spéculatif en Allemagne au XIVᵉ siècle,* which Eliot had merely placed on one of his three checklists of titles.

147

though Eliot did not date his note-taking, one can discern the change in his handwriting between the earlier and later cards.

As an example of the post-Paris hand, we have four cards of notes on Evelyn Underhill's *Mysticism*, which was first published in 1911. The notes on James are somewhat choppier than the Underhill; they lack the elegant fluidity of the later hand. Unfortunately, the Underhill cards are in ink and the James cards are in pencil, and this difference does affect comparison. But having studied Eliot's note cards on separate occasions, and having tested my findings against the facsimiles of dated manuscripts in the Berg Collection,[3] I see no cause to rule out this interesting possibility: that the notes on James are in the pre-Paris hand. If so, Eliot would have read James before he finished "The Love Song of J. Alfred Prufrock." And whether the cards antedate Eliot's year abroad or not, the poet may have read or flipped through James's book before he wrote his famous simile.

Eliot's notes on James derive solely from the chapter in *The Varieties of Religious Experience* entitled "Mysticism." In this chapter, James documents an experience called "Anaesthetic Revelation" through the writings of some of its prime exponents. He begins with Benjamin Paul Blood, author of "Tennyson's Trances and the Anaesthetic Revelation," who describes the experience: "no words may express the imposing certainty of the patient that he is realizing the primordial, Adamic surprise of Life." After a long note devoted to Mr. Blood (Blood, by the way, is the maiden name of Charlotte Eliot's mother, a fact that Eliot would certainly have noticed),[4] James subjoins another lengthy note, the testimony of "a gifted woman" who was "taking ether for a surgical operation." The woman refers to her "ether dream":

> A great Being or Power was traveling through the sky, his foot was on a kind of lightning as a wheel is on a rail, it was his pathway. The lightning was made entirely of the spirits of innumerable people close to one another, and I was one of them. He moved in a straight line, and each part of the streak or flash came into its conscious existence only that he might travel. I seemed to be directly under the foot of God, and I thought he was grinding his own life up out of my pain.

3. For a probable chronology of the Berg manuscript poems and an excellent discussion of the problems in dating them, see Ricks in *IMH*, xxxvii–xlii, and xvii–xviii, respectively.

4. William James, *The Varieties of Religious Experience*, 381. Eliot put the name of B. P. Blood on one of the three checklists.

> . . . He went on and I came to. In that moment the whole of my life passed before me, including each little meaningless piece of distress, and I *understood* them. *This* was what it had all meant, *this* was the piece of work it had all been contributing to do. (Her emphasis)[5]

On his note cards, Eliot refers to this section of James's chapter in detail, and singles out the experience of the "gifted woman" as especially interesting. Unlike the testimonies of Benjamin Blood, who speaks of "the wonder and assurance of the soul," and John Addington Symonds, who felt "the undemonstrable but irrefragable certainty of God," her mystical vision has a dark aspect: "Knowledge and Love are One, and the *measure* is suffering" (her emphasis).[6] Her account, descending perhaps from Ezekiel by way of Shelley's "The Triumph of Life," complicates the tone of James's chapter by its fatalism.

In general, though, James strikes a note of enthusiastic speculation. His own experiment with nitrous oxide had left him convinced "that our normal waking consciousness . . . is but one special type of consciousness, whilst all about it, parted by the filmiest of screens, there lie potential forms of consciousness entirely different." As corroboration of the existence of mystical consciousness, he points to lyric poetry's "beckoning and inviting" moments, to its power to open "vague vistas" and "irrational doorways." The chapter is infused with the excitement of intellectual and spiritual discovery,[7] and James colors and accents his discussion with the words of Shelley, Tennyson, Whitman, and Swinburne.

For Eliot and Prufrock, the "evening" doesn't properly belong to James's mystical atmosphere. The poem alludes to the kind of subjectivity that James describes: the evening, spread out, expansive, is like the patient under ether who will speak of intimations, of liminal states and unities that can be experienced if not fully expressed. But the "evening" is *like* that, and in likeness there is unlikeness. Eliot magnifies this unlikeness through the detail of the operating "table." The effect of the "table" is to insist that we are viewing the patient from the outside (as we would in fact view a corpse),

---

5. James, *Varieties,* 383.
6. Ibid., 382, 383, 384.
7. Ibid., 378, 374. Eliot would himself remark, "James has an exceptional quality of always leaving his reader with the feeling that the world is full of possibilities . . ." (T. S. Eliot, "William James on Immortality," 547).

to emphasize the precariousness and limitedness of the human state, and to disrupt the glow of spiritual realization that James conveys. Of course, James had cited the "gifted woman" and thereby qualified his metaphysical optimism; the woman's brilliant narrative reminds us of an irony that Eliot himself sometimes overlooked: in their concern with spirit and mind, such writers as Shelley and Whitman were aware of materialist and determinist philosophies. But the poet who attempts to make literary history must deal in a certain level of generality. It was Eliot's creative insight to turn the rich suggestiveness of a simile into a definitive expression of cultural unlikeness and the passing of nineteenth-century romanticism.

Works Cited

Abboud, Robert. "Jeremiah's Mad Again." *New England Quarterly* 69 (March 1996): 75–90.

Abrams, M. H. *Natural Supernaturalism.* New York: W. W. Norton, 1971.

Ackroyd, Peter. *T. S. Eliot: A Life.* New York: Simon and Schuster, 1984.

Adams, Henry. *The Education of Henry Adams.* 1907. Reprint, Boston: Houghton Mifflin, 1973.

Aiken, Conrad? [Editorial.] *Harvard Advocate* 86 (January 26, 1909): 130.

———. "King Bolo and Others." In *T. S. Eliot: A Symposium from Conrad Aiken (and Others),* ed. Richard March and Tambimuttu, 20–23. Chicago: H. Regnery, 1949.

———. "Prefatory Note" to "Anatomy of Melancholy." 1958. In *T. S. Eliot: The Man and His Work,* ed. Allen Tate, 194–96. New York: Dell, 1966.

Alderman, Nigel. " 'Where Are the Eagles and the Trumpets?' The Strange Case of Eliot's Missing Quatrains." *Twentieth Century Literature* 39 (Summer 1993): 129–51.

Altieri, Charles. "Eliot's Impact." In *The Cambridge Companion to T. S. Eliot,* ed. A. D. Moody, 189–209. Cambridge: Cambridge University Press, 1994.

Arnold, Matthew. *The Poetical Works of Matthew Arnold.* Ed. C. B. Tinker and H. F. Lowry. London: Oxford University Press, 1950.

———. *Prose Works.* 11 vols. Ed. R. H. Super. Ann Arbor: University of Michigan Press, 1961–1977.

Ashbery, John. *Self-Portrait in a Convex Mirror.* 1975. New York: Penguin Books, 1976.

————. *Three Poems.* 1972. New York: Penguin Books, 1977.

Asselineau, Roger. "The European Roots of *Leaves of Grass.*" In *Walt Whitman: The Centennial Essays,* ed. Ed Folsom, 51–60. Iowa City: University of Iowa Press, 1994.

Auden, W. H. Introduction to *The Faber Book of Modern American Verse,* ed. W. H. Auden. London: Faber and Faber, 1956.

Auerbach, Erich. *Mimesis.* Trans. Willard R. Trask. Princeton: Princeton University Press, 1953.

Babbitt, Irving. *Literature and the American College.* Boston: Houghton Mifflin, 1908.

Beehler, Michael. " 'Riddle the Inevitable': Levinas, Eliot, and the Critical Moment of Ethics." In *America's Modernisms,* ed. Kathryne V. Lindberg et al., 118–34. Baton Rouge: Louisiana State University Press, 1996.

Bercovitch, Sacvan. *The American Jeremiad.* Madison: University of Wisconsin Press, 1978.

————. *The Rites of Assent: Transformations in the Symbolic Construction of America.* New York: Routledge, 1993.

Bishop, Elizabeth. *The Complete Poems, 1927–1979.* New York: Farrar, Straus and Giroux, 1983.

————. *One Art: Letters.* Ed. Robert Giroux. New York: Farrar, Straus and Giroux, 1994.

Bloom, Harold. Introduction to *"The Waste Land": Modern Critical Interpretations,* ed. Harold Bloom. New York: Chelsea House, 1986.

————. *Poetics of Influence.* Ed. John Hollander. New Haven: Henry R. Schwab, 1988.

Bloom, Harold, ed. *"The Waste Land": Modern Critical Interpretations.* New York: Chelsea House, 1986.

Bly, Robert. *American Poetry: Wilderness and Domesticity.* New York: Harper and Row, 1990.

Breslin, James E. B. *From Modern to Contemporary: American Poetry, 1945–1965.* Chicago: University of Chicago Press, 1984.

Bromwich, David. *A Choice of Inheritance: Self and Community from Edmund Burke to Robert Frost.* Cambridge: Harvard University Press, 1989.

Brooker, Jewel Spears. *Mastery and Escape: T. S. Eliot and the Dialectic of Modernism.* Amherst: University of Massachusetts Press, 1994.

Brooker, Jewel Spears, ed. *The Placing of T. S. Eliot*. Columbia: University of Missouri Press, 1991.

Brooks, Van Wyck. *The Wine of the Puritans*. 1909. In *Van Wyck Brooks: The Early Years*, ed. Claire Sprague, 1–60. New York: Harper and Row, 1968.

Brooks, Van Wyck, ed. *Writers at Work: The "Paris Review" Interviews*. 2d ser. New York: Viking Press, 1963.

Burke, Edmund. *Reflections on the Revolution in France*. New York: Penguin Books, 1968.

Burke, Kenneth. "I, Eye, Ay—Emerson's Early Essay on 'Nature': Thoughts on the Machinery of Transcendence." *Sewanee Review* 74 (1966): 875–95.

———. "Policy Made Personal." In *"Leaves of Grass": One Hundred Years After*, ed. Milton Hindus, 74–108. Stanford: Stanford University Press, 1955.

Bush, Ronald. "Nathaniel Hawthorne and T. S. Eliot's American Connection." *Southern Review* 21 (October 1985): 924–33.

———. *T. S. Eliot: A Study in Character and Style*. New York: Oxford University Press, 1983.

———. "T. S. Eliot: Singing the Emerson Blues." In *Emerson: Prospect and Retrospect*, ed. Joel Porte, 179–97. Cambridge: Harvard University Press, 1982.

———. " 'Turned toward Creation': T. S. Eliot, 1988." In *T. S. Eliot: Man and Poet*, ed. Laura Cowan. Vol. 1. Orono: University of Maine, 1990.

Bush, Ronald, ed. *T. S. Eliot: The Modernist in History*. Cambridge: Cambridge University Press, 1991.

Butscher, Edward. *Conrad Aiken, Poet of White Horse Vale*. Atlanta: University of Georgia Press, 1988.

Clendenning, John. "Time, Doubt and Vision." *American Scholar* 36 (1967): 125–32.

Coleridge, Samuel Taylor. *Collected Works of Samuel Taylor Coleridge*. 13 vols. Ed. Kathleen Coburn. Princeton: Princeton University Press, 1985.

Costello, Bonnie. *Elizabeth Bishop: Questions of Mastery*. Cambridge: Harvard University Press, 1991.

Cowan, Laura, ed. *T. S. Eliot: Man and Poet*. 2 vols. Orono: University of Maine, 1990.

Crane, Hart. *The Letters of Hart Crane, 1916–1932.* Ed. Brom Weber. Berkeley and Los Angeles: University of California Press, 1965.

———. *The Poems of Hart Crane.* Ed. Marc Simon. New York: Liveright, 1986.

D'Ambrosio, Vinnie-Marie. *Eliot Possessed: T. S. Eliot and FitzGerald's "Rubáiyát."* New York: New York University Press, 1989.

Deiss, William. "William Greenleaf Eliot: The Formative Years (1811–1834)." Introduction to *William Greenleaf Eliot,* by Earl Holt. St. Louis: First Unitarian Church of St. Louis, 1985.

Derrida, Jacques. *Writing and Difference.* Trans. Alan Bass. Chicago: University of Chicago Press, 1978.

DiBattista, Maria, and Lucy McDiarmid, eds. *High and Low Moderns: Literature and Culture, 1889–1939.* New York: Oxford University Press, 1996.

Donoghue, Denis. *Being Modern Together.* Atlanta: Scholars Press, 1991.

———. "Eliot's 'Marina' and Closure." *Hudson Review* 49 (Autumn 1996): 367–88.

Dupee, F. W., ed. *The Question of Henry James: A Collection of Critical Essays.* New York: Henry Holt, 1945.

Edel, Leon, ed. *Collected Travel Writings [of Henry James].* New York: Library of America, 1993.

Eliot, Charlotte. "God's Kingdom Is at Hand. Repent!" Eliot Collection, Houghton Library, Harvard University, n.d.

———. *Savonarola.* London: R. Cobden-Sanderson, 1926.

———. "The Wednesday Club." Eliot Collection, Houghton Library, Harvard University, n.d.

———. *William Greenleaf Eliot.* Boston: Houghton Mifflin, 1904.

Eliot, T. S. *After Strange Gods.* New York: Harcourt, Brace, 1934.

———. "An American Critic." *New Statesman* 7 (June 24, 1916): 284.

———. "American Critics." *Times Literary Supplement* no. 1406 (January 10, 1929): 24.

———. "American Literature." *Athenaeum* no. 4643 (April 25, 1919): 236–37.

———. *Collected Poems, 1909–1962.* New York: Harcourt Brace Jovanovich, 1988.

———. "A Commentary." *Criterion* 2 (April 1924): 231–35.

———. "A Commentary." *Criterion* 12 (April 1933): 468–73.

————. "A Commentary: That Poetry Is Made with Words." *New English Weekly* 15 (April 27, 1939): 27–28.

————. "The Development of Leibniz's Monadism." *Monist* 26 (October 1916): 534–56.

————. "Disjecta Membra." *Egoist* 5 (April 1918): 55.

————. "A Dream within a Dream." *Listener* 29 (February 25, 1943): 243–44.

————. "Eeldrop and Appleplex," Part 1. *Little Review* 4 (May 1917): 7–11.

————. *Elizabethan Essays*. London: Faber and Faber, 1934.

————. Foreword to *Symbolisme from Poe to Mallarmé,* by Joseph Chiari. New York: Macmillan, 1956.

————. *For Lancelot Andrewes*. Garden City: Doubleday, 1929.

————. *The Idea of a Christian Society*. 1939. Reprint, with *Notes towards the Definition of Culture,* in *Christianity and Culture*. San Diego: Harcourt Brace Jovanovich, 1977.

————. "The Influence of Landscape upon the Poet." *Daedalus* 89 (Spring 1960): 420–22.

————. Interview by Donald Hall. 1959. In *Writers at Work: The "Paris Review" Interviews,* ed. Van Wyck Brooks, 89–110. Reprint, New York: Viking, 1963.

————. Introduction to *Ezra Pound: Selected Poems*. London: Faber and Faber, 1928.

————. Introduction to *Savonarola,* by Charlotte Eliot. London: R. Cobden-Sanderson, 1926.

————. Introduction to *The Adventures of Huckleberry Finn,* by Mark Twain. 1950. In *Huckleberry Finn,* ed. Kenneth Lynn. Reprint, New York: Harcourt Brace Jovanovich, 1961.

————. Introduction to *The Wheel of Fire,* by G. Wilson Knight. 1930. Reprint, London: Methuen, 1949.

————. *Inventions of the March Hare: Poems, 1909–1917*. Ed. Christopher Ricks. New York: Harcourt Brace, 1996.

————. "Isolated Superiority," *Dial* 84 (January 1928): 4–7.

————. *Knowledge and Experience in the Philosophy of F. H. Bradley*. 1964. Reprint, New York: Columbia University Press, 1989.

————. "The Lesson of Baudelaire." *Tyro* 1 (Spring 1921): 4.

————. *The Letters of T. S. Eliot, 1898–1922*. Ed. Valerie Eliot. San Diego: Harcourt Brace Jovanovich, 1988.

———. Letters to William Force Stead. Osborn Collection, Beineke Library, Yale University.

———. Letter to the Editor. *Sunday Times,* April 6, 1958, 4.

———. "Marianne Moore." *Dial* 75 (December 1923): 594–97.

———. "Mr. Leacock Serious." *New Statesman* 7 (July 29, 1916): 404–5.

———. "Mr. P. E. More's Essays." *Times Literary Supplement* no. 1412 (February 21, 1929): 136.

———. Note Cards on Philosophy. Fifty-nine four-by-six-inch cards. Eliot Collection, Houghton Library, Harvard University, ca. 1910.

———. "Notes on the Way." *Time and Tide* 16 (January 19, 1935): 88–90.

———. *Notes towards the Definition of Culture.* 1948. Reprint, with *The Idea of a Christian Society,* in *Christianity and Culture.* San Diego: Harcourt Brace Jovanovich, 1977.

———. "Note sur Mallarmé et Poe." Trans. Ramon Fernandez. *La Nouvelle Revue Française* 14 (November 1, 1926): 526.

———. "Observations." *Egoist* 5 (May 1918): 69–70.

———. "On Henry James." 1918. In *The Question of Henry James: A Collection of Critical Essays,* ed. F. W. Dupee, 108–19. New York: Henry Holt, 1945.

———. *On Poetry and Poets.* London: Faber and Faber, 1957.

———. *Poems Written in Early Youth.* New York: Farrar, Straus and Giroux, 1967.

———. "The Preacher as Artist." *Athenaeum* no. 4674 (November 28, 1919): 1252–53.

———. Preface to *This American World,* by Edgar Ansel Mowrer. London: Faber and Faber, 1928.

———. "Reflections on Contemporary Poetry." *Egoist* 4 (November 1917): 151.

———. "Reflections on Contemporary Poetry." *Egoist* 6 (July 1919): 39–40.

———. Review of *Israfel,* by Hervey Allen. *Nation and Athenaeum* 41 (May 21, 1927): 219.

———. Review of *Mens Creatrix,* by William Temple. *International Journal of Ethics* 27 (July 1917): 542–43.

———. Review of *The Wine of the Puritans,* by Van Wyck Brooks. *Harvard Advocate* 87 (May 7, 1909): 80.

———. Review of *The World as Imagination,* by Edward Fawcett. *International Journal of Ethics* 28 (July 1918): 572.

————. "A Romantic Patrician." *Athenaeum* no. 4644 (May 2, 1919): 265–67.

————. "A Sceptical Patrician." *Athenaeum* no. 4647 (May 23, 1919): 361–62.

————. *Selected Essays.* New York: Harcourt, Brace and World, 1950.

————. *The Selected Prose of T. S. Eliot.* Ed. Frank Kermode. New York: Harcourt Brace Jovanovich, 1975.

————. "Tarr." *Egoist* 5 (September 1918): 105–6.

————. "The Three Provincialities." *Tyro* 2 [(Spring 1922)]: 11–13.

————. *To Criticize the Critic and Other Writings.* 1965. Reprint, Lincoln: University of Nebraska Press, 1991.

————. "Turgenev." *Egoist* 4 (December 1917): 167.

————. *The Use of Poetry and the Use of Criticism.* 1933. Reprint, Cambridge: Harvard University Press, 1964.

————. *The Varieties of Metaphysical Poetry.* Ed. Ronald Schuchard. New York: Harcourt Brace, 1993.

————. *The Waste Land: A Facsimile and Transcript of the Original Drafts.* Ed. Valerie Eliot. New York: Harcourt Brace Jovanovich, 1971.

————. "Whitman and Tennyson." *Nation and Athenaeum* 40 (December 18, 1926): 426.

————. "William James on Immortality." *New Statesman* 9 (September 8, 1917): 547.

Eliot, T. S., ed. *Literary Essays of Ezra Pound.* London: Faber and Faber, 1954.

Emerson, Ralph Waldo. *The Complete Works of Ralph Waldo Emerson.* 12 vols. Ed. Edward Waldo Emerson. Boston: Houghton Mifflin, 1903–1904.

————. *The Letters of Ralph Waldo Emerson.* 9 vols. Ed. Ralph L. Rusk. New York: Columbia University Press, 1939.

Empson, William. "The Style of the Master." In *T. S. Eliot: Twentieth Century Views,* ed. Hugh Kenner, 152–54. Englewood Cliffs, N.J.: Prentice-Hall, 1962.

————. *Using Biography.* London: Chatto and Windus, 1984.

Fisher, Benjamin. "The Urban Scene and Edgar Allan Poe." *Publications of the Mississippi Philological Association* (1986): 40–50.

Folsom, Ed, ed. *Walt Whitman: The Centennial Essays.* Iowa City: University of Iowa Press, 1994.

Ford, Mark. "Nothing and a Lot." Review of John Ashbery, *Can You Hear, Bird. Times Literary Supplement* no. 4859 (May 17, 1996): 26.

Friedrich, Hugo. *The Structure of Modern Poetry.* Trans. Joachim Neugroschel. Evanston, Ill.: Northwestern University Press, 1974.

Frost, Robert. *Selected Prose of Robert Frost.* Ed. Hyde Cox and Edward Lathem. New York: Holt, Rinehart and Winston, 1966.

Fry, Paul H. *The Poet's Calling in the English Ode.* New Haven: Yale University Press, 1980.

Frye, Northrop. *T. S. Eliot: An Introduction.* Chicago: University of Chicago Press, 1963.

Gadamer, Hans-Georg. *Truth and Method.* New York: Seabury Press, 1975.

Gallup, Donald. "The 'Lost' Manuscripts of T. S. Eliot." *Bulletin of the New York Public Library* 72 (December 1968): 641–52.

———. "Mr. Eliot at the Churchill Club. Includes a transcription of T. S. Eliot's 1944 lecture, 'Walt Whitman and Modern Poetry.'" In *T. S. Eliot: Essays from the "Southern Review,"* ed. James Olney, 97–101. Oxford: Clarendon Press, 1988.

———. *T. S. Eliot: A Bibliography.* London: Faber and Faber, 1969.

Gardner, Helen. *The Composition of "Four Quartets."* London: Faber and Faber, 1978.

Gordon, Lyndall. *Eliot's Early Years.* New York: Farrar, Straus and Giroux, 1977.

———. *Eliot's New Life.* New York: Farrar, Straus and Giroux, 1988.

[Greene, William Chase]. Review of *Walt Whitman,* by George Rice Carpenter. *Harvard Advocate* 87 (May 7, 1909): 80.

Gross, Harvey. *Sound and Form in Modern Poetry.* Ann Arbor: University of Michigan Press, 1964.

Hamilton, Ian. *Robert Lowell: A Biography.* New York: Random House, 1982.

Hammer, Langdon. *Hart Crane and Allen Tate: Janus-Faced Modernism.* Princeton: Princeton University Press, 1993.

Harari, Josué V., ed. *Textual Strategies: Perspectives in Post-Structuralist Criticism.* Ithaca: Cornell University Press, 1979.

Hass, Robert. *Sun under Wood.* Hopewell, N.J.: Ecco Press, 1996.

Hawthorne, Nathaniel. *The Centenary Edition of the Works of Nathaniel Hawthorne.* 20 vols. Ed. William Charvat, Roy Harvey Pearce, and Claude Simpson. Ohio State Center for Textual Studies, 1962– .

Hindus, Milton, ed. *"Leaves of Grass": One Hundred Years After*. Stanford: Stanford University Press, 1955.

Hodder, Alan D. " 'After a High Negative Way': Emerson's 'Self-Reliance' and the Rhetoric of Conversion." *Harvard Theological Review* 84 (1991): 423–46.

Hoffman, Daniel. "Poetry." In *Harvard Guide to Contemporary American Writing,* ed. Daniel Hoffman, 439–606. Cambridge: Harvard University Press, 1979.

Hoffman, Daniel, ed. *Harvard Guide to Contemporary American Writing*. Cambridge: Harvard University Press, 1979.

Howarth, Herbert. "Charlotte Champe Stearns Eliot." In *Notable American Women, 1607–1950,* ed. Edward James, 1:568–69. 3 vols. Cambridge: Harvard University Press, 1971.

———. *Notes on Some Figures behind T. S. Eliot*. Boston: Houghton Mifflin, 1964.

James, Edward, ed. *Notable American Women, 1607–1950*. 3 vols. Cambridge: Harvard University Press, 1971.

James, Henry. *The American Scene*. 1907. In *Collected Travel Writings [of Henry James]*, ed. Leon Edel, 351–736. Reprint, New York: Library of America, 1993.

James, William. *The Varieties of Religious Experience*. 1902. Reprint, New York: Modern Library, 1936.

Jarrell, Randall. *Poetry and the Age*. New York: Vintage Books, 1955.

Jay, Gregory S. *T. S. Eliot and the Poetics of Literary History*. Baton Rouge: Louisiana State University Press, 1983.

Julius, Anthony. *T. S. Eliot, Anti-Semitism, and Literary Form*. New York: Cambridge University Press, 1995.

Kearns, Cleo McNelly. "Realism, Politics, and Literary Persona in *The Waste Land*." In *"The Waste Land": Modern Critical Interpretations,* ed. Harold Bloom, 137–52. New York: Chelsea House, 1986.

———. *T. S. Eliot and Indic Traditions: A Study in Poetry and Belief*. New York: Cambridge University Press, 1987.

Kenner, Hugh. *The Invisible Poet: T. S. Eliot*. New York: Harcourt, Brace and World, 1959.

Kenner, Hugh, ed. *T. S. Eliot: Twentieth Century Views*. Englewood Cliffs, N.J.: Prentice-Hall, 1962.

Kermode, Frank. *An Appetite for Poetry.* Cambridge: Harvard University Press, 1989.

———. *Romantic Image.* London: Routledge and Paul, 1957.

Laforgue, Jules. *Les Brins d'Herbes.* [Translation of passages from *Leaves of Grass.*] *La Vogue* 10 (June 28, 1886): 325–28.

Lasch, Christopher. *The Revolt of the Elites: And the Betrayal of Democracy.* New York: W. W. Norton, 1996.

Lewis, Wyndham. *Tarr.* 1918. Reprint, New York: Penguin Books, 1982.

Lindberg, Kathryne V., and Joseph Kronick, eds. *America's Modernisms: Revaluing the Canon: Essays in Honor of Joseph N. Riddel.* Baton Rouge: Louisiana State University Press, 1996.

Lobb, Edward, ed. *Words in Time: New Essays on Eliot's "Four Quartets."* London: Athlone Press, 1993.

Longenbach, James. "*Ara Vos Prec:* Satire and Suffering." In *T. S. Eliot: The Modernist in History,* ed. Ronald Bush, 41–66. Cambridge: Cambridge University Press, 1991.

———. "Elizabeth Bishop and the Story of Postmodernism." *Southern Review* 28 (July 1992): 469–84.

———. *Modernist Poetics of History: Pound, Eliot, and the Sense of the Past.* Princeton: Princeton University Press, 1987.

———. *Modern Poetry after Modernism.* New York: Oxford University Press, 1997.

Lopez, Michael. "De-transcendentalizing Emerson." *Emerson Society Quarterly* 34 (1988): 77–139.

Love, W. DeLoss, Jr. *The Fast and Thanksgiving Days of New England.* Boston: Houghton Mifflin, 1895.

Lowell, Robert. *Collected Prose.* Ed. Robert Giroux. New York: Farrar, Straus and Giroux, 1987.

———. *For the Union Dead.* New York: Farrar, Straus and Giroux, 1964.

———. *History.* New York: Farrar, Straus and Giroux, 1973.

———. *Land of Unlikeness.* Cummington, Mass.: Cummington Press, 1944.

———. Letters to Ezra Pound. Beineke Library, Yale University.

———. *Life Studies.* London: Farrar, Straus and Giroux, 1959.

———. *Lord Weary's Castle.* New York: Harcourt, Brace, 1946.

Manganaro, Marc. *Myth, Rhetoric, and the Voice of Authority: A Critique of Frazer, Eliot, Frye, and Campbell.* New Haven: Yale University Press, 1992.

March, Richard, and Tambimuttu, eds. *T. S. Eliot: A Symposium from Conrad Aiken (and Others)*. Chicago: H. Regnery, 1949.

Marchand, Ernest. "Poe as Social Critic." *American Literature* 6 (1934–1935): 28–43.

Mariani, Paul. *Lost Puritan: A Life of Robert Lowell*. New York: W. W. Norton, 1994.

Martin, Mildred. *A Half-Century of Eliot Criticism: An Annotated Bibliography of Books and Articles in English, 1916–1965*. Lewisburg, Pa.: Bucknell University Press, 1972.

Matthiessen, F. O. *The Achievement of T. S. Eliot*. 1935. Reprint, New York: Oxford University Press, 1959.

———. *American Renaissance*. London: Oxford University Press, 1941.

Mayer, John T. *T. S. Eliot's Silent Voices*. New York, Oxford University Press, 1989.

Menand, Louis. *Discovering Modernism: T. S. Eliot and His Context*. New York: Oxford University Press, 1987.

Meredith, George. *The Poems of George Meredith*. 2 vols. Ed. Phyllis Bartlett. New Haven: Yale University Press, 1978.

Miller, Perry. *Errand into the Wilderness*. Cambridge: Harvard University Press, 1956.

———. *Nature's Nation*. Cambridge: Harvard University Press, 1967.

———. *The New England Mind: From Colony to Province*. Cambridge: Harvard University Press, 1953.

Moody, A. David. "The American Strain." In *The Placing of T. S. Eliot,* ed. Jewel Spears Brooker, 77–89. Columbia: University of Missouri Press, 1991.

———. *Thomas Stearns Eliot, Poet*. Cambridge: Cambridge University Press, 1979.

———. *Tracing T. S. Eliot's Spirit*. Cambridge: Cambridge University Press, 1996.

Moody, A. David, ed. *The Cambridge Companion to T. S. Eliot*. Cambridge: Cambridge University Press, 1994.

Moore, Marianne. "The Accented Syllable." *Egoist* 3 (October 1916): 151–52.

More, P. E. Review of *Selected Essays,* by T. S. Eliot. 1932. In *T. S. Eliot: A Selected Critique,* ed. Leonard Unger, 24–29. New York: Rinehart, 1948.

Morse, Jonathan. "Sweeney, the Sties of the Irish, and *The Waste Land.*" In *Critical Essays on T. S. Eliot: The Sweeney Motif,* ed. Kinley Roby, 135–46. Boston: G. K. Hall, 1985.

Musgrove, Sydney. *T. S. Eliot and Walt Whitman.* Wellington: New Zealand University Press, 1952.

New, Elisa. *The Regenerate Lyric: Theology and Innovation in American Poetry.* Cambridge: Cambridge University Press, 1993.

Niebuhr, H. Richard. *The Kingdom of God in America.* Chicago: Willett, Clark, 1937.

Nordloh, David, ed. *American Literary Scholarship: An Annual, 1996.* Durham: Duke University Press, 1998.

Olney, James, ed. *T. S. Eliot: Essays from the "Southern Review."* Oxford: Clarendon Press, 1988.

Oser, Lee, and Alec Marsh. "Pound and Eliot." In *American Literary Scholarship: An Annual, 1996,* ed. David Nordloh and Gary Scharnhorst. Durham: Duke University Press, 1998.

Owen, W. J. B., ed. *Wordsworth's Literary Criticism.* London: Routledge and K. Paul, 1974.

Peake, Charles. "'Sweeney Erect' and the Emersonian Hero." 1960. In *Critical Essays on T. S. Eliot: The Sweeney Motif,* ed. Kinley Roby, 49–55. Boston: G. K. Hall, 1985.

Pearce, Roy Harvey. *The Continuity of American Poetry.* 1961. Reprint, Middletown, Conn.: Wesleyan University Press, 1987.

Perl, Jeffrey. *Skepticism and Modern Enmity: Before and after Eliot.* Baltimore: Johns Hopkins University Press, 1989.

Poe, Edgar Allan. *Essays and Reviews.* Ed. G. R. Thompson. New York: Library of America, 1984.

———. *Poetry and Tales.* Ed. Patrick Quinn. New York: Library of America, 1984.

Poirier, Richard. *Poetry and Pragmatism.* Cambridge: Harvard University Press, 1992.

———. *The Renewal of Literature: Emersonian Reflections.* New York: Random House, 1987.

Porte, Joel, ed. *Emerson: Prospect and Retrospect.* Cambridge: Harvard University Press, 1982.

Pound, Ezra. "Historical Survey." *Little Review* 8 (Autumn 1921): 39–42.

————. *Literary Essays of Ezra Pound.* Ed. T. S. Eliot. London: Faber and Faber, 1954.

————. *Selected Prose.* Ed. William Cookson. New York: New Directions, 1973.

Powel, H. W. H., Jr. "Notes on the Life of T. S. Eliot 1888–1910." Master's thesis, Brown University, 1954.

Powell, Grosvenor. "The Two Paradigms for Iambic Pentameter and Twentieth-Century Metrical Experimentation." *Modern Language Review* 91 (July 1996): 561–77.

Praz, Mario. *The Romantic Agony.* 1933. Reprint, Cleveland: Meridian Books, 1968.

Press, John. *A Map of Modern English Verse.* New York: Oxford University Press, 1969.

Price, Kenneth. *Whitman and Tradition: The Poet in His Century.* New Haven: Yale University Press, 1990.

Raleigh, John Henry. *Matthew Arnold and American Culture.* Berkeley and Los Angeles: University of California Press, 1957.

Read, Sir Herbert. "T. S. E.—A Memoir." In *T. S. Eliot: The Man and His Work,* ed. Allen Tate, 11–37. New York: Dell, 1966.

Richardson, Robert D., Jr. *Emerson: The Mind on Fire.* Berkeley and Los Angeles: University of California Press, 1995.

Ricks, Christopher. *T. S. Eliot and Prejudice.* London: Faber and Faber, 1988.

Ricks, Christopher, ed. *Inventions of the March Hare: Poems, 1909–1917,* by T. S. Eliot. New York: Harcourt Brace, 1996.

Riddel, Joseph. "Decentering the Image." In *Textual Strategies: Perspectives in Post-Structuralist Criticism,* ed. Josué V. Harari, 322–58. Ithaca: Cornell University Press, 1979.

Riquelme, John Paul. *Harmony of Dissonances: T. S. Eliot, Romanticism, and Imagination.* Baltimore: Johns Hopkins University Press, 1991.

Roby, Kinley, ed. *Critical Essays on T. S. Eliot: The Sweeney Motif.* Boston: G. K. Hall, 1985.

Rudman, Mark. *Robert Lowell: An Introduction to the Poetry.* New York: Columbia University Press, 1983.

Rydell, Robert. *All the World's a Fair: Visions of Empire at American International Expositions, 1876–1916.* Chicago: University of Chicago Press, 1984.

Santayana, George. *George Santayana's America.* Ed. James Ballowe. Chicago: University of Illinois Press, 1967.

———. *The Last Puritan.* New York: Charles Scribner's Sons, 1936.

Schuchard, Ronald. " 'If I Think, Again, of This Place': Eliot, Herbert, and the Way to 'Little Gidding.' " In *Words in Time: New Essays on Eliot's "Four Quartets,"* ed. Edward Lobb, 52–83. London: Athlone Press, 1993.

———. "T. S. Eliot as an Extension Lecturer." Part 2. *Review of English Studies* 25 (August 1974): 292–304.

Schuchard, Ronald, ed. *The Varieties of Metaphysical Poetry,* by T. S. Eliot. New York: Harcourt Brace, 1993.

Schwartz, Sanford. *The Matrix of Modernism: Pound, Eliot, and Early Twentieth-Century Thought.* Princeton: Princeton University Press, 1985.

Shusterman, Richard. *T. S. Eliot and the Philosophy of Criticism.* New York: Columbia University Press, 1988.

Sigg, Eric. *The American T. S. Eliot: A Study of the Early Writings.* Cambridge: Cambridge University Press, 1989.

———. "Eliot as a Product of America." In *The Cambridge Companion to T. S. Eliot,* ed. A. D. Moody, 14–30. Cambridge: Cambridge University Press, 1994.

Sinclair, May. "Two Notes." *Egoist* 2 (June 1, 1915): 89.

Smith, Grover. *T. S. Eliot and the Use of Memory.* Lewisburg, Pa.: Bucknell University Press, 1996.

———. *T. S. Eliot's Poetry and Plays.* Chicago: University of Chicago Press, 1956.

———. *"The Waste Land."* London: George Allen and Unwin, 1983.

Soldo, John. *The Tempering of T. S. Eliot.* Ann Arbor: UMI Research Press, 1983.

Southam, B. C. *A Guide to the Selected Poems of T. S. Eliot.* 6th ed. New York: Harcourt Brace, 1996.

Spender, Stephen. *T. S. Eliot.* New York: Penguin Books, 1976.

Sprague, Claire, ed. *Van Wyck Brooks: The Early Years.* New York: Harper and Row, 1968.

Stepanchev, Stephen. *American Poetry since 1945: A Critical Survey.* New York: Harper and Row, 1965.

Stovall, Floyd. *The Foreground to "Leaves of Grass."* Charlottesville: University of Virginia Press, 1974.

Symons, Arthur. *The Symbolist Movement in Literature.* 1899. Reprint, New York: Dutton, 1958.

Tate, Allen. *On the Limits of Poetry: Selected Essays, 1928–1948.* New York: Swallow Press, 1948.

Tate, Allen, ed. *T. S. Eliot: The Man and His Work.* New York: Dell, 1966.

Teres, Harvey. "Remaking Marxist Criticism: *Partisan Review*'s Eliotic Leftism, 1934–1936." In *High and Low Moderns: Literature and Culture, 1889–1939,* ed. Maria DiBattista and Lucy McDiarmid, 65–84. New York: Oxford University Press, 1996.

Thomas, Edward. Review of *Personae of Ezra Pound,* by Ezra Pound. *English Review* 2 (June 1909): 627–30.

Timmerman, John. *T. S. Eliot's Ariel Poems: The Poetics of Recovery.* Lewisburg, Pa.: Bucknell University Press, 1994.

Unger, Leonard. "Actual Times and Actual Places." In *The Placing of T. S. Eliot,* ed. Jewel Spears Brooker, 90–106. Columbia: University of Missouri Press, 1991.

Unger, Leonard, ed. *T. S. Eliot: A Selected Critique.* New York: Rinehart, 1948.

Vendler, Helen. "Contemporary American Poetry." In *The Harvard Book of Contemporary American Poetry,* ed. Helen Vendler. Cambridge: Harvard University Press, 1985.

Wendell, Barrett. *A Literary History of America.* New York: Charles Scribner's Sons, 1900.

Whicher, Stephen. *Freedom and Fate.* Philadelphia: University of Philadelphia Press, 1953.

Whitman, Walt. *Complete Poetry and Collected Prose.* Ed. Justin Kaplan. New York: Library of America, 1982.

Williams, Raymond. *Culture and Society, 1780–1950.* 1958. Reprint, New York: Columbia University Press, 1983.

Williams, William Carlos. *Spring and All.* 1923. In *Imaginations,* ed. Webster Scott. New York: New Directions, 1971.

Wordsworth, William. *Wordsworth's Literary Criticism.* Ed. W. J. B. Owen. London: Routledge and K. Paul, 1974.

Yeats, W. B. Introduction to *The Oxford Book of Modern Verse,* ed. W. B. Yeats. New York: Oxford University Press, 1936.

Index

Abrams, M. H., 92
Adams, Brooks, 88
Adams, Henry, 62n40, 70–71, 86, 88–91
Aeschylus, 53
Aiken, Conrad, 2, 6, 47n13, 60, 62n40
Alcott, Bronson, 72
Aldington, Richard, 68
Alexander VI, Pope, 105
American themes: Fourth of July, 87,
    90–91, 93; frontiers, 20–21, 24, 110, 124;
    imperialism, 7n12, 15, 24; individualism,
    46–47, 58–60, 62–64, 145; millennialism
    (prophetic history), 4–5, 35, 39–41, 63,
    79, 90–97, 101–2, 111–13, 118, 132–33,
    135–36, 144–46; the national character,
    2, 19, 62; rhetoric of optimism and
    progress, 5, 7, 8, 10–11, 15–16, 31–32, 56,
    91, 141. *See also* Democracy; Sermonical
    traditions
Ammonius Saccas, 47
Andrewes, Lancelot, 30, 71, 100
Aristotle, 59, 142
Arnold, Matthew, 17, 39, 45, 50, 54–55, 65,
    67, 69, 144
Ashbery, John, 126, 128–33
Auden, W. H., 65–66, 128
Augustine, Saint, 30

Babbitt, Irving, 58–59, 101n24
Barlow, Joel, 144

Baudelaire, Charles, 6–7, 10, 13, 32, 52, 77,
    93, 131
Beehler, Michael, 128
Bercovitch, Sacvan, 27, 30, 36, 58, 90n12
Bergson, Henri, 62
Bhagavad-Gita, The, 44, 52
Biblical references, 37, 38, 48, 52, 69, 71, 73,
    74, 90, 95, 101, 105, 124, 137. *See also*
    Ezekiel; Jeremiah; John the Baptist
Bishop, Elizabeth, 3, 8, 22, 126, 133–38
Blake, William, 101
Blood, Benjamin P., 148–49
Bloom, Harold, 22, 23n34, 46–47, 118n23
Borroff, Marie, 24n35
Boston doubt, the, 62n40, 108n8
Bradford, William, 28
Bradley, Francis Herbert, 81–83
Brathwaite, E. K., 135
Bromwich, David, 46–47, 139n21
Brontë, Charlotte, 97
Brooker, Jewel Spears, 88n5
Brooks, Van Wyck, 6, 28–31, 46, 102n24
Browning, Robert, 39–40, 92, 95
Bryant, William Cullen, 5, 36
Buddhism. *See* Indic religions
Burke, Edmund, 58
Burke, Kenneth, 63–64, 79n20
Bush, Ronald, 44, 51n22, 108n8, 116n21
Bushnell, Horace, 36